IDENTITY

SAGE was founded in 1965 by Sara Miller McCune to support the dissemination of usable knowledge by publishing innovative and high-quality research and teaching content. Today, we publish over 900 journals, including those of more than 400 learned societies, more than 800 new books per year, and a growing range of library products including archives, data, case studies, reports, and video. SAGE remains majority-owned by our founder, and after Sara's lifetime will become owned by a charitable trust that secures our continued independence.

Los Angeles | London | New Delhi | Singapore | Washington DC | Melbourne

IDENTITY

UNIQUE & SHARED

GLYNIS M. BREAKWELL

Los Angeles | London | New Delhi
Singapore | Washington DC | Melbourne

Los Angeles | London | New Delhi
Singapore | Washington DC | Melbourne

SAGE Publications Ltd
1 Oliver's Yard
55 City Road
London EC1Y 1SP

SAGE Publications Inc.
2455 Teller Road
Thousand Oaks, California 91320

SAGE Publications India Pvt Ltd
B 1/I 1 Mohan Cooperative Industrial Area
Mathura Road
New Delhi 110 044

SAGE Publications Asia-Pacific Pte Ltd
3 Church Street
#10-04 Samsung Hub
Singapore 049483

Editors: Amy Maher and Martin Perchard
Editorial assistant: Emma Yuan
Production editor: Imogen Roome
Copyeditor: Sarah Bury
Proofreader: Leigh Smithson
Marketing manager: Fauzia Eastwood
Cover design: Wendy Scott
Typeset by: KnowledgeWorks Global Ltd.
Printed in the UK

Library of Congress Control Number: 2022943480

British Library Cataloguing in Publication data

A catalogue record for this book is available from the British Library

ISBN 978-1-5297-7434-4
ISBN 978-1-5297-7433-7 (pbk)

At SAGE we take sustainability seriously. Most of our products are printed in the UK using responsibly sourced papers and boards. When we print overseas we ensure sustainable papers are used as measured by the PREPS grading system. We undertake an annual audit to monitor our sustainability.

DEDICATION

To Colin Rowett – invaluable, informant, interlocutor, and interrogator

CONTENTS

ABOUT THE AUTHOR

Dame Glynis M. Breakwell is Professor Emeritus at the University of Bath in the Department of Psychology and has Visiting Professorships at Imperial College, London and the University of Surrey. Her research focuses on identity process theory, social influence and social representation processes, leadership in complex organisations, and the psychology of risk management, perception, and communication. She has published more than 20 books, several of which are on research methods. She has been an adviser to both public and private sector organisations on the use of psychological methods and theories, especially concerning responses to public crises and major emergencies.

1

IDENTITY, UNIQUE AND SHARED

> Identity is the story that you tell yourself about yourself and share selectively with others.
>
> Identity is also the story that others tell about your self.

Building and defending a unique identity motivates thought, feeling, and action

This book describes how building and defending a unique identity motivates thought, feeling and action. This is one of the most powerful motivational forces in the human psyche. This book explores what we know about identity processes. It shows why knowing about them is important. There is a diverse social science literature on identity. This book is a new contribution to this literature because it provides a comprehensive review of contemporary developments in Identity Process Theory (Breakwell, 1986, 2015a).

It is worth beginning with some preliminary discussion of some basic questions:

- What is identity?
- What constitutes self-awareness?
- What purposes does identity serve?

The answers to each of these questions have always been the subject of great debate but this has been particularly true in psychology in recent years.

However, before getting into all of that, we can clear the decks of some conceptual clutter. Identity can be treated as a catch-all label for the constellation of characteristics that define a person uniquely. At its crudest, it can be the information on a passport that signifies to officialdom who you are: name, gender, nationality, date of birth, place of birth, and photograph of your face. In other contexts, it can be derived from the hallmarks that your body itself offers, for instance, fingerprints, voiceprint, DNA, or dental structure. Less certainly, it can be indicated by documentation associated with you over your lifetime, such as educational qualifications, occupational history, and medical records. It can be suggested by membership of, or affiliation with, particular groups or social categories (this includes a vast range of types of recognisable social classifications, e.g., from ethnicity to being a supporter of a specific soccer club). All of these features can be used as markers to differentiate a person from others. They are some of the physical and social markers that together suggest a person's uniqueness. It is worth noting that the changes in some of these markers dictate that the substance of a person's uniqueness changes over time. Most markers change, though some do not. For instance, while fingerprints do not change after the 17th week of pregnancy, DNA does change with age due to damage and mutations (even though the genetic sequence does not). Some of these changes are epigenetic. These affect how genes are turned on and off, or expressed, and thus help regulate how cells in different parts of the body use the same genetic code.

As used in psychological theory, the concept of identity is more than just the aggregation of such markers of uniqueness. Of course, those sorts of characteristic have a role to play in the construction of an identity, but they sit alongside other characteristics that make a person unique. These include attitudes, beliefs, values, knowledge, memories, skills, cognitive abilities, and personality traits (such as neuroticism, extroversion, curiosity, conscientiousness, and agreeableness). Evidently, many characteristics have to be included when describing a person's uniqueness, and thus their identity. Treating identity as an emergent property of the interaction of these varied characteristics necessitates looking at the identity as a whole, and not being satisfied with just delving into fragments of it. This is an important point to bear in mind when building a general theory of identity.

It should already be evident from what is said above that a person's identity is not just the aggregation of the characteristics acquired through living. That could merely be a biographical note, not even an autobiographical note. Identity is more than that. Identity is not just a product of experience. Identity is lodged in dynamic processes of thought, feeling, and action. Consequently, identity, when taken as a whole, is an actor in its own production. At the most basic level, identity affects choices that shape what experiences the individual has. At other levels, identity influences how an experience is interpreted and combined with others in constructing a landscape of information that individuals compile about themselves. This activity of identity is dependent upon the person having self-awareness. Self-awareness, basically, entails the person recognising their uniqueness and individuality and being conscious of the thought patterns and feelings in which they are rooted. We will return to the significance of self-awareness later.

So, what is identity?

Having hopefully cleared some conceptual clutter, it is sadly necessary to accumulate some more in the process of summarising some important definitions of identity that have been offered. In fact, identity is one of those concepts that are difficult to define incontrovertibly now because so many differing definitions have been offered by different academic disciplines, over time and across circumstances. As Berger et al. (1974) pointed out, definitions of identity vary with overall definitions of reality. Nevertheless, when considering them, it is useful to remember the importance of uniqueness and self-awareness.

Identity is regularly split into sub-categories, for instance, differentiating personal and social identity. Early definitions elided the concepts of 'personal identity' and 'the self'. For instance, in 1690, John Locke (2008 [1847]) considered personal identity (which he also sometimes referred to as the self or self-identity) to be founded on the repeated act of consciousness. He proposed that we are the same person to the extent that we are conscious of our past and future thoughts and actions in the same way as we are conscious of our current thoughts and actions. Thus, he believed that memory is fundamental to personal identity. In this context, memory is both the process of capturing a record of one's thoughts, feelings, and actions and the ability to retrieve material from that record.

The way Locke moved, somewhat erratically, between labelling this complex set of processes as the self, self-identity, and personal identity, finds echoes in the work of many later identity theorists. This may occur because theorists tend to differ in the aspect of identity that they focus on. Then these aspects of the identity concept as a whole are differentiated by being given different labels. For instance, the 'self-concept' is used to refer to certain aspects of identity (i.e., how people think about, evaluate, and perceive themselves). But the idea of the self-concept itself has been broken down into discrete components. For instance, Rogers (1947) said it has three components: self-image, self-esteem, and the ideal self. Subsequently, further components have been added, notably 'self-efficacy' (Bandura, 1982). This intense examination of the individual components of identity may be absolutely necessary for the detailed empirical examination of the multi-dimensional functions that it serves. However, it has tended to divert attention away from efforts to produce a wholistic theory of identity. If it were possible to produce in psychology a general theory of identity, it could have an impact on psychology akin to Einstein's (1922) general theory of relativity on astrophysicists' understanding of space-time. Relativity improved the science of elementary particles so as to allow the prediction of extraordinary phenomena, such as neutron stars, black holes, and gravitational waves. Having a wholistic theory of identity should improve the capacity of social scientists to predict the interactions between people that are fundamental to better understanding the nature of the social universe.

Contemporary philosophers tend to distinguish between two questions (known as the diachronic and synchronic) when defining the 'personal' aspect of identity: (i) what makes it true that a person at one time is the same entity as a person at another time; and (ii) what features and traits characterise a person at a given time? Psychologists have tended to focus on the second of these questions. Of course, the examination of what characterises the person at any one time has entailed work on intelligence, emotionality, cognitive style, neurological functions, biochemical and genetic makeup, besides broadly defined personality traits and behavioural patterns. At this point, it is possible to argue that the various definitions of personal identity morph to encompass all aspects of the person that psychologists choose to study.

Focusing on definitions of identity emanating from major theorists in psychology still reveals considerable diversity. For instance, in the Freudian psychoanalytic framework, the mind was composed of the id, driven by instinct and desire, the superego, driven by morality and values, and the ego which moderates the two and creates the identity (Freud, 2019, p. 48). Many factors are said to contribute to ego functioning, including insight, agency, empathy, and purpose. Also from a psychoanalytic perspective, Erikson (1968), in his theory of development, coined the term 'ego identity', which he regarded as the continuing and enduring sense of self that a person has. He argues that the ego identity serves to merge all the different versions of oneself acquired through development (for example, the child self, the parent self, the sexual self) into a coherent whole. Notably, both these theorists consider identity to be the wholistic product of psychological and social processes. They do not talk about the individual possessing 'multiple identities'. For them, the identity is singular and incorporates both the social and psychological characteristics of the person.

Other theorists in psychology clearly differentiate between personal and social identity. Notably, Social Identity Theory (SIT), first proposed by Tajfel (1978), defines identity in terms of group or social category memberships, each affiliation providing its own 'social identity', suggesting that most people can have several social identities (e.g., gender, age, ethnicity, occupation, etc.). Importantly, Tajfel was not trying to produce a theory of identity *per se*. He was producing a theory initially designed to explain intergroup differentiation and conflict by showing that people would try, by discriminating against other groups, to optimise the contribution of their own group memberships to their own self-esteem (i.e., the positive evaluation of the self). The debate about the relative roles of personal and social identity has been important in social psychology (Schwartz et al., 2011). There is now no doubt that the socially derived component of identity is vitally important. The challenge that has to be faced is how to theorise the relationships between all those components that make up the identity as a whole.

Interestingly, the American Psychological Association (APA) does not emphasise the personal identity – social identity dichotomy. The American Psychological Association's *Dictionary of Psychology* (2022) defines 'identity' as 'an individual's sense of self defined by (a) a set of physical, psychological, and interpersonal characteristics that is not wholly shared with any other person and (b) a range of affiliations (e.g., ethnicity) and social roles. Identity involves a sense of continuity, or the feeling that one is the same person today that one was yesterday or last year (despite physical or other changes). Such a sense is derived from one's body sensations; one's body image; and the feeling that one's memories, goals, values, expectations, and beliefs belong to the self'. This inclusive, wholistic definition is the one that is most in accord with the concept of identity used in Identity Process Theory (IPT), as described in this book.

With respect to the personal identity–social identity debate, IPT has staunchly argued that the assumed dichotomy is an artefact of temporal perspective. It is well documented that at a single moment in time personal and social identity can be separated; the person concerned experiences them as different. However, considered over time, they are not separated. Developmentally, personal identity is, partly, a residual product of the impact of social roles and influences, but one which is self-made by virtue of the active role it plays in assimilating, and then accommodating, the effects of social experiences. Personal components of identity (e.g., cognitive ability) will affect what social identities are available and how they are interpreted. Over time, the evolution of identity entails a continual and truly dialectical relationship between the personal and social components of identity. Breakwell (1983, p. 12) stated that: 'Current personal identity is the product of the interaction of all past personal identities with all past and present social identities. But the reverse is also true: current social identities are the product of the interactions of all past social identities with all past and current personal identities.' This argument would lead IPT to the abandonment of any reliance on the assumed personal–social identity dichotomy when explaining thought, feeling, or action over time. Instead, IPT incorporated the dynamic interaction of personal and social components of identity in predicting reactions.

To return to the question posed at the start of this section: so, what is identity? The simple answer is it's complicated. However, in IPT, 'identity is treated as a dynamic social product, residing in psychological processes, which cannot be understood except in relation to its social context and historical perspective' (Breakwell, 2015a, p. 9). From its first formulation in 1986, IPT has stressed that it is only possible to articulate the wholistic nature of identity by focusing, in turn, on:

- the structural components of identity over time;
- the processes underpinning identity and the principles that direct their operation;
- the structures and processes of the societal context in which the identity resides;
- the effects of social change upon identity;
- and the relationship of identity and action.

The definition that theorists give for identity depends upon the purpose and the philosophical and methodological foundations of their theory. IPT grew out of an attempt to model how people cope with threatening life events. It was, thus, quintessentially concerned with both personal and social changes and their interactions. Specifically, it was focused upon the opportunities for, and constraints upon, personal change. This resulted in a model of identity specified in a series of propositions. The first of these was that:

> The structure of identity is a dynamic social product of the interaction of the capacities for memory, consciousness and organised construal which are characteristic of the biological organism with the physical and societal structures and influence processes which constitute the social context. The identity resides in psychological processes but is manifested through thought, action and affect. It can therefore be described at two levels, in terms of its structures and in terms of its processes. (Breakwell, 2015a, p. 190)

Clearly, IPT is interested in identity as a whole. As suggested earlier, this general theory of identity relies on assumptions about people being self-aware and monitoring the status of their identity. It speaks of 'the identity' in the singular, not of 'multiple identities'.

What constitutes self-awareness?

There are some fascinating questions about the nature of self-awareness. To be self-aware, it is generally agreed that you need to be conscious. This does not help greatly since consciousness is an ill-defined, fuzzy concept. Sutherland (1989), cutting a swathe through centuries of argument, said simply that it is only to be aware of the external world, of what we experience through our senses. He also said it is impossible to specify what it is, what it does, or why it has evolved. It has not stopped people trying. That it entails having the neurophysiological and biochemical capacity to have perceptions, thoughts, and feelings (sometimes called 'qualia') that signal the existence of awareness seems a common assumption. However, consciousness is often described as having another type of dimension. It might be conceived as a director. It is a process that modifies attention or focus on what is sensed, it fits new experiences into the record of earlier ones, and it contributes to the interpretation of those experiences. These functions are purposive, they are not indiscriminate, and they are motivated. Once one gets to this stage in defining consciousness, it starts to sound like a generic co-ordinator of perceptual, cognitive, conative, and orectic processes. It is not surprising then that consciousness is a precursor of self-awareness. Self-awareness, at one level, is basically being aware that you are conscious and that your consciousness is operating to direct and co-ordinate. At another level, it is being cognisant of the products of consciousness that specifically apply to oneself. It entails being aware of characteristics that differentiate yourself from others. It also involves purposive examination and evaluation of your own attributes. Self-awareness is one of the key processes that shapes motivation and thus experience and acquisition of new information.

The next question has to be: what initiates the growth of self-awareness?

It begins with interaction, first with the physical environment. Self-awareness apparently starts with differentiating the bodily self from the non-self. Developmental psychologists have found that this begins with the newborn gradually recognising where his or her own body ends and the rest of the world begins. Thereafter, by a few months of age, they are learning the relationship between the proprioceptive information they receive from their body and the visual cues they gain from their environment (first-person self-awareness). By 18 months, on average, they begin to recognise themselves in photographs, reflections, and mirrors (reflective self-awareness). Shortly after, they typically develop the ability to recognise their own bodies in space and time that interact with other things (objective self-awareness). There is some evidence that self-awareness is not a uniquely human phenomenon. At least, this seems to hold for body self-awareness. Research using 'mirror tests', where animals are tested to determine whether they can recognise the reflected image of themselves in a mirror as different from those of others, have been used to assess body self-awareness. They indicate that chimpanzees and other apes, dolphins, and some birds (e.g., magpies) have this aspect of self-awareness. Self-recognition is treated as a marker for self-awareness. The findings suggest that we should not assume that all aspects of self-awareness are human-species specific. This should not be a surprise since many of the physical and social interactions that engender self-awareness in humans happen, perhaps in other guises, for members of other species. It raises the intriguing question of whether members of other species have their own unique identities. Many animal owners might argue that their pets do. However, conducting research on an animal's understanding of their unique identity would probably need more equipment than a mirror.

Turning quickly back to humans, in his theory of self-knowledge, Hegel (1977 [1807]) suggested that it is through practical activity that a person 'acquires a mind of his own'. By transforming things in the external world, the person gains self-awareness. By observing the effects of their actions, people achieve some appreciation of their own powers and grow to characterise their self in terms of the effects they have brought about. Interactions with other people can work similarly to modify self-knowledge. From active involvement with others, individuals come to know that they have perceptions, cognitions, emotions, and intentionality. In recognising this, individuals come to understand that other people must see them as also possessing these qualities. Thus, people gain self-consciousness by coming to understand how other people perceive them.

However, self-consciousness or self-knowledge is not the simple passive mirroring of what one believes others see in oneself. This is an iterative process, recognising that what the other perceives affects the object that is perceived and, thus, that object is influenced to change. It is important to note that Hegel does not say that self-knowledge is subject to external or objective validation. It is what you think about your 'self' after reflecting on what others perceive.

This is an interesting point when thinking about the development of identity. Individuals may determine through processes of self-awareness what they believe to be an accurate image of their identity. However, if the image of identity produced is inaccurate, then continued interactions with the object (physical or social) that stimulated it will highlight inconsistencies or contradictions. Hegel argued that the solution for such contradictions is the fulcrum of the development of the self from an undifferentiated whole to a highly differentiated system. Overcoming such contradictions is necessary for the growth of the mature differentiated self. Contradictions can be overcome by gaining a better understanding of their source and reflecting on it. Thus, contradictions are deemed remediable if new insight and information can be achieved. This can be a very positive picture when applied to identity development. The contradictions that self-awareness reveals in identity should be open to resolution through self-reflection or practical corrective engagement with the source of the inconsistency in the identity image.

This explanation of the development of self-knowledge (or identity) has at its centre a hermeneutical circle in which both parties to an interaction are changed by it, as both reflect on its meaning for the other. It is notable that humans develop the capacity to understand that others have their own unique perspective on the world gradually. This understanding that other people's thinking or feelings may differ from their own (what is known as 'theory of mind', see Sodian and Kristen (2016) for an overview, and Saxe (2013) for possible links with brain activity) grows as children gain greater experience across diverse social interactions with others of different ages (e.g., in play, make-believe, story-telling, and formal education). This is called 'theory of mind' because, since the mind of someone else cannot be directly observed, our understanding of the minds of others is based on inference and hypothesis. It is a theory that becomes more intricate and less fallible but probably also less falsifiable over a lifetime.

The key period for children to develop a theory of mind seems to be between 3 years and 5 years, and they acquire their understanding of the various aspects of the way other people's minds work (e.g., with regard to attentiveness, motives, beliefs, knowledge, falsehood, and deception) at different points in the process. More recent research on theory of mind has moved significantly away from its early conceptual roots in Piagetian concepts of childhood developmental stages (Piaget, 2000). It is suggesting that an individual's development of theory of mind does not cease with the end of childhood (Valle et al., 2015). People continue to develop more sophisticated and differentiated appreciation of how others differ from, and also agree with, their own thoughts and feelings through the lifespan (although in old age there is some evidence that this may be reversed). A key advantage of mastering the theory of mind is that it improves one's ability to predict how others will behave and to build hypotheses about why they behave in the ways that they do. Application of theory of mind can also be generalised. Earlier, the possibility of non-human species having self-awareness and even identity was mentioned. People are inclined to generalise theory of mind assumptions when predicting the behaviour of other animals. People may be tempted to speculate about the cognitive, emotional, and motivational reasons for the behaviour that individuals of other species exhibit. This need not be simple anthropomorphism – the theory of mind that they develop for their cat can be quite different from that they apply to their child. However, it may influence their own behaviour towards the cat and result in their pet maintaining or changing how it behaves. Such cats may develop an 'identity', not through acquiring their own theory of mind but through learning regimes shaped by their human.

In the case of humans, complexity in the theory of mind that one applies to others is reflected in what can be applied to oneself. It is worth considering the possible effects of having differing degrees of complexity in the theory of mind available to an individual in the process of developing an identity. The most obvious implication of having a complex theory of mind might be that choices between alternative identity development pathways become easier to make because it makes the prediction of other people's reactions and evaluations more accurate. Identity choices and manifestations can be attuned more effectively to the audience addressed. As a result, contradictions between aspects of the identity image can be avoided. Having a highly developed theory of mind may also support more effective coping when contradictions or inconsistencies in the identity image occur (as they are likely to if the complexity of social interactions grows either across time or at one time). The individual with the more complex, differentiated theory of mind has more latitude to reinterpret the social exchanges that stimulate a contradiction and, thereby, moderate, explain, or dismiss the contradiction.

Self-awareness, and its corollary 'other-awareness', have to be fundamental parts of any explanation of how identity works. This is particularly evidenced when there are deficits in self-awareness. Most of the studies of deficits in self-awareness emphasise that self-awareness is not a unitary phenomenon and that one can be aware of different aspects of the self at any one time. So, for instance, research suggests that in dementia, self-awareness dependent on higher-level cognitive processes, such as autobiographical memory and emotional regulation, may be impaired while capacities for bodily awareness and agency may be relatively preserved (Mograbi et al., 2021). Similarly, according to Williams (2010) in relation to autism, while awareness of the 'physical self' is maintained, a deficit is evident in recognising their own mental states ('the theory of *own* mind') and in recognising the mental states of others. In some forms of psychiatric illness, the lack of self-awareness is a defining characteristic. For instance, in schizophrenia, the very nature of the illness circles around the loss of any self-awareness that is founded in a connection to the reality outside their systems of hallucinations or unsubstantiated beliefs. In other forms of psychiatric illness, self-awareness is present erratically. For instance, in bipolar disorder, an illness which is characterised by shifts in mood and energy, the accuracy of self-awareness may vary as mood and ability to cope changes.

All of these examples serve to emphasise that self-awareness sadly cannot be treated as a given. They illustrate how the bases of identity construction and maintenance are at risk when self-awareness is diminished or undermined. Identity cannot be sustained without the operation of self-awareness. It is notable from the examples that many different physical, biochemical, and neurophysiological causes may be implicated in the diminution or loss of self-awareness. These causes may be seen as the ultimate source of the threat to a functioning identity. However, they work through, and are mediated by, self-awareness.

What purposes does identity serve?

In the next chapter, identity composition and expression are considered in detail. Before getting to that, it may be useful, briefly and in general terms, to consider the different types of purpose an identity serves. Understanding some of its key purposes may allow us to hypothesise why it may have evolved as a part of the human psyche, and, most particularly, why it continues to evolve as part of the human psyche. These purposes (or, more strictly, consequences) fall into two clusters: those that identity serves for the individual and those that identity in individuals serves for society. Identity serves both the individual and the society. Of course, these purposes intersect.

For individuals, identity can be:

- an ever-changing embodiment of their individuality;
- a sign and a way of expressing their ultimate uniqueness;
- a repository of attitudes, beliefs, values, emotions;

- a source of motives and desires;
- a specification of their social position, authority, and rights;
- a personalised and developing rationale for being, and for continuing to be, or for the reverse;
- a source of regret, fear, and anger, or of joy, hope, and pride (i.e., any emotion you can think of).

For society as a whole, that individuals each have their own unique identity means:

- they can be categorised, recorded, tracked, and thus become more controllable;
- they are self-interested (in the original sense of the word) and may be less controllable;
- they will seek to occupy different roles in the social world, and to some extent their choices will be predictable;
- their social processes will evolve to influence how individual identities are shaped;
- their identity characteristics, once identified, can be used to mobilise, or deter, individual action;
- their identity differences will be a source, as well as a product, of inter-individual and inter-group conflict.

This is not meant to be an exhaustive list of the purposes (or consequences) of identity. Those mentioned give a flavour of the complex interface between individual and societal purposes of identity. Identities are deeply dependent on the society in which they reside, but societies are driven in part by the identities they foster.

It may be easier to recognise the evolutionary role of societies in the development of the social (group membership-based) aspects of identity (Brewer & Caporael, 2006), but all aspects of individual identity are developed in the specific social milieu of their time period and will be impacted by it. It is useful to consider from an evolutionary approach how identity might become a fundamental part of the human psyche. Of course, the assumption made by evolutionary theorists is that identity emerged because it aids survival of the individual and those aligned to the individual. Basically, identity markers (whether physical, for example wearing particular garments, or behavioural, such as using particular forms of greeting) make recognition easier and, thus, the detection of threat, and its containment, more likely. Furthermore, identity markers can be very complex and revealed over time. For instance, repeating patterns of behaviour (e.g., always avoiding physical aggression) can become a marker of identity. Such identity markers facilitate prediction of the person's future reactions. The survival value for the individual of predictability may vary with context. However, without doubt, there is a survival value for a community that has the power to predict the behaviour of its members based on identity markers.

Natural selection would favour those who learned how to signal their identity optimally for personal gain in both interpersonal and wider social gatherings. In parallel, natural selection would favour those individuals and communities who attended to, and accurately interpreted, the identity markers provided by other people. The skills of expressing and reading identity markers are important in averting a wide spectrum of threat (from inconvenience through open challenge to assault). It is attractive to think of identity evolving as an integral property of the human psyche over millennia because it serves to improve the survival chances of the individual and their communities, and thereby the species. However, that really is too simplistic. The evolution of identity as a central human characteristic has had side-effects that significantly intensify the threats that the species has to face. Identity can motivate the denial of threat if to acknowledge that threat challenges identity, so militating against threat alert and response. Identity can motivate unjustified or unreasoned aggression against others. Identity can be used as a lever to change behaviour so as to harm the individual. Identity claims can lead to competition and conflict. There is a long list of the downsides from having identity as a defining characteristic of humankind. In evolutionary terms, it is hard to see where it might go next.

Unique and also shared

Most of what has already been said highlights that a person's identity is unique, particularly when treated as a whole rather than broken down into component slivers. What does it mean to say that identity is also shared? It is not meant to say that two or more people have the same identity as each other. It is not to imply copying. No one has exactly the same identity configuration as someone else because no two people share the same biological organism or have the same pattern of life experiences at precisely the same time. Even when two people do notionally share some component of identity, it is unreasonable to assume that it will be identical for both of them. For instance, they may both be members of the same group, say a tennis club, but the meaning of that membership for each will depend on many prior life events that they have not shared. For one, tennis has been a lifelong passion and she is very competitive; for the other, tennis is a recently discovered way of meeting people and every game is a social event. Each component of identity, as a part of the whole, interacts with all others, past and present, and possibly even prospective. Nominally, people may share an identity component – it has the same label (e.g., an ethnicity, gender, nationality, etc.). However, the meanings of that component to the individuals who share it can be vastly different. Indeed, even their self-awareness of that common identity component can differ across people.

To illustrate that self-awareness of a superficially common identity component will differ, it is useful to consider variations in the identity implications of gender. To make the variations that are possible stark, let's take an intergenerational comparison of two women. Assume that both of these people, when asked, identify as women. One is 70 years of age, the other 20. Would you expect that their self-awareness of their gender as a part of their identity was the same? Perhaps not. You might point to the changes in the societal representations of gender that have occurred during the 50 years that stand between them. Assuming that they both live in the same country in North America or Western Europe, most likely you would point to the fact that the 70-year-old had developed her awareness of her gender during an era of feminist awakening, would have had fewer opportunities than her male peers for higher education, entry into the professions, or high earnings and pension. In addition, you might think about the changes in the expectations of the roles of women in family life during that time. All this means that if we compare what being a woman meant to the 70-year-old when she was 20 with what it means to a woman aged 20 now, there are going to be differences. What is more, the 70-year-old has been exposed over a lifetime to the changing social images and positioning of women. Currently, she might share the same context as the 20-year-old, but she experiences it against the backdrop of accumulated memories of past images and positions. The two women perceive the meaning of being a woman differently as a consequence. Membership of the social category 'woman' has a different impact on their identities. Of course, then it is necessary to add in a further complexity in predicting the implication of this shared category membership. Age interacts with gender to create the contribution the latter can make to identity. To state the obvious, being a woman who is 70 is very different from being a woman who is 20. Not only are their positions in societal expectations different; they have significant bodily differences. Some of these bodily differences can alter the way that being a woman fits into the whole identity. The menopause can be one such difference. This illustration of the difficulties of treating gender as a 'shared' component of identity would become even more vivid if the comparison was between two women drawn from different cultures or politico-religious regimes. Woman is a conceptual group (Breakwell, 1979) as well as a social classification, and its conceptualisation is infinitely diverse, like that of most social classifications.

The value of this illustration lies in the fact that these two people apparently do share a membership of a social category. Yet:

- their experience of that category membership differs because their position in it varies;
- the social meaning of the categorisation changes over time and these changes impact on them differentially;
- the import of one ongoing category membership can interact with another category membership (i.e., age with gender) to result in a change in the subjective meaning of either or both.

The commonalities in the identities of these two women that are attributable to their gender alone are slender. Sharing membership of a social category is not the same as sharing the meaning of that membership for identity. Certainly, it does not mean that identity is shared.

So, is there a way in which identity is shared? Most definitely, yes. However, this is sharing of a different sort. This is not about two people sharing the same thing, apportioning some of it to one and some to the other (for instance, each having a slice from the same cheesecake). It is closer to seeing sharing as using or experiencing something jointly with another or others (for instance, sharing good news). This is essentially what people do with their identity. They share it with others. They may not share all of it, or not all of it at one time, but they do share it. That is one of the prime reasons that it exists. Think back to the evolutionary explanations for the existence of identity. Identity signals who you are (in the broadest sense) and what you are likely to do. Knowing about your identity makes you less threatening and more useful to other people. Identity cannot fulfil this prime function unless it is exposed to them (i.e., shared with them). This sharing may be circumscribed, of course, since your identity has prime functions to serve for you that may be disrupted if everything about your identity is shared.

Sharing your identity, when carefully controlled, can be advantageous. Yet it may be hard to conceive the sharing of identity as a deliberate act. The unique part of you that is the product of all you have experienced, and which directs and motivates you, is not to be shared lightly. Of course, sharing material from the periphery of your identity or something that is to all intents and purposes already obvious might not seem problematic. Sharing other aspects of identity that you regard as more important, particularly if they undermine how others evaluate you, might seem less likely. The real questions that then emerge are:

- How is sharing achieved?
- Under what conditions does it occur?
- What is shared?
- With whom is it shared?
- What types of implications does sharing have?

The answers to each of these questions is dependent on the others. There are many answers to each question, so it is worth bearing these questions in mind as you read the rest of this book. They appear as recurring themes throughout, in one guise or another. Sharing, in all its forms, is an essential ingredient of identity processes.

When considering the questions, it soon becomes evident that sharing your identity (or aspects of it) may or may not occur intentionally. You might disclose or recount things about yourself deliberately. This might be motivated by a desire to stimulate a reaction in your audience. You might know what reaction you aim to achieve but, equally, you may be uncertain, and a range of reactions might be acceptable. Often, the motive for deliberate identity sharing is associated with seeking from others confirmation or ratification of identity claims. Alternatively, you might purposefully share something about your identity not because of the effect it may have on others, but rather, because it has an effect on you. Effectively, this sort of identity disclosure has yourself as the primary or 'real' audience, and this is made possible through the presence of some other person or persons.

Identity disclosure of this sort, which is self-directed, is often important in securing a component in the whole configuration of the identity. For instance, if an emerging or newly assimilated aspect of your identity is something that you feel ambivalent about, or something that you think is ill-defined, articulating it to others, and thus to yourself, may be a route to facilitating its better assimilation. Of course, it may also make you realise it is not something that fits well with your whole identity now or the one you want in the future. Using sharing of your identity with others in order for you to become your own primary audience has effects different from those you might achieve through self-reflection or introspection. Two factors are at play: marshalling the narrative about your identity that is needed during sharing makes you think more fully (and perhaps more systematically) about your own hopes, doubts, or uncertainties; and, once you 'go public', the things you externalise have a different status in relation to you, they are less permeable and less ignorable. Deliberate identity sharing, whether initially aimed at others or at yourself, always has a feedback loop to yourself. The process of deliberately sharing inevitably has consequences for the ongoing development of the whole identity.

Incidental (unintended) sharing of identity also occurs. This is not deliberate (though it can be argued that it may be unconsciously motivated). The point is that we all leave a trail of small clues about our identity in every interaction that we have. Since our identity is expressed, intentionally or unintentionally, in our every thought, feeling, and action, we litter the world with our identity traces. Consequently, in this sense, our unique identity is continually shared, whether we know it or not. It is part of the fabric of our social world.

Any general theory of identity must encompass how this deliberate and incidental sharing occurs and its implications for identity processes.

A general theory of identity

The objective of Identity Process Theory (IPT) is to contribute towards the development of a general theory of identity that will help social scientists to understand the social universe. IPT models identity as a whole: the personal and the social components. It focuses on the complex matrix of psychological and social processes that shape the identity of a person. Identity is treated as a motivational system, residing in psychological processes which cannot be understood except in relation to their socio-historical milieu. It is very difficult, perhaps impossible, to describe a dynamic system, which exists to motivate and enable change, using words, sentences, and paragraphs that impose linearity.

Breakwell (1986, p. 9) talked about needing to describe a general model of identity in terms of each of its parts, but also about the need to view the framework as an integrated whole. Breakwell used the analogy of making a film. The director can focus on different details in a rapidly shifting landscape: a fast car flashing through a panorama, panning before and after it; then widening the view to see more of the ever-changing backdrop; and making the car itself (its windows open or closed) or its occupants (the same or joined by an unknown hitchhiker) change. The film records it all. The director largely dictates where the eye and mind will rest during the ongoing story by shifts in focus (sometimes locational, sometimes temporal). The finished film seen by the public is the integration of all the footage, shots, and scenes that are retained from those that are initially filmed. Sometimes this is the 'director's cut', sometimes commercial and other considerations mean that it is not. A theorist is akin to a film director in that they both make decisions about the details to capture, the form of their representation, the sequence in which they are presented to an audience, and the narrative that they unfurl.

To extend the analogy, presenting the structure of a theory needs to be done scene by scene; all the articulating parts explained; and the integrated whole brought together, hopefully seamlessly. The charm of this analogy is that the original film can be re-cut and sequels can be produced. Theory-building also requires a willingness to revisit and redevelop models so that they can remain true to the evidence base and relevant to their users. Since its original formulation, Identity Process Theory has been significantly adapted and evolved (e.g., Breakwell, 2021; Jaspal & Breakwell, 2014), particularly with regard to incorporating the findings from cognitive psychology on the malleability of memory, the bases and effects of identity resilience, the nature and role of identifications with groups or social categories, and the consequences of social representational and influence processes.

In subsequent chapters, some of the psychological and social dynamics that underpin identity uniqueness and sharing are described through the lens of current developments in IPT. The emphasis is on elaborating further the integration of individualistic and social models of identity through examining the processes underlying identity rather than simply the substantive components that comprise it. It particularly aims to show the relevance of a general theory of identity when trying to explain how people respond when things change or go wrong in either the private or public realms that they inhabit. The chapters in this book each focus on different aspects of identity processes. They cover the acquisition and expression of identity components. They describe how stability and change in identity are managed, especially in relation to the makeup and role of identity resilience, and the way other people and organisations provide the social support that works to stabilise, secure, and develop identities. They examine how identity processes respond to public crises and personal attack, including their interactions with cognitions and emotions. The dynamic relationships between group identifications and group conflict are considered and their implications for identity processes and identity structure are outlined. Inevitably, identity processes do not always succeed in stabilising and developing identity positively; the conditions that precipitate their failure and its consequences for thought, feeling, and action are described. The final two chapters of the book examine the practical and policy implications of a wholistic theory of identity processes. In doing so, they emphasise that all theories should adapt and evolve in response to challenge and to use.

Chapter 2 begins this exposition of identity processes. It starts by suggesting how a complex theory of identity processes may be visualised and by discussing how people express their identity intentionally and incidentally.

2

IDENTITY COMPOSITION AND EXPRESSION

> The identity cannot be compartmentalized; it cannot be split in halves or thirds, nor have any clearly defined set of boundaries. I do not have several identities, I only have one, made of all the elements that have shaped its unique proportions. Maalouf (2000, n.p.)

Issues addressed in this chapter

This chapter starts with the difficulties of producing a valid and useful description of the structure of identity. It is driven by the Identity Process Theory approach to modelling the whole identity. Undoubtedly, any description is inherently difficult because identity is complex. But description is made more problematic because there is no consensual linguistic or mathematical code that has been developed to depict the whole structure of identity. There is no comprehensive visualisation technique that is dynamic and detailed enough to capture what is happening to allow identity to exist psychologically, inside the person, and socially, outside the person. Consequently, the tendency is for models of identity to focus on fragments of the whole. It is worthwhile having a look at some of these partial representations in this chapter in order to understand some of the issues they highlight. This will include discussing how Identity Process Theory originally figuratively depicted the identity structure and processes, and how and why these representations need to be revised. Consequently, the chapter addresses the issues of identity composition and expression from both historical and current perspectives. It outlines key aspects of the intrapsychic processes and societal processes that interact to compose an identity. It goes on to examine forms and functions of identity-expression. It also looks at the way societal processes shape the expression of identity.

Visualising identity

Most theories of identity acknowledge that the identity has more than one component, whether these components are reflecting bodily characteristics, psychological traits, or social category memberships, or something else, such as beliefs or values. The task then becomes to depict how these components relate to each other. Various approaches have been adopted that are to visualise these relationships. Typically, they are bound by the medium of their communication (in the past, usually print) and end up being two-dimensional images. They sometimes manage a third dimension. Here, some of the common types are described, primarily in order to illustrate how the representation limits what is said about the complexity and dynamism of the relationship between identity components. Types of identity representations that are used include the following:

1. Pie chart (Figure 2.1)
2. Nested concentric circles (Figure 2.2)
3. Venn diagram (Figure 2.3)
4. Cluster diagram (Figure 2.4)
5. Hierarchical figure (Figure 2.5)
6. Honeycomb chart (Figure 2.6)

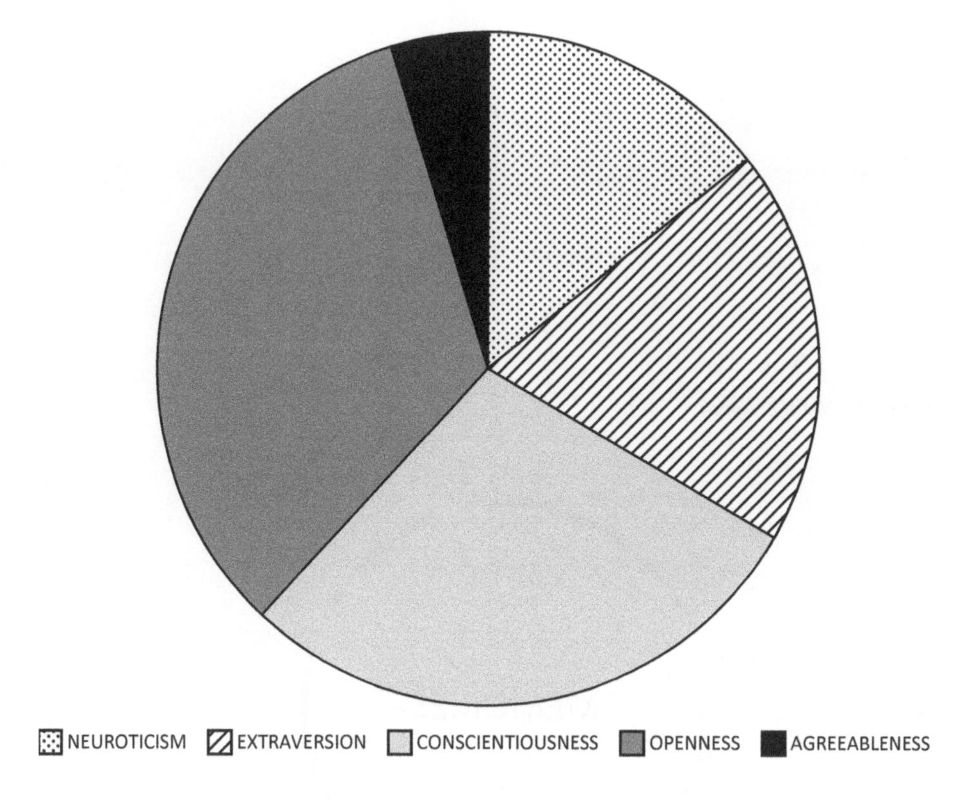

Figure 2.1 Pie chart

These illustrative figures are not taken from specific theories of identity. The identity components that are mentioned in them are included purely to reflect the broad range of concepts that are used to describe components of identity. The figures here are merely used to highlight the visualisation approaches that can be used.

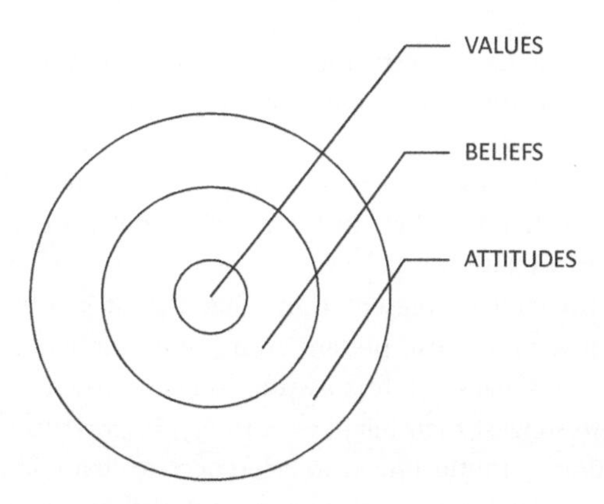

Figure 2.2 Nested concentric circles

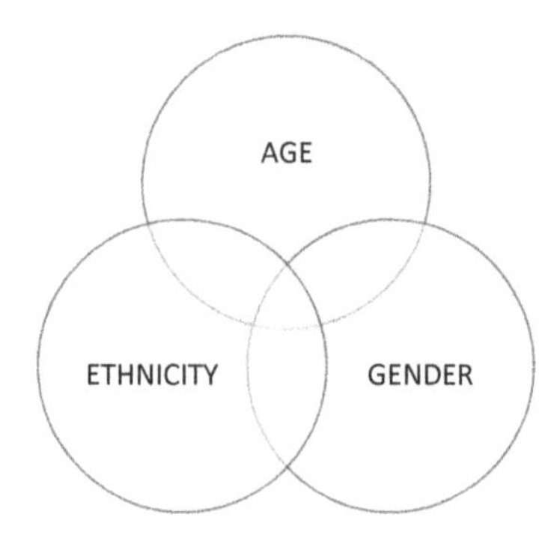

Figure 2.3 Venn diagram

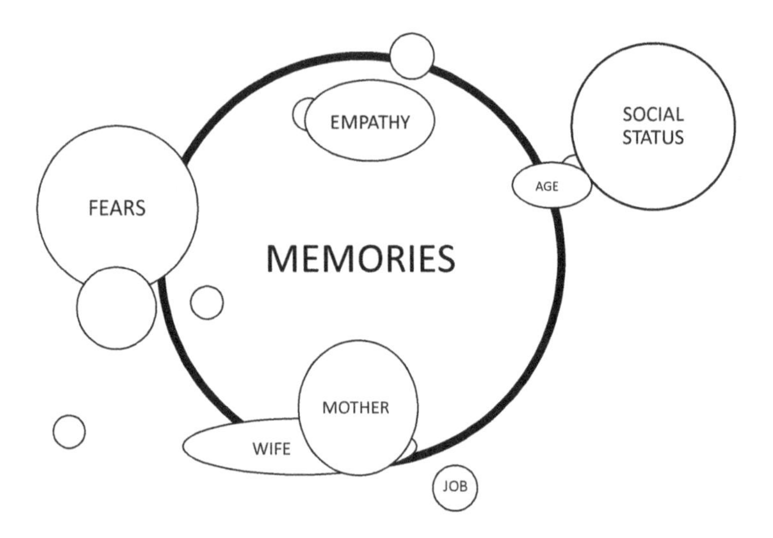

Figure 2.4 Cluster diagram

Each representation type has its own story to tell about what resides in identity. The pie chart basically tells us two things: which identity components are present and what proportion of the whole identity each component occupies. It tells us nothing about their relationships, unless size is equated with salience within the theory that underlies the representation. The position of a slice relative to others in the chart is rarely, if ever, used to indicate the nature or closeness of their relationship.

The nested concentric circles representation suggests that identity has layers of various thicknesses that encircle a core. It can present an infinite number of layers (although most often only a few layers are suggested). It is used to indicate which identity components are present but often also to suggest their relative centrality, importance, or developmental primacy. This representation is found linked to references to 'core' and 'peripheral' identity components. Again, the figure is not speaking about interactions or change in identity components. It implies no permeability of boundaries or interpenetrations.

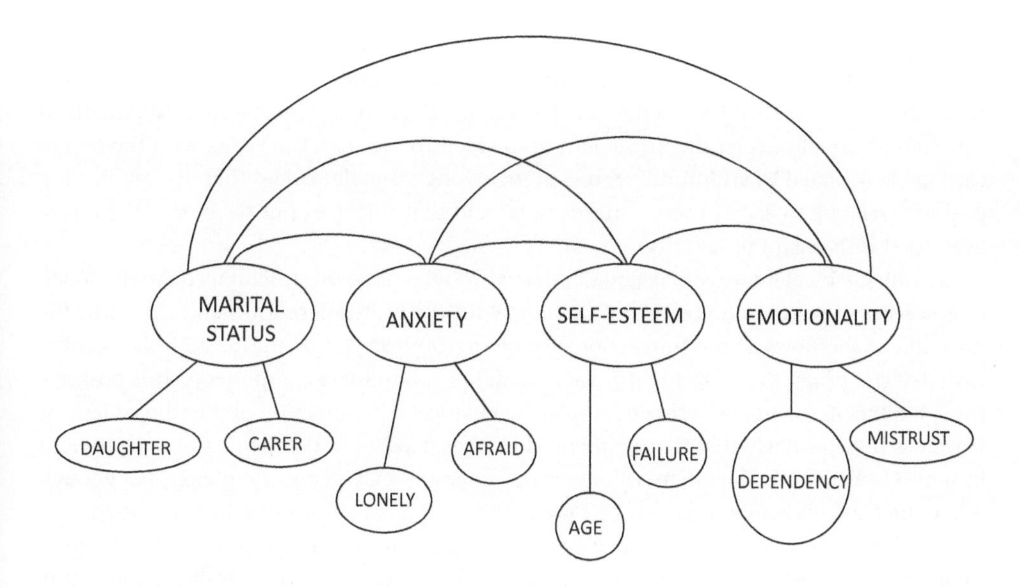

Figure 2.5 Hierarchical figure

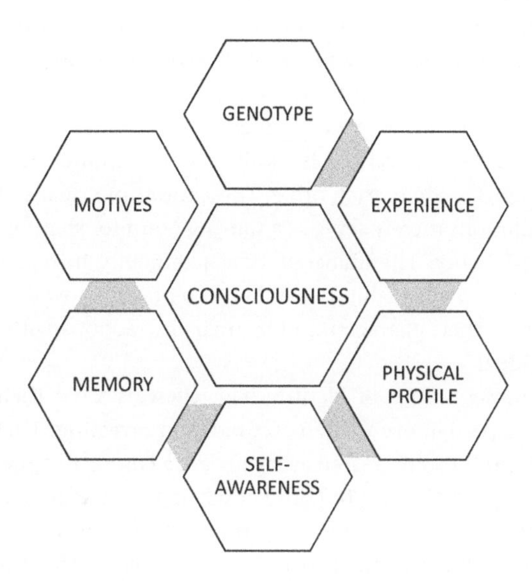

Figure 2.6 Honeycomb chart

The Venn diagram goes one step further because it depicts the overlaps between components. It can be used to show the closeness and similarity between components. The standard Venn diagram does not indicate size differences between components, but more complex versions can be constructed to do this.

The cluster diagram is more complex and more useful. The size of the circle can be used to symbolise any of a number of properties of the component (e.g., importance, stability);

the thickness of the line of the circle can be used too (e.g., permeability); the positioning of the circles can signify, for instance, their conceptual similarity, the frequency of their co-occurrence, or their interdependency. The cluster diagram is a flexible tool. Notionally, it can even be used to depict the movement of the identity through time (e.g., with the trail of each circle depicted in an infinite regress of increasingly smaller circles that occupy shifting positions relative to each other). It needs to be said that this does not seem to date to have been tried with regard to identity.

The hierarchical figure will be familiar to anyone who has used structural equation modelling. It shows the key components of the model (in the illustration, four) and can show the direction of the flows of the interactions (or influence) between them. It also indicates that each key component is a product (in some sense) of subordinate components. It is possible, though difficult, to imagine a super-complex hierarchical representation of the whole identity. However, it seems likely that this would need to be a snapshot of the identity at one moment in time. Over time, the hierarchy will inevitably change – maybe not completely, but enough to require new representations to reflect the nature of the transitions that have occurred.

The honeycomb chart is included here because it attempts to capture the sequence of influence by one identity component on another. It also can be used to indicate the nature of a 'core' property of identity (in the illustration, consciousness), which all the rest encircle. For instance, the core property can be treated as personal agency that deliberately manages the interactions of the other components of identity (like the non-volatile operating (NVO) system of a computer – the read-only memory (ROM) is an example of an NVO). Alternatively, it can be considered more akin to the accumulated product of those interactions (like the random-access memory (RAM) in a computer).

The honeycomb, like all the others, is too limited to capture the real dynamism of the way identity components relate to each other. These forms of visualisation are too static, too linear. These representations merely serve as a starting point for sharing how identity is being conceptualised in any theory. They have particular difficulty in representing how identity changes over time. They also have limited ability to represent how identity components are influenced iteratively in their character and in their interactions with each other by forces external to the individual.

Diagrammatic representations of identity have their uses but their resemblance to the thing they represent is partial, even when accurate and revealing. Their inadequacies often become a problem when they are treated as if they are a complete representation of identity. This may not be such a problem with the simpler schematics; like the caricature of a beautiful woman, they are seen to say something about their subject but not mistaken for the whole story. At one level, the problem is much greater when the representation is very complex, like the Da Vinci painting of the Mona Lisa, which seems to say so very much about its subject that it begs the viewer to believe that it captures everything that she is. An effort of will is needed to remember that it does not and needs to be treated as what it is – a rendering, fixed in time, that symbolises the woman.

When dealing with two-dimensional representations of the relationships between components of identity, it is necessary to remember:

- they are poor at representing change over time;
- they are weak at representing two-way or iterative interactions between components;

- they tend to include various types of components (e.g., personality traits, attitudes, motives, social category memberships, etc.) without indicating how they differ from each other in their substance (e.g., their origins, functions, longevity) and consequently in the role they play in the identity as a whole;
- they tend to omit how and when the external influences that affect identity have their effects upon identity components.

Hopefully, this should not matter if the theory that is represented deals with these issues in some other way; for instance, in textual explanations or using more dynamic media (e.g., immersive interactive virtual reality platforms). It would be easier, of course, if we had an agreed language for representing identity, especially if we had mathematical tools that would permit the dynamics of identity to be captured. It really is important for identity theorists to get better at creating virtual, interactive models of both identity structures and processes. It is frustrating that science can give us dynamic visualisations of the movement of the asteroid Vesta, of the shifting lunar surface, and of the landing of the Perseverance rover at the Jezero Crater on Mars, and we have made so little progress in mapping and representing identity systems. Of course, as an astrophysicist friend once said to me, identity is more complex than the solar system. She could have added something about black holes as well. But there is no need to despair. The enormous growth of information sources and data on human beings means that sophisticated models of identity processes will be produced eventually.

Diagrammatic representations of Identity Process Theory

The basic structures

Before looking at the diagrammatic or schematic representations of Identity Process Theory, an outline of what it says about the structure of identity is necessary. IPT acknowledges that the capacities for memory, consciousness, and organised construal that are characteristic of the biological organism are the foundations for identity structure. Since the biological organism changes across the life course, it has to be acknowledged, and included in representations of identity structure, throughout. From its inception, IPT spoke of the identity structure as having two planes: the content dimension and the value dimension. The content dimension consists of the characteristics which define identity: all the properties, psychological and social, which, taken as a constellation, mark the individual as unique. The content dimension has structural features. The relationships between its components were initially described in terms of:

- the degree of centrality of each component;
- the hierarchical arrangements of its components;
- the relative salience of components.

More recent developments of the theory have suggested that there are other structural features that should be considered; for instance, the relative permanence or transience of components and the authenticity of components.

The organisation of identity components is not static and is responsive to changes in various sources, including:

- the person's attempts to assimilate and accommodate new components;
- changes in the demands on the individual from the social context regarding the expression of identity; variation in circumstances may mean an identity component becomes more or less salient (maybe temporarily);
- changes in the cognitive or conative capacity of the individual to maintain the prior organisation of identity components.

In addition, IPT proposes that the individual is continually managing the organisation of identity content to optimise it in terms of certain preferred states (IPT refers to the motives driving this as *identity principles*, which are described in detail later). The important point here is that IPT assumes agency on the part of the individual. They are the artist painting their own identity, even though they have forces bearing upon them that will change the oils they have available and the steadiness of their brushstrokes.

Each component in the content dimension of identity has some subjective value attached to it on a positive–negative spectrum. Taken together, these evaluations constitute the value dimension of identity. The value of each component will change as:

- its position or function in the organisation of the whole identity shifts;
- the social value attributed to the component changes;
- the individual's position in relation to such social value systems is modified, making the meaning of its values for the individual different.

The actual relative contribution that any one identity component makes to the value dimension is difficult to gauge. No simple mathematical weighting formula has been proposed from IPT. Of course, for any one individual, at any one time, it is possible empirically to assess how each component is valued and how these values relate to the individual's general self-assessment of identity value. It would be interesting to do this for a large sample of people with repeated measures longitudinally. Research that has been done on coping strategies when the value of an identity component is challenged with being eroded suggests that a marked decline in the value of one component can have a disproportionate impact on the self-evaluation of the whole identity or there can be compensatory re-evaluation of other components and no reduction in the value of the whole.

However, these issues of the relationship between the value of a component and the value of the whole identity need further investigation. What can be said is that the value dimension itself is a dynamic property of the identity as a whole. It may even be inappropriate to expect to be able to give it a single score on one metric. The original formulation of IPT did not consider this. The way the sum value of identity to the individual at any one time is constituted does need much further research. Some of the factors that need to be considered are raised below when discussing the figurative representation of IPT.

Since IPT is a theory which builds the role of social context into the model, it is necessary to include here a mention of the assumptions that it makes about the social structure. These assumptions are limited, but they have always been present in the diagrams used to describe the model. As far as the individual is concerned, IPT describes social context as comprising interpersonal networks, group and social category memberships, and intergroup relationships. Clearly, theories that are primarily concerned with social structure offer far more detail about its elements. It is notable that the research literature that has evolved around IPT, especially recently, has been re-examining the features of the social context that need to be considered in detail. We will return to this in subsequent chapters when dealing with the effects of social support, public crises, and group dynamics on identity.

The basic processes

The original diagrams representing the IPT model of identity included two types of processes: those operating at the intra-psychic level and those operating at the interpersonal and societal level.

At *the intra-psychic level*, the structure of identity is established by the dynamic processes of accommodation-assimilation and evaluation. The accommodation-assimilation process entails the absorption of new components into the identity structure. The accommodation process entails the adjustment of the existing structure in order to reconcile it either to the introduction of new components or to respond to modifications in the external demands being made on the identity (e.g., if circumstances change so as to make a particular component of identity undesirable or unsustainable).

Accommodation-assimilation is an information-processing and storage system that is mandated to serve the motives that drive identity construction and maintenance (the 'identity principles' mentioned earlier). It is consequently selective. It not only adds new material to the identity structure and reorganises what is already there, it can also delete or alter what is already there. It is a logical possibility that it can also fail to admit new material. In this sense, accommodation-assimilation can be considered not just a compiler but also a censor working to established rules. The censorship role of accommodation-assimilation was not to the fore in the early work on IPT, but it has become increasingly apparent that this is an important part of its activity. People do refuse to accept and will eject identity components that would damage the identity as a whole.

It is evident from this that the accommodation-assimilation process works hand in hand with the second of the intra-psychic processes, the evaluation process. The process of evaluation entails the allocation of meaning and value to identity components, new and old. Like the accommodation-assimilation process, it also is guided by the identity principles that define desirable states for the value as well as the structure of identity. However, the evaluation process is also guided by factors external to the individual; by the standards of identity worth which are established by that individual's society. The evaluation process is an important interface between the individual and society.

The two intra-psychic processes are conceptually distinct but, in practice, they are inseparable. No identity component can be value neutral. The value allocated to a component will both affect where it is located in the identity structure by accommodation-assimilation and will be affected by each new position it has in that structure. The value of an identity component will thus inevitably change to some extent over time because accommodation-assimilation is continual and change in the identity structure is the norm. It will also change because societal standards applied to the evaluation of identity worth will vary over time. The value it has when it was first assimilated may inflate or collapse, rather like the value of a share in a stock market. It is notable that such changes in value are particularly important, or, at least, noticeable developmentally. This is probably most evident in transitions during adolescence, led both by physical changes in the body and by changes in an individual's social status. The more we understand the evaluation process, the more we recognise how complex the value dimension of identity composition is.

At *the interpersonal and societal level*, the many processes that operate to shape identity can be given a generic label, social influence. Social influence processes (e.g., education, propaganda, religion, politics, peer expectations, social media messaging, etc.) establish, channel and direct systems of values and beliefs that are communicated in social representations, norms, and attributions. Such social influence processes build the ideological milieu in which an identity is composed and expressed. Recent developments of IPT have been particularly concerned with the interactions between social influence processes, particularly social representational processes and identity processes. These developments are considered in later chapters.

Basic diagrammatic representations of the IPT model

The original diagrammatic representations of the structure of identity (Breakwell, 1986) were attempts to create an image of growth of identity over the lifetime, acknowledging the continuing role that the characteristics of the biological organism play and encompassing the influence of the social context. Figure 2.7 is an amalgam of three figures used originally to represent elements of the IPT model. It tries to capture the dynamic development of the individual's identity through the lifetime within social time. The individual's identity structure is represented by the central object that is outlined with greater weight. The image is two-dimensional but attempts to signal the growth of the content and value of the identity structure over time, the omnipresence of the processes of assimilation-accommodation (through which identity content is captured and arranged as part of the ongoing identity configuration) and evaluation (through which identity content is allocated value and, more broadly, psychological meaningfulness). Figure 2.7 is designed to indicate that these two processes are dependent on social influence processes and available ideologies, and societal structures (such as interpersonal networks or intergroup relations). The bi-directional arrows are there to acknowledge that individuals, in interacting with the social context that surrounds them, while they are influenced by it, are also playing their part in creating that social context.

Such an attempt to visualise some of the basic tenets of IPT is certainly inadequate now, and probably was at the time it was first proposed. It may have been better to stay with textual descriptions of the dynamism of the identity system. Referring to it as an identity system, rather than just an identity, is also probably apt. IPT was never about the composition of identity alone; it has always been about the psychological and social processes that plant, tend, and threaten an individual identity in a society filled with other unique identities. It seems that is it actually possible to surface many features of a theory by examining the weaknesses in the basic diagrammatic representations of it. It is important not to let the diagram supplant or trammel the underlying theory.

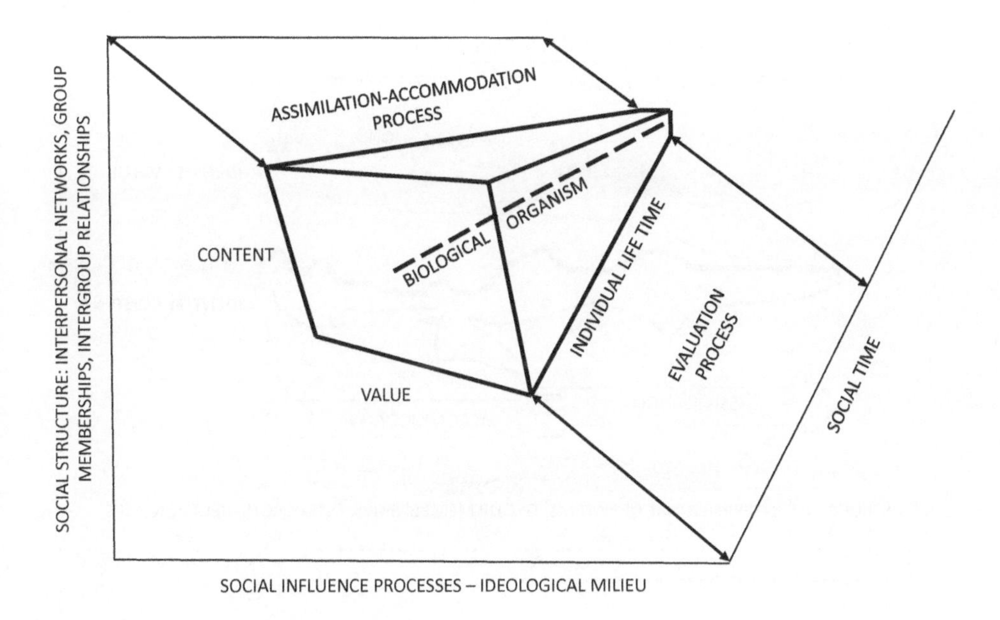

Figure 2.7 Identity Process Theory (1986)

Another representation of the IPT model

IPT has developed since 1986 on a number of fronts and some of these are described in detail in later chapters. However, it has not found a particularly effective diagrammatic representation of its main arguments. Given that such diagrams often serve less as an accurate exposition of a theory and more as a memorable image to symbolise the theory, it may be sensible to design one now. Figure 2.8 is an attempt to condense the initial theory into a single graphic.

The new diagram has a certain chaotic quality. It may not be as memorable as one might wish. It is certainly not what one expects to see in a psychology diagram. However, it does some things that its predecessors failed to do:

- The biological organism is indicated as an erratic undulating line to symbolise that it does not continue as the same structure throughout and does experience changes that can be linked to modifications in the content and value dimensions of identity.
- The content of identity does not simply grow bigger over time – there can be erosion/excision/retrenchment of identity components – and the content line does not simply move forward in one direction – there can be revisiting/reprising of earlier identity components to change the way they are accommodated in the newly developing identity structure.
- The value of identity similarly is not assumed to have a simple trajectory. One issue with using a single line to represent identity value is that it suggests we are dealing with moves in the aggregate value of the whole identity over time. That does not

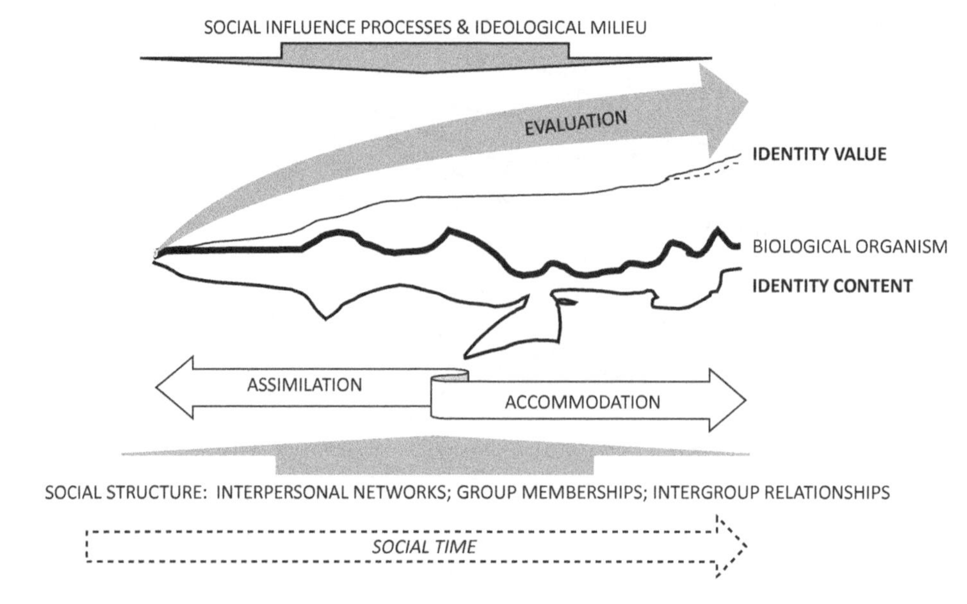

Figure 2.8 Identity Process Theory (1986) revisited

capture the possibility that a single aggregate value is meaningless because the individual is simultaneously harbouring several evaluations of identity. This possibility is acknowledged in the diagram with the dashed line that appears across the latter half of the value line.

- The theory proposes that two processes are ongoing perpetually: evaluation of identity contents, and assimilation of and accommodation to identity contents. The new diagram suggests that through the life course the evaluation process gets bigger (i.e., more elaborated and sophisticated as the person develops cognitively and emotionally; and having to deal with more inputs as the person is exposed to more diverse experiences). The evaluation process does not just provide a value for current identity, because to do that in a way that produces an acceptable and satisfying result for the individual will often mean amending the values attached to earlier identity content. Similarly, it suggests that the assimilation-accommodation process needs to operate concurrently across identity content from the entire life course. The process will be adjusting the identity content configuration retrospectively as well as contemporaneously. The complexities of these two processes will be revisited in later chapters more fully.
- The diagram pinpoints the importance of social influence processes and social structures. It is meant to suggest that they are continually at work through the construction and maintenance of identity since they are inevitable constituents of the social context. It is necessary later to consider the way social structures and social influences interact. This is particularly important as social influencing has moved also to work outside traditional social structure channels and into a virtual world.

The advantages of this diagram for representing IPT is that it blows away the idea that a model of identity composition and development can be both dynamic and tidy. It is still a 2-D diagram that relies on the textual interpretation accompanying it. It is a compromise representation waiting to be supplanted by some medium of communication that can be more dynamic. Nevertheless, it transmits quite a few messages about the composition of identity. The rest of this chapter seeks to elaborate further on some of the key ingredients that are signposted in the diagram. At the end of this book, in Chapter 10, there is another diagram which represents the IPT model as it was formulated in 2022, reflecting some of the significant evolution and adaptation of the theory that is described in the course of this book.

Dynamics of identity composition and expression

Composition

IPT does not specify the substance of the actual identity components. It says they are derived from life experiences, mediated by perception and cognition, and embodied in self-awareness. It allows that they will come in many forms (e.g., beliefs, values, attitudes, social roles, group memberships) and many labels (e.g., traits, habits). It notes that identity components are defined in different ways in different cultures and that identity components will change as the person grows from baby to old age. However, IPT does not propose that cultural or developmental variations change the underlying dimensions of the identity structure (i.e., content and evaluation), nor does it assume that they change the identity processes (assimilation-accommodation and evaluation). Nevertheless, IPT does argue that culture may influence the nature of the identity principles that motivate and target these principles.

Detailing the actual composition of identity in terms of individual components has been seen in IPT research to be an empirical exercise. The theoretical task has been to describe the processes whereby the identity composition or structure is created and renovated. The specific substance of the identity component has been regarded as important only in so far as it impacts on the way these processes operate.

This approach in IPT should be seen in the context of the important work of many theorists who have sought to describe the actual constituents of the content dimension of identity. Early theorists mapped the constituent parts of the self, rather than talking about identity, although it does appear that they were concerned with the entity that is here called the whole identity. William James (1890), who was heavily influenced by the works of Descartes, Hume, Locke, Kant, and Schopenhauer, among others, distinguished between the self as subject (the I) and the self as object (the me) but stated that they are merely discriminated aspects of the singularity of the process of experience which comprises the 'global self'. James' way of identifying the components of the global self was to differentiate within it types of self: the spiritual self (entailing thinking and feeling); the material self (entailing one's possessions); the social self (entailing reference to those individuals or groups whose opinions matter); and the bodily self (entailing the physical organism). Essentially, James was detailing what Allport (1955, p. 38) called 'all the regions of our life that we regard as ultimately and essentially ours'.

James was not simply concerned with listing types of self. He was interested in how these selves are experienced. He argued that the process of knowing or experiencing these distinguishing features of the global self was inextricably bound to the process of evaluating them. Furthermore, according to James, the value of any aspect of self can only be understood in relation to the person's pretensions. Such pretensions are basically described as the aspirations or expectations which establish how the person judges success or failure. It seems that James is expressing the existence of the complex dynamic between the content and value dimensions of the global self. He is also indicating that the way content and value is established and experienced is determined in part by the end states for the global self that the person is motivated to achieve. This assumption is echoed in IPT in the proposed role of the identity principles.

While the IPT model of the 'whole identity' owes a lot to the thinking of James and his successors (particularly, Mead, 1910; Mead & Mind, 1934), it has abandoned the search for a definitive list of different types of self or of identity. Of course, looking for types of identity is different from looking for components of identity. The components of the whole identity are not treated in IPT as identities in themselves. However, it is commonplace in social psychology research currently to talk about a person having multiple identities. Typically, in such work, an identity is equated with a role (e.g., being a spouse) or a social category membership (e.g., being a pensioner) occupied by the individual. Much of the interest in the multiplicity of identities revolves around the way they relate to each other (Graumann, 1983) and how this can change when circumstances change (Brewer, 1999; Josselson & Harway, 2012). This focus on multiple identities has largely been informed by Social Identity Theory. However, there has been little progress in building a general theory that explains how the phenomena of multiple identities can be modelled separately from seeing their role in the whole identity (having just described James' global self, it is tempting to call this the global identity). Once one starts to model their role in the whole identity, they may as well be called components of that identity rather than identities in their own right.

The work that has been done on multiple identities has been useful in highlighting how important it is not only to examine the individual components of the whole identity as separate features; it is also important to examine their interactions with each other. These changing patterns of interactions are fundamental in the production of a unique identity. Even if the components in two identities were actually the same (and the probability of this tends to infinity), then the way in which they interact with each other, and with their social context, could still differ. The uniqueness of an identity grows from the multiplicity of its component parts.

In emphasising the assimilation-accommodation process, IPT has always pointed to the significance of this dynamic relationship between identity components. In describing the way that the identity principles motivate and direct the assimilation-accommodation and evaluation processes, IPT is also indicating how the relationships between identity components are determined. Further, IPT postulates that social structures and social influence processes impact on the intra-psychic processes, and, thus, on the interactions between identity components. This suggests that IPT may be useful in reinterpreting the findings of research on multiple identities – as long as they can be treated as components of the whole identity.

Expression

In some respects, everything we do is an expression of some component of our identity. But it is worth thinking about the different types of expression. There are three primary categories:

- Intended

This category of identity-expression covers deliberate efforts to communicate something about your identity. It can be explicit or implicit in something you say or do (or refrain from saying or doing). The representation of identity (referred to here as the identity image) that you express is most likely to be just a small fragment of your whole identity. It may not be even all of one component of your identity. It may be an amalgam of more than one fragment from different components of your identity. Intended identity-expressions are usually targeted at chosen audiences and are designed to yield particular effects. Sometimes the audience is primarily oneself, rather than other people. We will return later to the various sorts of function served by identity-expression.

Take an example of intended identity-expression: you are to meet a prospective employer, you want her to recognise that you are qualified for the job, reliable, well-organised, a leader of people; you marshal the evidence (your educational record, your proofs of past achievements in other jobs, you work out how you can casually mention that you have a lot of experience working in teams and enjoy it, but especially when you can be in charge, etc.); and you present the evidence through various media (the certificates of courses completed, glowing references from previous employers, you arrive on time and well-dressed, you illustrate your identity through the content of what you say and the way that you say it, and through your body language, your background, and your projected self-assurance).

You might argue that the example is a very structured situation where all participants know the rules of the game that they are playing. The interviewee is expected to be calculating in identity disclosure or identity claims. The interviewer is primed to judge how much to take at face value. The interview may develop into an arena where the two players spar to thrash out or negotiate the 'real' identity of the candidate. Real in this context means the version that the two players are willing to acknowledge for the purposes of their business together. More often, an interview will not get that far. The interviewer does not fully reveal how far she is persuaded about the identity image that is being paraded before her.

Intentional expressions of identity are often expected in ritualised or habitual social contexts (e.g., at large family gatherings, at a sports competition, or when building new relationships). Indeed, the social context usually will alert you to which bits of your identity need to be presented and the ways in which you should express them. For instance, at large family gatherings you might be expected to express how you are a good daughter, a high achiever in college, and a bit of a rebel. Failing to deliver the identity-expression expected can make you and/or others feel uncomfortable, uncertain, even threatened.

There are sophisticated systems of social norms and expectations that exist to delimit the appropriate expression of identity. These rules are learnt early and elaborated throughout life as experiences become more varied and demanding. It could be argued that the start of this learning is coterminous with the growth of self-awareness that was discussed in Chapter 1.

As you become self-aware, you also become aware of the expectations that other people (notably parents) have about the way you should show self-awareness. This establishes an alertness to the social cues that signal what forms of identity-expression are accepted. Knowing the rules of identity-expression that apply in your own era and culture (or the culture in which you reside at any one time) is at the heart of achieving your intended goals whenever you decide to present an identity image. Successful intentional identity-expression is also dependent upon having developed a good working theory of mind. You need to be able to imagine how other people see you, and how they make sense of, and will evaluate, the identity components that you present to them. Intentional identity-expression is a complex business. Three issues need to be considered:

1. First, even at its most complex, it will be partial. The whole identity cannot normally be served up at one sitting. Components of the identity may be expressed serially and slowly over time in the context of long-term relationships. Simultaneously, the identity is changing, so the characteristics that are expressed at one time may be attributed a different meaning at another time. The entity that is being expressed is itself changing. What's more, the act of expressing it may also initiate change in it. Notably this occurs when the reaction aroused by the identity-expression is not the one expected or desired.
2. Second, an inaccuracy in the image of one or more identity components may be embedded in the identity-expression. The inaccuracy may be deliberate or unintentional. Inaccuracies in identity-expression can be motivated by the same identity principles that direct the assimilation-accommodation and evaluation processes. The inaccuracy usually entails the omission of some feature of one's identity that would be negatively evaluated by the audience. But inaccuracies can be the product of ongoing reinterpretations or change in the identity structure and value dimensions. In this case, the audience is misled because the identity-expression is lagging behind, or alternatively anticipating, the evolution of the identity. This possibility highlights the fact that the individual may not know how to express accurately the complexities of a changing identity. The nature of inaccuracies in identity-expression has to be revisited in a later chapter where identity failure is considered.
3. Third, intentional identity-expression sometimes involves deliberate fabrication. The person delivers a narrative of his or her identity which is doctored to achieve particular effects. People do this sometimes for the effects it has on themselves as much as for the effects it has on other people. These fabrications can be elaborate. Sometimes, the identity portrayed represents an alter ego, an alternative version of the persona. For the individual, acting out, or embodying, this expression of an alternative identity can be enormously important. It is not in existence just to fool others; it exists to allow the individual to cope with threat to their basic identity. There are some interesting cases of well-known musicians who present an alter ego when they go on stage (see Anderson, 2022). Alter egos may function in different ways for different artists. They may act as a mask that draws the line between the artist and their work. For instance, David Bowie, through various alter egos, most notably the intergalactic alien rock star Ziggy Stardust, explored and shared his perceptions

of his own life while distancing himself from it. Alter egos may also provide a certain freedom for breaking away from earlier identity images and asserting change. For instance, in 2008, Beyoncé, who had already achieved acclaim as a member of the band Destiny's Child and as a solo artist, sought to express what she called her more sensual, more aggressive, more outspoken, and more glamourous side. She created Sasha Fierce to do this, and by 2016 her album 'I am ... Sasha Fierce' had sold 8 million copies worldwide. This alter ego represented a staging post. By 2010, Beyoncé was able to move on to present an expression of her identity with the characteristics of Fierce as an integral part, assimilated and accommodated.

4. Fourth, at first sight, you may think that the creation of elaborate alter egos is the preserve of the rich and famous who live in communities and work in jobs that permit (and sometimes reward and even demand) such fabrications. However, the digital age has opened up possibilities for almost anyone to present some component of a faked identity to other people online. The expression of identity digitally is considered later in this chapter.

- Incidental

Identity-expression does not necessarily have a preordained target audience. Incidental identity-expression happens as a minor accompaniment to something else. It occurs when you are about your business, not engaged in intentional efforts to communicate any particular thing about your identity, but something you do or say makes someone else realise something about your identity. Usually, this involves behavioural cues to identity. This could be having a recognisable regional or national accent. If you do, as soon as you speak, a probable part of your identity is signalled (as long as your listener knows what the accent indicates). Displaying a noticeable habit could act in the same way. For instance, regularly carrying the latest copy of the *Racing Times* could suggest you are a gambler (or a racehorse owner). Other habits reveal state of mind, rather than social roles or statuses. For instance, when sitting in a public space being restless, fidgeting, or continually watching the door, or the clock over it, it can be perceived as indicating anxiety or fear. If this behaviour was habitual rather than specific to a particular occasion, it might be seen as indicating a trait. Reading the cues to identity that are made available incidentally varies in difficulty. Some cues need minor detective skills (such as when someone arrives wearing the sweatshirt of the university they attended). Some cues are more subtle. For instance, not talking about one's family or childhood can speak volumes. Omitting to say or do something can reveal identity to those who are attuned to the significance of evasion or avoidance.

It is evident that incidental identity-expression depends very much upon the motivation and skills of the audience. People vary in their sensitivity to such incidental identity-expression. However, because understanding the identities of others with whom you interact is so important to being successful in interacting with them, people are usually alert to incidental identity images. In addition, there are strong stereotypes in any culture that focus them on some incidental identity cues (such as accent, type of clothing, food preferences, religious emblems, expenditure patterns, or friendship networks). Subtle incidental clues to identity may be missed but those linked to social stereotypes are hard to ignore.

Since some incidental clues to identity do tend to be linked to commonly understood stereotypes and implicit theories of personality, it must also be assumed that the person providing these incidental expressions of identity will know how they are likely to be interpreted. For example, if my accent is associated with people from a working-class background, I am unlikely not to know that. I will realise that my accent will imply my class, and possibly the region where I grew up. If I do, and yet I still retain that accent, it could be argued that, by doing so, I am actually choosing to disclose some components of my identity. It could just mean, of course, that I do not care if they are disclosed, and I deliberately choose not to hide them. Not vetting the availability of incidental clues to one's identity can thus become a form of self-aware identity-expression. Put like that, it makes what is regarded as intentional or incidental identity-expression a matter of interpretation of the specific circumstances in which it occurs.

Incidental identity-expressions may also be treated by an audience as revealing some of the more authentic or 'real' identity components because they are believed not to be shared deliberately. They can consequently be given greater credence and weight. This may be a mistake. Unless they are independently verified, the conclusions drawn from incidental identity clues can be very misleading. In this case, the individual is not deliberately faking an identity; the error (if there is one) lies in the inferences that the perceivers make.

- Accidental

This category of identity-expression occurs without deliberate intent and is not incidental to some other activity. It is an identity image which is expressed by chance or unexpectedly. It may be something that the individual has hidden previously that in error is revealed. It can be something of which the individual has not previously become conscious. For now, ignore the possibility that this is a motivated error such as what has been called a Freudian slip (in psychoanalysis, a Freudian slip, also called parapraxis, is an error in speech, memory, or physical action that occurs due to the interference of an unconscious, subdued wish, or internal train of thought (Freud, 2021)).

An accidental expression of identity can be a minor affair if the identity component revealed is not deemed to be significant by the identity principles that motivate the processes of assimilation-accommodation and evaluation. However, it can be very dangerous or damaging. This is most evident where an individual has kept part of what he knows about himself completely hidden. He has chosen not to express it to others. This is more frequent than might be suspected when the hidden component of identity is subject to social opprobrium or shaming. In some cultures, in some time periods, this might apply to suffering a mental illness (Corrigan et al., 2014) or to being LGBTQ+ (Parker et al., 2018). It is hard to envisage how a component of identity that has been long-hidden, but which is invested with great psychological importance, can be accidentally expressed. Of course, it may happen if the individual misunderstands the beliefs or value system of the audience. The accident then amounts to making the mistake of telling the wrong people. It can also happen if the identity-expression was never meant to be available to any but a very narrow audience but was then accidentally released more generally. This is easier now because of the existence of social media platforms. The danger of such accidental identity-expressions is vested in a number of factors: it is not planned or anticipated and the individual cannot prepare thoroughly for the likely effects it has on others; something previously deliberately hidden, once public, is more likely to evoke an aggressive rejection or some other negative reaction; and the position of the revealed component within the identity composition is changed by the revelation and accommodations must be made, probably quickly and against a condemnatory backdrop.

Primary functions of identity-expression

The three types of identity-expression have different effects on the person and on the audience involved. Identity-expression is not usually purely an individual process. It is fundamentally dependent on there being a language of identity-expression that is shared, promulgated through processes of social influence. Identity-expression effectively has two audiences: the person whose identity is expressed and the people who receive the identity image that has been portrayed. Moreover, these two audiences in effect co-produce the identity image that is crystallised through their interaction.

The primary functions for the individual of engaging in identity-expression are to gain authentication from the audience for the identity claims made; to understand how the identity as expressed is evaluated by the audience and, thus, to learn how to ascribe value to the identity components; to learn what different opportunities for identity development might be available or socially condoned; and to establish their specific position in a social context and to gauge what challenges are associated with that position.

The primary functions for the people receiving the identity image are to have an opportunity to shape future identity development and, thus, the position and contribution of the individual in their social context; to gain feedback on their own effectiveness in influencing sustainable identity management; and to gauge the extent to which the individual is similar to others in their social context. The functionality of the identity-expression process for the receiving audience is enhanced when what an individual presents is then pooled with identity-expressions from others. It becomes a way of testing the stability of relationships within the social context. Where the identity-expression is essentially between two people interacting, rather than involving a larger group, the function for both is more likely to involve a mutual exchange of identity images. Both see it as an opportunity for identity verification and support. Of course, this does not always materialise and is dependent on the initial motives of those involved. We return to this in Chapter 4, which discusses some of the ways social support structures work to stabilise, secure, and develop identities.

Besides these primary functions, identity-expression has other purposes. One needs to be mentioned here and it has to do with imagination. Charles Horton Cooley (1902) coined the label 'the Looking Glass Self' to describe our reflection of how we think we appear to others. Social interaction acts as a mirror that offers us the wherewithal to imagine how others are perceiving our identity. It also allows us to imagine how they feel about us because of what they think about our identity. The 'Looking Glass Self' analogy is actually misleading. Unlike the mirror image we see of ourselves on the bathroom cabinet door, social interaction provides us with an identity image that is permeated by our imagination and our own identity motives. We are capable of seeing what we wish to see in the response of others to us. Discounting the feedback from others about our identity-expression is an important part of protecting the stability of identity in stressful or challenging social contexts.

In fact, identity-expression can be used even when a negative response from an audience is anticipated. In some contexts, continuing to present an identity component despite knowing that there will be rejection is itself a very forceful affirmation of the importance of that aspect for the identity as a whole. When viewed in this way, the function of identity-expression as a potential means of social or interpersonal protest is clearly evident. Identity-expression is not inevitably a search for social verification. It can be an attack on discrimination, or any other form of social degradation. Such identity-expressions often have an important function in bringing about social change.

Psychologists in the past have often talked about the way seeing ourselves as other people see us (or 'taking the role of the other'; Mead, 1910) conditions our view of our own identity. Too little attention has been paid to the possibility that 'having taken the role of the other' we decide it is unjustified and choose to dismiss it. The likelihood of this happening increases significantly as the number of arenas in which identity can be expressed grows. When there are a variety of audiences for identity-expression available, it is possible that there will be differences in their reactions to the identity image presented. Where audience reactions are inconsistent or incompatible with each other, the scope for the individual to exercise choice and some imaginative concatenation grows.

Identity-expression in cyberspace

A century ago, the issue of multiple audiences for identity-expression was not perhaps as significant as it became in the social media era. There has been a fascinating, burgeoning literature on identity-expression in cyberspace (e.g., Kaakinen et al., 2020; Warburton, 2012). The availability of the digital world changes the whole social contract that surrounded erstwhile identity-expression.

Cyberspace allows you greater power over the choice of your audience and the form of the feedback it gives you. The cyber environment allows relatively unfettered claims to be made about identity. You can change your age, gender, ethnicity, geographical location, tastes, attitudes, family background, education qualifications, fears, and loves (and the list could go on). One function of expressing a cyber alter ego is to test what might be the reaction to it. It is a low social-cost experiment. You can run several such alternative identities simultaneously (if you have the time and patience). It can become a sort of game with an infinite number of anonymous (or pseudonymous) players. The rules on some social media platforms may limit the expression of some identity images, but there is still enormous scope for flights of fancy. Acknowledging the minor airbrushing out of physical or personality flaws, it is actually interesting that mostly the identity-expressions that appear online are ordinary enough to appear attempts at accurate self-description.

There is a question about the relationship between such cyber alter egos and the non-cyber identity. There can be effects of expressing a cyber identity on the self-awareness and the evaluation of the non-cyber identity. For instance, in the most extreme cases, the distinction between the cyber and non-cyber identities can become blurred (Wang et al., 2019). Also, when a cyber alter ego is greeted with praise by the audience, it may undermine the value of the non-cyber identity. In so far as activity in cyberspace is a low-risk opportunity to experiment with identity-expression, it can also stimulate new identity assimilation and accommodation. For instance, professing that you possess a radical political belief system on social media may start as a fake or lie, but the process of presenting it, interacting about it, and, perhaps, going through the motions of defending it, can encourage you to accept it as an actual component of your identity. A strange sort of self-persuasion can occur. There is a venerable literature in social psychology on persuasion that shows that arguing a case in public that is counter to your own beliefs is likely to see you shift your own beliefs towards the position that you have been told to adopt (Cialdini, 2001a). Most fake facts about identity that a person proselytises, whether in person or digitally, can initiate some degree of self-persuasion and the consequent possibility of identity change.

The role of social media in identity-expression is now much more complex than just as a forum for the presentation of alter egos and fake personas. Efforts to present what one believes to be a genuine reflection of one's own identity are common. Social media offer unending space-time for self-revelation. Virtually every aspect of one's thoughts, feelings and actions can be recorded and transmitted. The instantaneous and simultaneous transmission to varied audiences makes this very different from earlier forms of identity-expression. There is also less opportunity for the representation of identity to be accompanied by the specific interpretation that is preferred by the sender.

Consequently, the negotiation of identity via social media is very different from that occurring face to face or through more linear channels. The identity image created, while initially in the individual's control, is soon at the disposal of myriad users. The misuse and abuse of identity revelations on the internet is a very real threat to the non-cyber identity. It is an arena where incidental and accidental identity-expressions can be very costly because they are attributed meaning by many audiences, and most of these have no reason to be kind or caring in their interpretations. Any rules that have been constructed by societies to ensure mutuality, reciprocity, confidentiality, or the use of agreed identity symbols, have not been predictably transposed into cyberspace. Therefore, there is a stressful fluidity about the types of negotiation that can take place between the sender and receivers of the identity-expression. One consequence may be that the sender gets on a never-ending treadmill of continuing identity explanation and revelation while in parallel seeking to reconfigure and re-evaluate the identity itself.

Never completely voluntary; never totally determined

In closing this chapter, it is worth emphasising that the individual is not spontaneously or voluntarily undertaking identity composition and identity-expression. These processes are never in the conscious control of the individual. An identity is a societal requirement. Identity has functions to serve for society, just as it has functions to serve for the individual that it marks as unique. Social processes, which start to have an impact on the foetus before birth, influence what composition that identity will have and what expressions it will be allowed. Social influence processes and social structure, mediated often through material contexts, will establish the context within which the individual will construct an identity that is unique and built to be shared. Identity Process Theory stresses that there is not even a hint of determinism hidden in this assertion. Individuals have agency. Their biological makeup readies them for active construal of their surroundings and provides the foundations for self-awareness. The complexity of the social world in which they live offers ample opportunity for individual choice and self-determination in identity creation and maintenance. However, people will differ in the extent to which they can be resilient and maintain their identity when threatened. The next chapter deals with identity resilience.

3

IDENTITY RESILIENCE

You may not control all the events that happen to you, but you can decide not to be reduced by them. Maya Angelou, *Letter to My Daughter* (2008)

Issues addressed in this chapter

Some people prove themselves more able to cope with stress and challenge than do others. In part, this is because people differ in the level of their identity resilience. In this chapter, we explore the psychological foundations of identity resilience. Essentially, the chapter is concerned with how people manage identity stability and change. It starts by describing the identity principles, proposed in Identity Process Theory, that motivate and direct the processes of assimilation-accommodation and evaluation that construct a unique and wholistic identity. It considers how and why these identity principles have developed to serve societal and personal functions. It examines how complying with these identity principles results in an identity content and value that is resilient. The implications of variations in identity reliance for thought, feeling, and action are illustrated.

What is identity resilience?

Identity resilience has two facets, and both should be part of its definition. Identity resilience refers to the ability of a person's existing identity structure to retain its integrity and worth when experiencing threats that challenge its constitution or value. At the same time, identity resilience refers to the effects that having such an identity can have on the individual's thoughts, feelings, and actions when faced with other types of threat that are not specifically or immediately directed at identity itself. Thus, a resilient identity protects itself but also supports more broadly better adaptation to threats or stressors of all sorts. In effect, it is a classic example of the virtuous circle: what benefits the identity, benefits the person.

Having identity resilience is not dependent on the individual refusing or resisting identity change. It is about the individual seeking continually, under all circumstances, to minimise identity damage and to optimise identity adaptation. Resilience, on occasion, will require identity changes. These can be long-lived or, more often, temporary accommodations. Resilience, in this sense, supports the individual in bouncing back from undesired identity change.

IPT treats level of identity resilience as a relatively stable characteristic of the individual (akin to a trait). There are significant individual differences across subsets of populations in their habitual levels of identity resilience. However, there is also evidence that the identity resilience that is manifested varies across situations and forms of stress (e.g., from highly personal and individualised threat to generalised risk). This leads to a possibility that there can be a distinction drawn between 'global' and 'specific' identity resilience. A measurement tool for assessing identity resilience is referenced later. It focuses on global identity resilience. IPT proposes that identity resilience depends on the operation of the identity principles.

Identity principles

As described in earlier chapters, in Identity Process Theory the structure of identity is postulated to be regulated by the dynamic processes of accommodation-assimilation and evaluation, which are deemed to be universal psychological processes. The two processes interact to determine the changing content and value of identity over time, with changing patterns of assimilation requiring changes in evaluation, and vice versa.

These two identity processes are guided in their operation by principles that define desirable states for the structure (both content and value) of identity. While the actual states considered desirable, and consequently the guidance principles, are possibly temporally and culturally specific, the original formulation of IPT claimed that at that time in Western post-industrial cultures the three prime guidance principles evidenced were desire for continuity, distinctiveness, and self-esteem. Following a series of studies, some involving longitudinal cohort sequential designs (Banks et al., 1992), a fourth guidance principle was added. This is efficacy (after Bandura's work on self-efficacy; Bandura, 1997). These four principles were said to vary in their relative and absolute salience over time and across situations (including across cultures).

These four identity principles are each described in some detail later. It is worth saying here that there has been some debate about whether they should be called 'principles' or motives. Breakwell (2014) acknowledged that they might be called motives. Originally, I did not label them 'motives' because the term previously had been too often used in a circular argument: the existence of the motive being inferred from the action it was assumed to explain. I went on to say that a principle or motive explanation can only ever be an interim explanation, and that this may not be a problem in so far as all theories are interim approximations to a full explanation. It may be fit for some purposes but actually represents a staging-post *en route* to also explaining why the principle/motive is present. In relation to identity principles, the superordinate explanation could include the operation of cognitive, conative, interpersonal, and societal processes over significant time periods. Those processes might, for instance, be able to be described and to be modelled in the way they predispose, say, self-esteem to emerge as a fundamental guiding principle (or motive) for identity construction and maintenance. Articulating the variety of principles/motives that are at work is important, but it is then necessary to ask whether we can explain why those principles/motives are present. In fact, IPT goes on from describing a number of principles to talking about the routes whereby they come into existence. It describes the societal processes (including social representation processes) through which the identity principles and processes are evolved.

Without ignoring the motivational functions of the identity principles, purely for the sake of simplicity and consistency, in this book the label 'identity principles' will generally continue to be used when describing the IPT model.

The second debate has circled around how many principles there are. The early formulation of IPT never suggested that the four constituted an exhaustive list (Breakwell, 1988). Various researchers have posited the existence of further identity principles. For example, Marlowe et al. (1996) argued for additional principles of *authenticity/integrity* and *affiliation* while studying the coming out process among lesbian women; Vignoles et al. (2000) identified possible additional principles of *purpose/meaning* and *closeness to others* in interviews with Anglican parish priests (and later proposed 'motivated identity construction theory';

Vignoles, 2011); and Jaspal and Cinnirella (2010) suggested a *coherence* principle, based on their research into identity conflict among British Pakistani Muslim gay men. Each of these suggestions is derived empirically from studies of particular populations facing identity challenges. Other empirical work is likely to suggest that there are other principles. It will be important not to assume that a motivation that can be identified in a particular situation can be generalised to be of universal significance. It will be interesting to establish whether the motivations identified can be arranged in some hierarchy based on their specific or global relevance to guiding identity processes. The task that will remain is to show how each improves the explanatory power of IPT and how they relate to each other in their effects.

Mapping the actual empirical relationships between the identity principles is fundamentally important because they do relate to particular aspects of the whole identity in different ways. For instance, self-esteem and efficacy are often significantly correlated with each other, which is not surprising since both are related to positive personal worth. Yet they have been shown to differ in the way they co-vary with identity components (e.g., with employment status and political affiliation; Breakwell et al., 1989; Fife-Schaw & Breakwell, 1990, 1991). These studies showed that the two principles were doing different work in predicting responses to changes in various components of identity. Similarly, Ginting et al. (2018) showed that the identity principles most closely linked to affiliation with a particular place (often referred to as 'place identity'; Twigger-Ross & Uzzell,1996) were self-esteem and distinctiveness, while self-efficacy and continuity had much weaker connections to it.

As we think further about the nature of identity principles, it is important to differentiate between a desired state for identity and the actual structure of identity. For instance, it is possible, at any one time, to distinguish between how motivated one is to gain self-efficacy and how much self-efficacy you have. Identity principles can be measured in terms of both what intensity and direction of motivation they arouse and what effect they have on the structure (content and value) of identity. It has to be said that sometimes this distinction is not maintained in empirical studies. It really should be.

In fact, an identity principle can be operationalised in three different ways: first, in terms of how much the individual desires (is motivated) to achieve a specific identity state that is an expression of the principle (e.g., an ability to overcome barriers acting as an expression of self-efficacy); second, in terms of the level of effort that is being expended to gain the desired identity state (e.g., the amount of persistence shown in seeking to find ways of overcoming barriers); third, in terms of the extent to which the desired identity state has been achieved (e.g., the self-reported ratings of self-efficacy). Essentially, these distinctions are between motive strength, goal-oriented action, and identity state. Distinguishing between these three types of indexing is important when considering the measurement of identity resilience.

Four identity principles

Distinctiveness

Identity Process Theory asserts that positive distinctiveness is one of the key identity principles. This involves differentiating yourself from others in ways that are regarded as worthy by you and the people that matter to you. So, the objective is not just any distinctiveness, it has to be the right sort of distinctiveness. The significance of positive distinctiveness, at least in part, accounts for the way identities are constructed to be unique. IPT treats the distinctiveness principle as operating in most cultures (Vignoles et al., 2000).

IPT treats any component of identity as a potential basis for distinctiveness claims. Other theories have pinned the source of distinctiveness on social group memberships. For instance, Brewer (2003), who argues for a separation of the personal self (concerned with integrity and continuity) and the collective self (concerned with connectedness to social groups and security), produced the 'optimal distinctiveness' model of self. In it, she assigns primacy to the role of group memberships and collective identity as the forces driving the creation of optimal distinctiveness. The focus on optimising distinctiveness is important. If distinctiveness is based in social group memberships and the collective self that the individual derives from them, then a balance must be struck between conforming to the expectations of group membership and expressing individualism. It implies being distinctive but not too distinctive, and being distinctive in an acceptable manner. Brewer is concerned with optimal distinctiveness derived from group memberships and expressed in groups. However, IPT proposes that distinctiveness is not just derived from group memberships, it can be based on any type of identity component (e.g., intellect, creativity, fearlessness, or achievements). IPT refers to this as positive distinctiveness. Doubtless, people do seek to optimise the positivity of their distinctiveness, but not only in relation to their group memberships.

While IPT is concerned with the desire for positive distinctiveness as a motive force for identity processes, it has to be acknowledged that avoidance of being indistinguishable from others also motivates identity change and this can mean accepting negative distinctiveness sometimes because it is the only alternative to sameness or vanishing into the collective other. Cases where people settle for negative distinctiveness because nothing more positive is available are very numerous. The search for distinction gives way to the acceptance of notoriety. For example, children who cannot gain positive distinctiveness in school from their ability in lessons may become disruptive (e.g., playing the fool or bullying brighter children). The irony is that notoriety can have its own prestige within some sub-groups, so it might end up as positive distinctiveness in the end.

There are many ways to achieve distinctiveness: most often, it can occur by ascription (someone attributes to you some difference without you seeking it because they believe you have certain identity characteristics, usually because these are manifest); through effort (you take action to assimilate or reject an identity component, or you make sure people are aware of certain aspects of your existing identity); or through error (you misread the requirements of the social context and accidentally set yourself apart).

It is notable that distinctiveness is intrinsically a product of social comparisons. You cannot establish your distinctiveness without a comparator. There is a tendency to think of distinctiveness solely in terms of comparison against others. However, the comparator can be internal. You might be seeking positive distinctiveness from a previous image of yourself. Your earlier self as your comparator is common. For instance, in eating disorders, such as anorexia, the sufferer is sometimes motivated by the determination never again to have that hated body image they had before. In such cases, the positive distinctiveness that they derive in psychological terms from changing their body is rarely accompanied with positive distinctiveness in their social context.

Self-esteem

Self-esteem is the individual's subjective evaluation of their own worth. It reflects the degree to which the components of a person's identity are perceived to be positive. The concept has been used since the 18th century, when David Hume proposed that thinking well of oneself serves to motivate people to strive to fulfil their full potential (see Hume, 2019). Various ways of explicitly and implicitly accessing a person's self-esteem have been developed (notably by Rosenberg, 1965) and this has made it possible to assess the significance of self-esteem for many aspects of thought, feeling, and action. For instance, self-esteem is generally positively correlated with mental health (e.g., low self-esteem is associated with depressive symptoms; Sowislo & Orth, 2013). It has been shown to influence causal attributions (e.g., concerning failure; Fitch, 1970), and to predict persistence in a task in the face of threat (e.g., Di Paula & Campbell, 2002).

There have been many studies of the development of self-esteem over the life course (e.g., Trzesniewski et al., 2013) which typically suggest it is operative in very young children and heavily dependent on the social environment of the child (especially the parents or caregivers). Robins et al. (2002) explored age differences in self-esteem from age 9 to 90 years using cross-sectional data collected from 326,641 individuals over the internet. Self-esteem levels were high in childhood, dropped during adolescence, rose gradually throughout adulthood, and declined sharply in old age. This trajectory generally held across gender, socio-economic status, ethnicity, and nationality (US citizens vs non-US citizens). Overall, these findings support previous research. Variations in the level of self-esteem across the lifespan occur; however, it is not established that there are parallel variations in the significance of self-esteem in determining thought, feeling, or action. It seems unlikely that there would be.

Rosenberg et al. (1995) explored the distinction between global self-esteem (i.e., the subjective assessment of the worth of the whole identity) and specific self-esteem (i.e., the subjective evaluation of part of the identity) and their relationship. They present evidence that the two types of self-esteem may have strikingly different consequences, global self-esteem being more relevant to psychological well-being, and specific self-esteem being more relevant to behaviour. Their findings show that, while global self-esteem is more strongly related to measures of psychological well-being, specific (academic) self-esteem is a much better predictor of school performance. Other findings indicate that the degree to which specific academic self-esteem affects global self-esteem, particularly the positive component of global self-esteem, is a function of how highly academic performance is personally valued. This work is important for understanding how the value of the whole identity relates to the values attached to its specific components. The value (or importance) attributed to any one identity component can influence how the identity principles operate in motivating assimilation-accommodation and evaluation processes.

The weight of research that has been conducted on global self-esteem and specific self-esteem has made self-esteem appear a 'super' identity principle, important for all aspects of identity. In IPT, self-esteem is not automatically assumed to operate as the prime identity principle. Instead, it is assumed that the four identity principles will vary in their salience according to the specifics of the individual's identity structure and according to the immediate circumstances. This is an important caveat when examining the bases of identity resilience.

Self-efficacy

Bandura (1997) originally proposed the concept of self-efficacy. It refers to the individual's belief in their own ability to attain their goals. Self-efficacy reflects the extent to which an individual feels competent and powerful enough to achieve desired objectives even in the face of obstacles. Bandura emphasised that self-efficacy is distinct from the commonplace concept of confidence. Confidence refers to general self-assurance, whereas self-efficacy is more specifically linked to subjective expectations of goal-attainment.

The self-efficacy concept is central to Bandura's broader social cognitive theory. This focuses on the role of observational learning and social experience in the development of personality. The idea is simple: we observe others in social interactions and our own experiences with them, and, through this, we learn about ourselves and what others think about us and expect of us. Our understanding of our own self-efficacy is derived from observational learning. We develop a self-representation that includes a perception of how effective we are in achieving the outcomes that we desire. Of course, this echoes what William James had to say about the development of self-awareness (see Chapter 2).

Being established through social observation, as the input from experience changes it is reasonable to predict that self-efficacy will change too. Consequently, expression of self-efficacy may vary across situations and over the lifespan. However, self-efficacy levels determined by observational learning early in life may condition behaviour in, and interpretation of, subsequent experiences. As a result, the level of self-efficacy may become less sensitive to changes in the external environment over time; it is, in effect, self-reinforcing.

There is evidence that self-efficacy does generalise across situations. Feeling competent in facing one challenge may lead to an expectation of being competent in others. Yet, as empirical evidence on self-efficacy has grown, researchers have chosen to distinguish general self-efficacy from specific self-efficacy, the latter being tied to feelings of task-competence in particular situations or types of tasks. The parallel with the evolution of the distinction between global self-esteem and specific self-esteem is unmissable.

In health psychology, a large number of studies have shown that level of general self-efficacy and level of specific self-efficacy may be related to behaviours in response to the same disease in complex ways. Jackson et al. (2014) performed a meta-analysis to evaluate overall strengths of the relation between self-efficacy and functioning (pain severity, functional impairment, affective distress) in samples of people with chronic pain, as well as the potential moderating effects of socio-demographic characteristics and methodologic factors on these associations. In total, 86 samples ($N = 15{,}616$) fulfilled selection criteria for analysis. Self-efficacy had negative overall correlations with impairment, affective distress, and pain severity, although considerable heterogeneity was observed for all effect sizes. Age, pain duration, specific self-efficacy sub-scale content (i.e., self-efficacy for functioning despite pain vs self-efficacy for pain control vs self-efficacy for managing other symptoms, such as emotional distress) and type of impairment measure (self-report vs task performance) had significant moderating effects on self-efficacy–impairment associations. The self-efficacy and affective distress relationship was moderated by employment status and self-efficacy sub-scale content. Finally, moderator analyses of data from studies having longitudinal designs indicated that associations between baseline self-efficacy and each outcome at follow-up remained significant. Hence, self-efficacy was found to be a robust correlate of key outcomes related to chronic pain and a potentially important protective factor, with implications for subsequent functioning in affected groups.

It is evident that self-efficacy has various effects on thought, emotion, and behaviour. Low self-efficacy can result in people believing that tasks are harder than they actually are, resulting in higher stress levels and less systematic or appropriate planning of activities aimed at fulfilling the task. People with high self-efficacy levels stay focused, are more determined to persist when faced with obstacles, and are less likely to attribute any failure to themselves and more likely to blame external factors. Self-efficacy has been shown to be associated with self-preferential biases in attribution (e.g., dissociating oneself from socially stigmatised actions). Under these conditions, it is not surprising that lower self-efficacy is more associated with lower psychological well-being, particularly with more depressive or anxiety reactions. There is also evidence that higher levels of self-efficacy are linked to greater resilience against negative social influence pressures (Schwarzer & Warner, 2013). For instance, in adolescents, high self-efficacy is associated with an ability to resist peer pressure towards drug abuse or eating disorders. This suggests that higher self-efficacy may result in some anticipation of risk or danger, and avoidance of them.

Continuity

The fourth identity principle is continuity. People are motivated by a desire to establish and maintain the continuity of their identity. Defining what is meant by continuity in this context is quite difficult. We are not dealing with an objective or necessarily rational basis for defining identity continuity. First and foremost, we are dealing with the individual's own subjective perception of what constitutes continuity for their identity through time. The conception of identity continuity can be idiosyncratic; it will certainly vary across people. There are common underlying themes in what people say about the continuity of their identity over time:

- My identity is not the same now as it was in the past, but my identity now has incorporated what it was in the past into what I am now.
- There is a seamless connection between my identity in the past and my identity now.
- I have lived through events that have changed my identity, but somewhere in my heart I still know the old me. I am still the same person, as well as being a changed person.
- I have never really changed underneath the show I put on for other people.

The sort of reflections collected in response to the question depends on the age of the respondent and the sort of experiences they have had. Yet the underlying motif is that identity continuity is about feeling the same person while seeing there have been changes. 'Same and different' captures it. Moreover, like beauty, continuity is in the eye of the beholder. While a person may see themselves as possessing identity continuity, someone looking at them may see something quite different.

As an agentic motivational force of the identity, the continuity principle operates at two levels:

- It motivates people to seek to achieve continuity in their actual identity structure as long as that structure is perceived to satisfy the requirements of the other three principles.

- When the identity structure is called to change in accordance with modifications in social context (social influence processes or structures), the continuity principle influences the assimilation-accommodation process to optimise any change in such a way as to protect continuity of the identity. It will simultaneously stimulate attribution processes that explain the changes in such a way as to make them appropriate and consistent with what was previously there.

Thus, the continuity principle potentially has an important effect on the structure and evaluation of identity. Of course, it may fail or only partially succeed in either or both of these efforts.

Identity continuity seems to be valued and sought cross-culturally. One of the fascinating illustrations of how it works occurs in the cross-cultural prevalence of nostalgia (Sedikides & Wildschut, 2018). Reminiscences and narratives of the past are ways of maintaining the image of identities from the past, especially when they are shared (Wildschut et al., 2010). It is interesting how nostalgia can be a route for retrofitting past identity structures to engineer their consistency with a current identity (Vess et al., 2012). The nostalgia allows new shades of meaning to be attributed to the past identity components, but it also contextualises speculations about potential, but not yet assimilated, identity components.

Despite what appears to be a universal concern with identity continuity, communities and individuals will vary in both how much they value continuity and in the level of continuity that they believe they have achieved. It is notable that most measures of identity continuity focus on the person's estimate of its level, rather than on how much they want it. In relation to identity resilience, it is important to do both.

Given that IPT considers identity continuity to be a subjective product of the individual, it is allowing for idiosyncrasies in the decisions about what constitutes continuity. What matters is that the individual perceives their identity to exist and operate in an unbroken and consistent way over time. This means that the stability or consistency that is perceived can be based on some superordinate conception or property. For instance, someone might believe her identity to have continuity even though she knows that it changes erratically; she perceives such change as a consistent, continuing characteristic of her identity. Objective indexes of identity continuity can be widely at variance with the subjective experience of continuity.

The functions of the continuity principle for the individual are primarily the following:

- Self-prediction – believing your identity structure (content and value) to have continuity over time provides you with the basis for predicting what you are likely to think, feel, and do.
- Planning – identity continuity improves how you plan your future based on your past.
- Retaining kudos from the valued identity components – within the assimilate-accommodation process the continuity principle motivates retention of identity components that have long-term value.
- Reassurance in uncertainty – when circumstances change and the individual is faced with unexpected challenges or with high levels of uncertainty concerning the appropriate response, the continuity principle steers the individual to see current uncertainties in the context of their past identity development.

For society, the function of the continuity principle is relatively simple. Social structures and social influence processes rely on individuals fulfilling their allotted roles in predictable ways. Continuity in identity, despite inevitable developmental and experiential change, enhances predictability. This points to another function of continuity for individuals. It increases their chances of fulfilling the expectations of, and obligations to, their society. Indeed, IPT emphasises that the specific form that each of the four principles takes at any particular time will reflect what is then socially desirable. They are specified and articulated in different ways across cultures and over time. For instance, continuity may change its form if a culture experiences large-scale, multiplex uncertainty. However, it is hard to know which way its form would change. Perhaps it would change in saliency as well as form.

Identity principle states: personal and reflected

In describing the four identity principles, we have distinguished between the desire to gain distinctiveness, continuity, self-esteem, and self-efficacy and the level of each that has been achieved. Recent developments of IPT refer to the level achieved in a particular principle as the 'state' of that principle. The state of the principle will vary, in some circumstances quickly and significantly. It is not envisaged that the level of desire (or motivation) for each of the four principles is so labile.

One index of the principle's state depends on the subjective estimate of it by the individual concerned. Another index could rely on how other people would infer the principle's state based on observation of the individual. This would allow for disparities between the personal and the reflected estimates. There is a suggestion here that subjective estimates of continuity, self-esteem, self-efficacy, or distinctiveness can be 'unrealistic' when compared with some external indicators. The possibility of such divergence is inevitable. Individuals are motivated to achieve continuity, self-efficacy, self-esteem, and distinctiveness in their identities. This is likely to influence how they perceive the states of their identity. Their perceptions of themselves will sometimes be at variance with the attributions that other people make about them. Actually, an individual's identity is viewed from many perspectives in addition to their own. This is another product of the 'shared' nature of identity. There is absolutely no assurance that the sharers will agree on what they see or what it means.

However, it is important to note that individuals' estimates of their own identity status on the four principles do not always err on the side of inflating the positivity of their identity compared to what others think. In fact, subjective assessments of principle states are frequently less positive than estimates reflected by others. We will return to the effects of 'unrealism' in subjective assessments of principle states in Chapter 8.

Identity resilience in IPT

The concept

There are many existing measures of general resilience that have been reviewed elsewhere (Windle et al., 2011). The concept itself refers to the individual's ability to 'bounce back' in the face of various challenges that they face across the life course, such as ill-health. General resilience tends to be focused on the individual's capacity to deflect the impact of the challenge. Many of the measures focus almost exclusively on personal agency when exposed to a stressor, but the underlying psychological traits that facilitate such 'bounce back' are implicit and left to be inferred. In contrast, in Identity Process Theory, it is explicitly hypothesised that subjective feelings of self-efficacy (one's own subjective construal of control and competence, which is akin to personal agency) as well as distinctiveness, continuity, and self-esteem are collectively central to determining not only immediate responses to a stressor but also the ability to cope effectively subsequently. The identity resilience construct goes beyond any exclusive focus on personal agency (or self-efficacy) and incorporates the resilience of the identity structure itself (characterised in terms of all four identity principles and influenced by the effectiveness of the identity processes that respond to them).

Thus, identity resilience reflects one's subjective belief in one's capacity to interpret and overcome challenges as they occur, one's self-worth and value, certainty of who one is and will remain despite individual and social changes that occur, and one's self-construal as unique and positively distinctive. It is conceptualised in Identity Process Theory as a relatively stable self-schema, akin to a trait (Breakwell, 2021a; Breakwell, Fino & Jaspal, 2022). Over the life course, the individual will develop a sense of their identity resilience, and this reflects the extent to which their whole identity structure is characterised by the four principles. Identity resilience is said to be high when individuals perceive their identity to be characterised by a high overall combined rating of their self-efficacy, self-esteem, continuity, and distinctiveness. Identity resilience operates, through the processes of assimilation-accommodation and evaluation, to marshal dynamic adjustments in the identity structure that allow the implications of challenges and stressors not simply to be deflected but, more importantly, to be reconceptualised and re-evaluated and become contributions to the evolving identity. Identity resilience can be thought of as a superordinate state of identity. It is dependent for its maintenance on the effectiveness of the identity processes.

Seen in this way, identity resilience has three facets:

- Identity resilience refers to the extent to which an individual possesses an identity that facilitates adaptive coping in the face of threat or uncertainty.
- Identity resilience refers to the extent to which a person's identity configuration is capable of absorbing change while retaining its subjective meaning and value for that person.
- Identity resilience refers to the extent to which an individual conceives of herself or himself as capable of coping with threat or uncertainty without permanent negative effects on identity. Having high identity resilience does not equate to not feeling a threat in an objectively threatening situation. Instead, high identity resilience is associated with knowing oneself able to cope with the threat. Consequently, the threat is perceived as less 'threatening'.

The identity resilience concept, while based squarely in IPT, can be used alongside a number of other theoretical models that are currently utilised to explain how people react to risk and threats. For instance, it is compatible with the approach of Ritchie et al. (2016), who characterise a 'strong' sense of identity in terms of the self-regulatory goals of esteem, continuity, and meaningfulness. People reporting higher identity resilience respond more favourably to, and cope more effectively with, events and situations that question or threaten their identity (e.g., Breakwell & Jaspal, 2022). This is hardly surprising since the four identity principles that are the foundations for identity resilience have been shown individually to be instrumental in facilitating favourable coping responses to stressors (Brewer, 1991; Dumont & Provost, 1999; Sadeh & Karniol, 2012).

Once generated, identity resilience creates the platform for being able to defend identity more effectively in the future. In being an agent of identity defence, it is useful for identity resilience to be malleable – the combination of the four principles means that, when one is under pressure, the others can be brought to the fore to adjust against the threat. Differential prioritisation over time and circumstances is to be expected (Breakwell, 2015a). Resilience is also about 'bounce back', that is, recovery – the higher the identity resilience, the greater the capacity to reconstruct an identity configuration which is personally satisfying and defensible in the future.

While identity resilience is not fleeting or highly situation-specific, it is expected that it will vary because it is dependent on the states of the identity principles, and they will be subject to change as the identity structure changes or identity process effectiveness varies. Variability will reflect the success of coping strategies used to manage any emerging threats to identity. For instance, faced with having to recall a particularly negative memory of rejection by significant others, the individual, at that moment, may experience some challenge to self-esteem. Higher identity resilience would result in the individual being less likely to perceive any actual decrement in self-esteem. The coping mechanism at work might be intra-psychic denial or interpersonal self-justification. If successful, the state of self-esteem would stabilise, and identity resilience would be maintained.

The dynamics of identity resilience

The level (state) of an individual's identity resilience is usually measured in terms of the aggregate of the levels (states) of each of their identity principles. The state of identity resilience at any one time is a good predictor of the individual's capacity to adapt effectively to challenging changes in the physical, social, and psychological contexts. The psychological context is included because identity resilience levels are relevant to reactions to unwanted variations in the way the individual is thinking or feeling (e.g., in reactions to grief, disappointment, or fear).

While overall identity resilience at any one time is the product of the state of all four identity principles at that time, it is important to look beneath the aggregate score in order to understand the complex dynamics involved in identity resilience processes. The aggregate score masks any differences in weighting between the principles; they may not be contributing equally to the score. Also, at different times, the same aggregate score can be achieved by different combinations of the estimates for the four principles. Moreover, it is to be expected that the relative contributions of each of the principles will vary between individuals, even though they appear on aggregate to have the same level of identity resilience. There may also be systematic differences cross-culturally in the weighting of the importance of the four principles when constructing identity resilience. For instance, some cultures might be characterised by systems of social representation that favour a focus on continuity and not distinctiveness. This would mean that the same aggregate identity resilience score in, say, India and the US would be underpinned by a different profile across the identity principles.

So, it is possible that the overall level of identity resilience is the same, but the underlying constituents contribute to it differentially. This matters because it is likely to affect how the individual actually manages any change that is perceived as threatening. For instance, if distinctiveness is weighted heavily in the composition of identity resilience, it may be more likely that, in responding to a challenge, the individual will rely on their distinctiveness to reinterpret the significance of the threat for their identity. An illustration of this type of coping occurs during public health crises, when individuals claim that the illness is not something they will be concerned about because they are set apart from the potential sufferers by some distinctive set of characteristics (e.g., not old, not immunodeficient, not poor, etc.). Whether they are right in their claim that their distinctive profile reduces their risk of the disease or not, making the claim, even if they believe it only partially, is a way to reduce their immediate stress levels.

IPT postulates that the identity principles interact to shape responses to changes, particularly change that induces threat or uncertainty, guiding the operation of the accommodation-assimilation and evaluation processes to protect the identity structure. If the existing identity structure subjectively satisfies the individual in terms of the levels (states) of the four identity principles, identity resilience will be high, and change will be resisted unless it can be made to comply with the motives established by the identity principles. Yet IPT also emphasises the resourcefulness of the individual constructing a sense of identity, and it is thus possible that, in specific cultural contexts, individuals will accentuate some principles over others in order to derive an individually acceptable sense of identity resilience (Breakwell, 2015a).

The form and effectiveness of coping strategies used during threatening change depend on the level of identity resilience and the levels of each identity principle within it. Coping will also depend on the way identity resilience interacts with other components of identity. The individual's value system certainly interacts with their identity resilience to shape decisions. Bardi et al. (2014) report how an individual's values influence how important an identity component is felt to be. Value systems may channel identity resilience to preferentially protect certain aspects of identity, even when they are not natural foci for the identity principles.

The four identity principles are used in combination in assessing identity resilience because, while they are each conceptually distinct constructs, together they explain more of what motivates identity processes. It is recognised that they have somewhat different aetiologies and have been shown empirically to predict behaviour, thought, and affect differentially. Yet they do overlap. Significant correlations between self-esteem and self-efficacy are regularly found (Gardner & Pierce, 1998; Lane et al., 2008; Lightsey et al., 2006), and both correlate with continuity and positive distinctiveness (Sharma & Sharma, 2010; Sharma et al., 2005; Sharma et al., 2021; Wang & Xu, 2015). Introducing the identity resilience construct makes it possible to capitalise on the synergies of the four in predicting responses to stressors. Identity resilience is a superordinate construct that links the four components. This is analogous to the way general intelligence (the 'g' factor) is the overarching construct that links the various aspects of cognitive ability. Indeed, in developing a scale to measure identity resilience that incorporated the four components, Breakwell, Fino, and Jaspal (2022) established the existence of a superordinate factor that explained variance across the four sub-measures.

There is, however, an enormous amount of empirical work to do to determine the way the four components interact to shape coping strategies and, thereby, identity structure.

The emerging model of identity resilience

Breakwell (2021a) summarised the emerging model of identity resilience that can be based on Identity Process Theory and that has introduced an extension of that theory:

- An individual's resilience when dealing with stressful or threatening circumstances depends partly on identity processes.
- Resilience is a structural feature that differentiates between identity configurations. Some identity content configurations are more resilient to change than are others and some may provide greater scope for effective or adaptive coping strategies when facing changing situations (Breakwell, 2015b).
- Identity resilience refers to the capacity of the identity to resist its own invalidation, devaluation, or fragmentation.
- Identity resilience influences the form of cognitive, emotional, and behavioural reactions to uncertainties or threats. In this sense, identity resilience refers to the capacity of identity to influence responses to threat that are not directly concerned simply or solely with protecting itself.
- Identity resilience rests on having an identity structure that is characterised by levels of self-esteem, self-efficacy, positive distinctiveness, and continuity that are subjectively satisfying (i.e., 'optimised').
- The assimilation-accommodation and evaluation processes assemble, over the life course, an identity structure that is mandated by the four identity principles. However, identity resilience also depends on how intensely the person is motivated to continue to enhance or maintain these four properties of identity. An identity configuration that embodies high levels of self-esteem, self-efficacy, distinctiveness, and continuity is defined here as resilient, but it would not stay resilient if it was not regenerated and reaffirmed through continual effort. The distinctions between motive strength, goal-oriented action, and identity state were described earlier. In relation to identity resilience, their significance is emphasised. Identity resilience at any one time depends on all three. Contemporary identity state, motivation to defend or adapt that identity, and being able to take relevant action to manage threat are all parts of identity resilience.
- Identity resilience is a dynamic property of the individual, subject to change over the lifespan and in response to experience. It is a product of experiences and the way the individual interprets, but also chooses, them. Experience is a product of active construal. Level of identity resilience will influence the construal process but will also be influenced by it. Similarly, identity resilience at one moment in time may shape the choice of a particular coping strategy against adversity or the course of action taken against a hazard. However, identity resilience is itself a product over time of deploying those strategies.

Breakwell (2021a) argues that, given the definition of identity resilience used here, all of the theories that explain each of the four identity principles may have a role to play in describing how an individual comes to develop a resilient identity. Bandura (2005), in summarising the evolution of his social cognitive theory, provides a description of the processes that allow self-efficacy to be developed. This encompasses a model of social learning that adopts a perspective on self-development, adaptation, and change, which emphasises that the individual has agency. Models of self-esteem that stem back to Rosenberg (1965) incorporate the notion that it is a product of social support, which includes social reinforcement and recognition. The sources of optimal distinctiveness are more often focused upon symbolic interactions (interpersonal, intragroup, and intergroup) that influence how individuals know what constitutes approved distinctiveness, and how they learn to express their own distinctiveness (Leonardelli et al., 2010). The origins of continuity of identity also lie in different levels of social engagement, but its maintenance is fundamentally dependent on the capacity of, and interactions between, individual and collective memory (Licata & Mercy, 2015).

These general explanations of the way self-esteem, self-efficacy, distinctiveness, and continuity arise and are maintained share many common features. All, in their own way, explain why people will inevitably differ in the extent to which they have these four qualities. Since they share some of their sources, it is not surprising that the four identity principles tend to be correlated, even though they are distinguishable in their effects. The origins of identity resilience may be found in the sources of the four identity principles. However, although there has been wide-ranging research on the precursors of resilience in aversive conditions (see Atkinson et al., 2009, for a review of this literature), there is limited data on the particular constellation of factors that would result specifically in the development of identity resilience. There is a need for empirical research that maps the development of identity resilience across the lifespan. Equally, there is a need for studies of how identity resilience that may have been relatively stable for many years can decline precipitously. Work on the effects of identity resilience in ageing and dementia is particularly needed (Cosco et al., 2017; Hayman et al., 2017).

Identity resilience, threat perception, and identity change: two illustrative empirical studies

The Identity Resilience Index (IRI), developed by Breakwell, Fino, and Jaspal (2022) as an aggregate measure of identity resilience, has been used to explore how identity resilience is related to threat perception and identity change. This work assumes that individuals may not be spontaneously or continually conscious of their own identity resilience. However, when asked to reflect on how they think about and evaluate themselves, it predicts that they are able to describe a relatively stable 'self-schema' that subjectively reflects their identity resilience. It also predicts that individuals may become aware spontaneously and more acutely of the extent of their identity resilience when they are called upon to focus on a threat. The two studies described here both involve an experimental manipulation that is designed to increase respondents' attention to a threat. The first involves the recollection of a past threat and the second involves the consideration of a current threat. Neither study involved any o increase or change the threat; the object was simply to have respondents focus ntion on it.

Study 1: Identity resilience and internalised homonegativity

In this study, the moderating effects of identity resilience on identity change following threat were examined. Breakwell and Jaspal (2022), in a between-participants experimental study involving 333 gay men, investigated whether the baseline level of identity resilience moderates the impact that the recall of a negative coming out experience has on perceived identity threat in gay men. They found that identity resilience was negatively correlated both with distress during recall of the coming out experience and with internalised homonegativity. Both distress during memory recall and internalised homonegativity were in turn positively correlated with feeling contemporaneous identity threat (i.e., feeling their self-esteem, self-efficacy, continuity, and distinctiveness were being undermined or eroded). As a result of its dampening effects on distress and internalised homonegativity, identity resilience reduced the immediate identity threat that recollecting a negative coming out experience could create. Essentially, individuals representing themselves as having higher identity resilience did not become so distressed by the negative recollection and they did not report that their identity was changed as much by it. The broader significance of identity resilience for psychological well-being is also evident in this study. Internalised homonegativity (which entails directing stigmatising stereotypes of homosexuality towards oneself) can cause grave psychological distress (Jaspal, Lopes, & Rehman, 2021). Identity resilience and internalised homonegativity were negatively correlated. This illustrates how encouraging the development of identity resilience can be advantageous. Possessing identity resilience is associated with resisting the assimilation of negative stereotypes into the structure of identity.

Study 2: Identity resilience and perceived risk and fear of COVID-19

The possible role of identity resilience in responses to health hazards has also been studied. Breakwell and Jaspal (2021) examined the identity processes that influence emotional and attitudinal responses to COVID-19. Survey data were collected online from 251 adults in the UK during July 2020. Identity resilience, trust in science and scientists, fear of COVID-19, and perceived own risk of infection were measured. Respondents then watched a video clip designed to focus their thinking further on the disease. Immediately after viewing the video, levels of feeling afraid, uncertainty about self-protection, mistrust of anyone offering COVID-19 advice, and perceptions of identity change were indexed. A structural equation model of the relationship between these variables was tested and proved a good fit for the data.

The study found a complex network of relationships. Identity resilience was found to be negatively related to fear of COVID-19. Fear of COVID-19 was strongly positively related to perceptions of own risk of COVID-19 and to feeling afraid after viewing the video. Identity resilience was negatively related to uncertainty and to feeling afraid after viewing the video. Greater identity change after seeing the video was associated with higher mistrust, uncertainty, and feeling more afraid. Trust in science and scientists correlated positively with

perceived own risk of COVID-19 and negatively with mistrust of those offering advi
preventative behaviour. Any effect of identity resilience on identity change was me
through its negative effect on fear of COVID-19, and feeling afraid, and being uncertain after viewing the video. Through these effects, it militated against identity change. It is also worth noting that higher identity resilience was related to lower uncertainty concerning how to protect oneself from the disease.

The takeaway messages from this study are as follows:

- Greater identity resilience is associated with lower fear and less perceived personal risk.
- Greater identity resilience is associated with more certainty about how to protect oneself.
- Greater identity resilience is associated with less identity change after considering the risk of COVID-19.

In addition, this study shows that it is worth examining how identity resilience is linked to the emotional response to major health hazards such as COVID-19. Through this emotional response, in those studied, it is linked to perceived risk and to perceived identity change. Too often, the role of affect is ignored in modelling responses to hazards. Beliefs and attitudes are included but emotions are often demoted. Since identity processes are expressed through emotion as well as through cognition, it seems timely to refocus.

Building identity resilience in the interest of system resilience

The model of identity resilience, derived from IPT, which has been described here and operationalised with the IRI measure, predicts responses to threat. The empirical evidence thus far suggests that having greater identity resilience is associated with being able to cope better with threat, whether that threat is highly personalised (as in the case of negative coming out experiences for gay men) or societal (as in the case of a major health hazard in relation to reactions to risks of COVID-19). Identity resilience has been shown to be linked to adaptive and constructive cognitive, emotional, and behavioural responses. In both of the illustrative studies above, identity resilience was associated with less negative emotional reactions to threat and with more proactive resistance to damaging identity change.

Identity resilience is thus advantageous for the individual. Also, it may be useful for other people who gain collateral benefits. However, identity resilience is not necessarily associated with prosocial or altruistic beliefs or actions. In order to maintain itself, identity resilience is essentially selfish. Indeed, the coping strategies it relies on may inculcate mistrust of others (Breakwell, 2021b). Challenging the motives of others seems to be an important weapon in building self-protection. This does not exclude the possibility that prosocial behaviour in some circumstances will occur because it is serving the individual's drive towards self-esteem, self-efficacy, distinctiveness, and continuity.

Considerable further research is needed to test this model of identity resilience. The availability of the IRI is already encouraging empirical studies that will share a common operationalisation of the concept. It would be particularly valuable to have data on the way levels of identity resilience vary across the lifespan (using cohort sequential designs that would allow for the disambiguation of cohort and age effects). Also, it would be useful to have more evidence on the variability in the importance of each of the four principles contributing to identity resilience over sources of threat and over subcultures. Exploratory work on this has begun (Breakwell, Jaspal, & Wright, in press). This study examines how the four identity principles relate to factors that result in vaccine hesitancy.

The IRI measures identity resilience in terms of the individual's assessment of how far they perceived themselves to be characterised by self-efficacy, self-esteem, positive distinctiveness, and continuity. Yet it was pointed out earlier that the identity principles can be operationalised in three different ways: motive strength, goal-oriented action, and identity state. The IRI focuses on identity state. As further research develops, it will be valuable to develop tools that measure identity resilience in terms of goal orientation and motive strength. It will then be possible to examine more closely how these three types of measure relate to each other.

Further research should deal also with the role that the dynamics of identity resilience may have in therapeutic contexts. It is possible that identity resilience is a moderating factor in the impact of psychological therapies. Currently this is purely speculation, but given the significance of cognitive behavioural therapy approaches, it may be worth examining systematically.

Individual identity resilience has importance not just for individuals. For societies that are facing macro-existential threats and that wish to build system resilience, the big question is how to marshal individual identity resilience in the interests of the whole. One tactic might be to identify those who have greater identity resilience and place them strategically in the system (i.e., organisation) that is tackling the threat. Individual identity resilience could be used to bolster or even foster system resilience. Another tactic would be to develop greater identity resilience in key existing members of the system through training or coaching. Some organisations do this now (e.g., some military and health professions). The American Psychological Association (APA, 2020) has stated that resilience involves behaviours, thoughts, and actions that anyone can learn and develop. So, people may be able to learn resilience. While this may not be quite the same as identity resilience as defined by IPT, it may support the idea that systems can gain greater resilience by supporting their members to gain greater resilience. More general learning of resilience skills may also coincidentally further develop the self-esteem, self-efficacy, distinctiveness, and continuity of those individuals involved. The task of the system is then to retain for the benefit of everyone the adaptive and constructive contributions that people with high identity resilience can offer. Achieving resilience in physical and social systems is now recognised in science and politics as a fundamental necessity. By working together, the social and physical sciences should be able to design more effective and resilient systems. Such designs must incorporate the insights offered by an integrative model of identity resilience linked to a theory of identity processes.

4

IDENTITY AND SOCIAL SUPPORT

Social support is a psychological necessity.
Thoits (1985)

Issues addressed in this chapter

Throughout this book so far, the significance of social interactions to the composition and expression of identity has been emphasised. It is time to examine how social structures and social influences, as manifested in social support processes, work to stabilise, secure, and develop identities. So, this chapter focuses upon the role of social support. While often positive in its impact on identity, social support also can have its downsides. Both of these types of impact are considered here.

What is social support?

Social support is a fuzzy concept. It is used in myriad different ways in psychology. Virtually any sort of interaction between people can be designated social support. One might think that it has to have an element of one party providing 'support' to the other, and this suggests the transaction involves the transfer of something useful (material or psychosocial) to the other. Frequently, social support is said to occur when the receiver is facing stress or threat, or some other negative situation. Yet in fact, social support can also be given in positive or neutral contexts, not only *in extremis*. Social support is a habitual process that just becomes more visible in crises. Nevertheless, people do differ in the amount of social support that they have available to them and the conditions under which they receive it.

So far, so good. The devil is in the detail. The devil might be captured best by asking some questions:

- Who are the parties involved?
- What is the nature of their relationship?
- Who decides the transaction is necessary? Who decides support is necessary?
- Who decides that the transfer involves something useful? One of the parties involved, or some outside observer?
- Does the transfer involve reciprocation? Do all parties gain something useful to them?

The questions reveal that understanding social support requires consideration of the power relationship between the parties involved. They also suggest that there are many varieties of social support.

Stroebe and Stroebe (1996) raised the question of whether social support should be considered a unitary concept or several related concepts. Considered from a social psychological perspective, social support can be seen to have a variety of functions. Internally for groups, these include establishing attachment and retention, indicating comparative strength or usefulness of members, reinforcing hierarchies, and establishing or maintaining interdependencies. Social support has functions for groups externally, in their intergroup relationships.

These include differentiating the group positively from others by signalling its care for its members, and the values or beliefs associated with it. Such variation in functions suggests that it is a multiplex concept. This is emphasised when the social and psychological functions for the individual receiving social support are considered. Perceiving oneself to be socially supported is often associated with better mental and physical health, with self-report of higher quality of life, and with higher self-esteem, self-efficacy, positive distinctiveness, and continuity (in effect, with the ingredients of identity resilience).

Social support in the early development of identity

Some sorts of social support are fundamental during the early years of development of identity. Parents, siblings, and the extended family are typically the primary suppliers of social support as a child's identity is established. The child's relationship with these significant others usually entails all of the typical forms of social support that have been described by psychologists. These include the following:

- *Emotional or personal worth support*: empathy, concern, affection, love, trust, acceptance, intimacy, encouragement, or caring (i.e., providing emotional support can let the individual know that they are valued).
- *Material support*: concrete, direct sustenance, for example food, clothing, a place to live (i.e., providing the physical necessities for maturation and social experience).
- *Informational support*: advice, guidance, information, and explanation (i.e., facilitating both cognitive development and problem-solving skills).
- *Normative support*: instruction on the standards of behaviour, attitudes, and emotions that people expect to be followed, rule-setting, and boundary-marking (i.e., facilitating social conformity and social acceptability, but also development of values and beliefs).
- *Companionship support*: sharing social activities and modelling what prosocial behaviour involves (i.e., inculcating a sense of belonging).

These forms of support cover pretty much the whole socialisation process. Of course, family–child relationships vary, and some children have non-familial caregivers. Not all families or caregivers will offer all of these types of social support, and they vary in the level to which they deliver those forms that they do provide. They also vary in how successful they are in communicating their social support to the child. They may try, but fail.

Researchers also commonly make a distinction between perceived and enacted support. Perceived support refers to a recipient's subjective judgement that providers will offer (or have offered) effective support. Enacted support refers to the actual supportive actions provided. Young children are unlikely initially to recognise that they are the recipients of social support, let alone understand the type of support that is involved. However, recognition grows quickly (probably coterminous with the development of theory of mind). Children then become aware of the social support processes that encompass them.

Moreover, the residual memories of these perceptions of early life social support are retained as the individual matures, and can be fundamentally important to the long-term structure of identity. In later life, sometimes these memories of early experiences of social support from the family or other caregivers are revisited, revised, and rehearsed. This retrieval and reconceptualisation of early socialisation experiences and their implied consequences for identity can be highly motivating later to serve the identity principles, reinforcing a sense of personal worth and continuity.

Familial social support (or that offered by other caregivers that substitute for the family) is key in a child's early identity development, in respect of both content and structure. Most psychological theories (whether behaviourist, evolutionary, psychodynamic, or socio-cultural) of cognitive or emotional development point to the origins of the individual's self-awareness and identity content and value in their early experiences of social support. However, they also acknowledge that the child's understanding of the meaning of the social support offered will be limited by their stage of cognitive development.

Piaget (1965) argued for them moving through six stages, each dominated by reactions differentiated by their level of complexity and their access to formal propositional reasoning. These were: reflexes, primary circular reactions, secondary circular reactions, co-ordination of reactions, tertiary circular reactions, and early representational thought. Vygotsky (Vygotsky & Cole, 1978) suggested something similar: the sensorimotor stage, the preoperational stage, the concrete operational stage, and the formal operation stage. Bruner (1997, p. 65) contrasted 'Piaget's emphasis on the invariant logic of growth with Vygotsky's emphasis on the centrality of culturally patterned dialogue in the enablement of growth'. Both of these great theorists apparently wanted to understand cognitive development itself, rather than the impact of cognitive development on the capacity of the child to develop an identity with the input available from their social milieu. Yet Vygotsky does seem to have been more likely to acknowledge the role of the developing identity itself in influencing cognitive development. Nevertheless, the cognitive developmental stage of the child must be assumed to be of great importance in the way social support can shape identity structure. Depending on their stage of cognitive development, children will process the meaning of social support efforts quite differently. With greater cognitive complexity, and the development of theory of mind, the perception of social support is likely to be accompanied by the growth of assumptions about the motives or goals of the person providing it.

Social support and identity across the lifespan

The significance of social support to identity processes does not end once early childhood has passed. Erikson (1994) argued that identity formation begins at birth and develops in order through eight stages of psychosocial development, from infancy to adulthood and old age. During each stage, the person experiences a psychosocial crisis which can have a positive or negative outcome for identity development. For Erikson (1950, 1968), these crises are of a psychosocial nature because they involve the psychological needs of the individual conflicting with the needs of society. Successful completion of each stage results in a healthy growth of identity and the acquisition of what Erikson calls 'virtues' that the individual will be able to use to resolve subsequent crises. Failure in a stage can undermine the ability to complete further stages, but retrieval and resolution are possible. Erikson's model has been enormously

Table 4.1 Erikson's psychosocial crises

Stage	Psychosocial Crisis	Basic Virtue	Age
1.	Trust vs Mistrust	Hope	0–1½
2.	Autonomy vs Shame	Will	1½–3
3.	Initiative vs Guilt	Purpose	3–5
4.	Industry vs Inferiority	Competency	5–12
5.	Identity vs Role Confusion	Fidelity	12–18
6.	Intimacy vs Isolation	Love	18–40
7.	Generativity vs Stagnation	Care	40–65
8.	Ego Integrity vs Despair	Wisdom	65+

influential, and it is worth exploring it in some detail. An attempt is made here to show some of the model's links to IPT, but also to consider the weaknesses of a stage model of identity development. Table 4.1 describes the full list of eight stages.

Erikson is explicit that in each stage the developing individual is dependent on some form of social support. The correct forms of social support are vital for successful transitions through each stage:

- In Stage 1, Trust vs Mistrust, the infant looks to the primary caregiver for stability and consistency. If this is available, they learn to trust and this is generalised to other relationships, resulting in lower anxiety and a greater sense of security. The infant learns to 'hope' and trust that people will provide social support, rather than to mistrust them. Erikson places this sort of trust at the heart of successful development of identity.
- By Stage 2, Autonomy vs Shame, children are focused on developing a sense of independence and of their control over physical skills. If children in this stage are encouraged and supported in their increased independence, they become more confident and secure in their own ability to survive in the world. If children are criticised, overly controlled, or not given the opportunity to assert themselves, they begin to feel inadequate in their ability to survive, and may then become more dependent upon others, lack self-esteem, and feel a sense of shame or doubt in their abilities. Success in this stage endows the child with 'will'. It is notable that effective familial social support is seen to allow the child independence within safe bounds, such that trial and error is an opportunity rather than a danger, and failure is not inevitable or persistent. This illustrates how complex it is to offer social support effectively. During this stage, children are learning how to express 'will', while at the same time learning to trust themselves.
- In Stage 3, Initiative vs Guilt, things get even more complex for the social support giver and there are more agents involved in the provision of social support. In this stage, the child has more contact with more people, especially with other children, and becomes more assertive and willing to initiate interactions and practise their social skills, often planning, making decisions for themselves, or leading others (e.g., in play). Punishment for, or restriction of, this desire to express 'will' through taking initiatives

or seeking information (and asking questions) can lead the child to feel guilty. The control function of social support surfaces more clearly than earlier and is perceived by the child. The social support provider has to strike a careful balance between encouraging the child to acquire self-control and suppressing the child's creativity and self-determination. Success in this stage is marked by the development of a sense of 'purpose'. Failure is associated with feelings of guilt. It can also be a time when the child develops scepticism or doubt about the trustworthiness of others.

- Stage 4, Industry vs Inferiority, is longer than the first three. The child is typically in formal education and the social support function is less focused on the family. Approval from the child's peer group becomes important for identity development, especially for self-esteem. Being able to evidence 'competence' in specific skills (e.g., sports or ballet) that are highly valued by their peers, or significant others, leads to the development of pride, but failure leads to a sense of inferiority. Success in this stage leads to the growth of a belief in one's own 'competence' (perhaps the start of later self-efficacy). The adequacy of social support during this stage will depend upon the ability of providers to understand how the peer group dynamic (or interaction with others who are influential) is operating. It is easy for the social support provider to misunderstand which competencies are important or to misread ways in which the child believes that they should be displayed. It is not easy to support children appropriately so as to correct for their actual skill or competency deficits.
- Stage 5, Identity vs Role Confusion, occurs during adolescence and creates the greatest demand on social support providers. Erikson says this is a stage in which the individual is conscious of being in search of a unique identity, exploring the values, beliefs, and goals that will or should characterise it, and trying to find a distinctive place in society. The adolescent is said to be seeking out the roles that will characterise him or her as an adult. This is a stage involving the intense re-examination of the identity developed thus far. Particular attention, according to Erikson, is given to the sexual and the occupational roles to be adopted. If things go well, the stage ends with an identity structure that incorporates an adult body image and a set of role expectations that are clear. Success at this stage is associated with 'fidelity' (i.e., the ability to commit to accepting others even when they are different from oneself). Failure can result in 'role confusion', which involves uncertainty about one's place in society. Erikson refers to role confusion as an 'identity crisis' and suggests that this might lead to experimentation with different, alternative lifestyles in the search for certainty. Social support during Stage 5 has been shown to be important. That is, if an adolescent feels that they have appropriate social support, the transition is likely to be more successful. However, getting to know in advance what the adolescent actually will regard as appropriate social support is not simple. Rebellion against standard forms of social support seems to be commonplace. Rosenberg (1989), in his work on the adolescent self-image, also emphasises the importance of social integration during adolescence on the development of self-esteem. He defined social integration in terms of 'place in the social fabric'. In this, he included roles in the family, educational setting, workplace, and religious community, and also beliefs and value systems adopted. By Stage 5, the 'identity crisis' that the individual is facing is fundamentally the task of assimilating and accommodating extraordinary volumes of new identity components, and is also

having to reconcile this process with how the whole identity structure is evaluated. IPT would not define this as an identity crisis, but rather in terms of the series of threats to identity that the adolescent has to manage.

- Stage 6, Intimacy vs Isolation, in young adulthood is focused on forming intimate, long-term, loving relationships with other people outside the family. Success leads to finding 'love'. Successful completion of this stage can result in happy relationships and a sense of commitment, safety, and social support within a relationship. Failing to build such an intimate relationship has serious knock-on consequences for the availability of future social support and identity. This seems like a rather crude dichotomy and may be reflecting the cultural expectations of a particular historical period or specific communities. Erikson may have been defining the social norms prevailing at one time and in one place. Some sort of universal requirement for intimacy in young adulthood is plausible, but it depends on what is meant by intimacy and how long-term it needs to be. Does serial intimate, loving commitment or coterminous multiple intimate relationships have the same capacity to ward off isolation and identity crisis? IPT would suggest that the nature of the relationships that prove nurturant during these years will significantly depend on the prior development of the identity structure. The need to resolve the intimacy vs isolation opposition may not arise at this age because it may not even be perceived to exist by some individuals (e.g., in those who have constructed an identity that does not value long-term commitment to other people). The interesting question then becomes, can such people be regarded as psychologically isolated? It seems unnecessary to assume they would feel themselves to be so.
- Stage 7, Generativity vs Stagnation, occurs in middle adulthood and the virtue associated with this stage is 'care'. By generativity, Erikson is taken to mean the attempt to create something that will outlast oneself. Erikson suggested that, in middle-age, individuals experience a desire to nurture or establish things that will outlast them, often benefiting others. After making a societal contribution by raising children, being a productive worker, supporting the community through charitable and other works, generativity is an urge to secure a place in the future (maybe even posterity), to be remembered but also to achieve something important. Social support in this stage would appear to be focused on, first, facilitating the establishment of the thing for which the person is remembered and, second, being an audience that expresses recognition of the importance of the thing that is made. The individual is typically highly dependent on this social support for success. The nature of the thing which outlasts the person can vary in scale and social significance. What matters is the subjective importance it has for the person's sense of personal worth (self-efficacy, self-esteem, and positive distinctiveness) and continuity (a continuity of identity that is projected beyond the precincts of the longevity of the bodily self). Failure leads to feeling stagnant, unproductive, even pointless. Failing individuals may feel disconnected or uninvolved with their community and with society as a whole. Whether this stage is significant or has to be located at this time in life can be debated. It rather depends on what already has been achieved earlier. For instance, would the person who won 23 Olympic gold medals as a swimmer before the age of 30 still feel the motive to make a mark in middle age? Of course, early success may motivate

attempts for even greater achievements, perhaps in another field of endeavour. Even the serially successful can exhibit an evident desire to avoid or escape stagnation. It could be argued that the motive to avoid stagnation, and be generative, is simply another indicator that the individual is motivated to achieve continuing self-efficacy, self-esteem, and positive distinctiveness. If so, it would suggest that the search for generativity may be a more ubiquitous part of the processes of identity development throughout the lifespan, and not just in middle age.

- Stage 8, Ego Integrity vs Despair, occurs from the mid-60s onwards. It is during this time that Erikson says that people contemplate their accomplishments and can develop integrity if they see themselves as having led a successful life. Individuals who reflect on their life and regret not achieving their goals will experience feelings of bitterness and despair. Erikson describes ego integrity as a sense of coherence and wholeness. Success in this stage is said to lead to 'wisdom', which enables people to look back on their life with a sense of closure and completeness, and also accept death without fear. 'Wise' people are not characterised by a continuous state of ego integrity. They may experience shifts between feeling ego integrity and despair. Thus, according to Erikson, late life is characterised by the need to balance both integrity and despair. The role of social support in this stage, if it to be valued by the individual, has to be a complex mixture: affirming that the individual's life has been and continues to be valued, while also rejecting the individual's reasons for despair. Finding and retaining social support that is valued at this stage of life is difficult unless the foundations have been laid throughout other stages. For instance, a person who finds it hard to trust others, perhaps as a consequence of failures in the first three stages of development, may find believing what social supporters say about the value of their life hard.

Erikson has had a major effect on the way identity development in adulthood is regarded. He contributed an approach to understanding psychosocial development across the entire lifespan. Intuitively, people tend to find his model attractive, perhaps because it resonates with some of their personal experiences. Indeed, McAdams (2001) provided support for the proposed sequence of developmental stages. However, Erikson (1994) acknowledged that his theory is primarily a descriptive overview of social and emotional development and that it does not adequately explain what factors will predict how this development occurs. In this sense, it is not a falsifiable theory.

There is also doubt about the proposition that these eight stages are actually discrete (e.g., Costa & McCrae, 1997). The model could be seen as presenting one way of chunking what is a continual process of identity growth across the lifespan, in which the same psychological and social processes are always at work but producing differing outcomes as the context for their operation changes. Perhaps it is timely now to focus less on the description of these developmental stages and their consequent phenomena (such as identity diffusion, identity foreclosure, moratorium, and identity achievement) and to focus more on the psychological and social processes that might explain them. IPT does not describe discrete stages in identity development. Rather, it is concerned with the ongoing dynamics of construction and maintenance of identity across the lifetime.

The potential importance of social support has been highlighted throughout the outline description of the Eriksonian stages provided above. The form and function of social support across the stages clearly varied. In fact, the differing constituents and impact of social support on identity structure and processes across the whole lifespan need to be explicitly modelled. Social support can be treated as a generic factor in determining identity structure and changes in it.

Social influence and social control

IPT treats social support as important in explaining identity change throughout the lifespan. Social support is a key determinant of how far the identity principles can be satisfied. This is to say that social support is not just relevant to understanding how identity changes in crisis or under threat, it is central to the everyday operation of the identity processes of assimilation-accommodation and evaluation. The analogy of the mechanic that is used to both repair and service a motor vehicle springs to mind. Social support is sought when the identity is either broken down or showing signs of imminent breakdown, but also is regularly responsible for the ongoing performance of the identity. Just like a good garage, the social support structure in which the individual is located will not necessarily wait to be asked to offer help or advice. It prompts and reminds that things need to be done to keep identity moving forward appropriately. Social support providers are not just reactive, they are proactive. Social support providers have their own motives for engaging with the individual and for trying to shape his or her identity development.

Social support is crucially a bundle of social influence and social control processes, which are integrated by the many feedback loops between them. Many types of social support providers operate in ways that influence identity change across the lifespan. From Erikson and other personality and identity theorists, a list of key social support providers can be compiled that includes family; age, gender, educational, and occupational peer group members; long-term friends and sexual partners. Beyond that list, there are in addition many organisational and institutional social support systems that have a role to play (e.g., governmental social welfare provision). The relative influence of these various providers of social support for identity development varies over the lifespan.

Throughout the lifespan the individual is situated in a dynamic social support network. The network is never still. Its constituents change, their objectives shift, and their activities alter. Once social support is seen as an interactive network that is responsive to many demands, the multifaceted and variable nature of the impacts that it will have on identity structure content and evaluation over the lifespan becomes evident. The great unpredictability of the consequences for identity change also becomes more inevitable.

The active, rather than passive, role of the individual within this social support network also needs to be considered. IPT proposes that the individual will strive selectively to elicit from the network inputs that support self-esteem, self-efficacy, positive distinctiveness, and continuity. This will entail the following:

- *Rewarding*: showing gratitude for social support that satisfies the identity motives – reinforcing the provider to continue giving the same sort of support. Even infants do this, providing cues (such as smiling) that encourage their parents to behave as desired.

- *Positioning*: moving into social situations where desired social support is available and leaving ones where it is not.
- *Asking*: requests for social support can be explicit or implicit and can take many forms on a continuum from supplication to demand with menaces.

The fact that the individual is an agent in determining what social support is provided highlights the issue of control. Social support that is imposed without consent might be regarded as social control rather than support. There is a shadowy middle ground between social support and social control where they appear to be indistinguishable in practice to the external observer. Of course, if the definition of social support rests only on whether it is perceived by the recipient as support and not control, then the issue is moot. In either guise, social influence processes are vitally important for the effect upon identity.

Bases of social influence

Cialdini (2001b) argued that, in order to exert social influence and induce someone to conform or comply (i.e., to do, feel, or think as you wish), six 'weapons of influence' can be used:

- *Friendship*: using the fact of friendship/closeness/being related as a basis for the legitimacy of the request for compliance and people tend to be more easily swayed by others they like. The threat of losing a close relationship can also induce compliance.
- *Reciprocation*: offering explicitly or implicitly to do or give something in return for the compliance. Failure to comply might then be associated with the withdrawal of some desired reciprocity.
- *Authority*: using power differentials to legitimate or enforce the request/demand for compliance. The power claim made might be based in social role, information control, or some sort of punishment (e.g., physical, emotional, or psychosocial).
- *Consistency/commitment*: requests/demands for compliance are likely to be more persuasive if they are presented persistently and appear to be consistent. People are also motivated to be consistent once they commit to some course of action or way of thinking. Calls for conformity in the interests of personal consistency can be influential.
- *Social validation/proof*: using evidence that compliance is necessary or required can improve influence. Often this evidence is not based on some objective proof but rather on social exemplars or norms. Compliance can be a product of social modelling (copying others).
- *Scarcity*: having someone believe that some opportunity is in limited supply (e.g., allowing a small window of time for complying, or stressing that only a few people will get this chance) can increase the attractiveness of complying.

Cialdini and Goldstein (2004) reviewed research on the principles and processes underlying a target's susceptibility to outside influences. They found that targets are motivated to form accurate perceptions of reality and react to influence attempts accordingly; to develop and preserve meaningful social relationships; and to maintain a favourable self-concept.

They argue that these goals interact with external forces to engender social influence processes that are subtle, indirect, and largely outside awareness.

The desire that people have to form accurate perceptions of reality affects the form that most social influence activities take. It finds particular effect in the way information and its channels of dissemination become central to social influence processes. Key features are:

- the control of information flow – timing and sequencing of information provision;
- the selectivity of information provision – both omitted and included;
- the contextualisation of information – accurate information but with its meaning altered by surrounding information;
- misinformation – incorrect or misleading information shared without the intent to deceive;
- disinformation – information shared with the intent to deceive.

The meaning of any of these types of information can be modified by changing the apparent source from which they originate. The source alters the perceived truthfulness but also the persuasive power of the information and its interpretation (Breakwell, 2021b).

The basis for social influence also has to be seen from the perspective of group dynamics. Cialdini's six weapons are embedded in the intra- and intergroup contexts where they are deployed. The effectiveness of each weapon is dependent on where its user sits in the group dynamics that are important to the target of their influence attempts. Desire to retain group membership or conform with group identification requirements can either diminish or exaggerate the impact of attempts at social influence. A source of social influence associated with one's own significant group memberships may have a higher chance of exerting social influence. Cialdini and Goldstein (2004) speak of the external forces engendering social influence processes that are subtle, indirect, and largely outside awareness. One external force is group dynamics. It is a force at work in most aspects of identity development. We return to it further in Chapter 7.

In recognising the variety of social influence techniques and the factors that affect their use and effectiveness, their use in social support and their potential impact on identity development becomes somewhat clearer. Social support providers typically exert social influence. This influence may be a corollary of the prime objective when this is perceived by the support provider as being to give help. In this sense, it can be a collateral effect, not intended. More often support is about giving help to achieve particular effects, either for the provider or for the recipient. Once that happens, support is inevitably accompanied by social influence and the use of at least some of the tactics in the social influence arsenal that Cialdini described.

The motivation of social support providers can be ranged on a continuum from self-less altruism to self-centred control. By no means are all social support efforts purposefully aimed at bringing about particular changes in identity. The effect on identity can be collateral from support that is aimed at changing specific conditions for the individual (e.g., financial stability, different foster parents, or addiction therapy). The relationship between the specific social support provider and the individual can be described on a series of continua: from personal to institutional, from long-term to transient, from real-world to virtual, and from individualised to generalised.

The way the individual perceives the position of the social support provider on these continua may affect its power to influence identity processes because it may alter the interpretation of the provider's actions and intentions. It would be predicted, on the basis of general patterns of social influence success rates, that a social support provider that has a relationship with the individual that is personal, long-term, real-world, and individualised would have a greater effect on identity processes. Even so, IPT would predict that the impact would be moderated by prior levels of self-efficacy, self-esteem, positive distinctiveness, and continuity that characterise the identity. It is harder to use social influence to change identity if the identity is already resilient.

Channels of social influence: social media

The emphasis above on the lifespan development of identity tends to focus upon large-scale and long-term movements in the identity structure. It has also focused on traditionally significant sources of social support and social influence, such as the family or institutions (e.g., schools or employers). However, the continual and day-to-day reconstruction and growth of identity, with the imminent advent of the metaverse, has many other significant channels of social support and the influence that it exerts.

It is hard to know how to label the environment that now exists in our material world (lodged within our technologies) but which has been created in order to be a parallel, virtual reality. Using labels like 'digital world' or 'internet' does not capture the full complexity of this environment that is both part of the erstwhile real world and beyond its constraints. The metaverse is defined essentially as a virtual reality space in which users can interact with a computer-generated environment and with other users. The finished metaverse, as envisaged by technology companies, is currently a prospect rather than complete. But the functionality provided within augmented and virtual reality is growing rapidly, creating new means of connections (e.g., the internet of things, extended reality headsets, and cloud technologies) and new sources of making money and gaining power or influence (e.g., online gaming, blockchain, and nonfungible tokens).

Social support and social influence processes are rushing to inhabit the metaverse. In particular, they pervade social media. Unlike earlier public mass media channels for information transmission, social media are heavily interactive, allowing multi-way communication. They consequently open up greater opportunities for the social influence weaponry described earlier. Most importantly, they make it possible for more and different types of sources of social support and influence to establish themselves. An intrinsic ingredient of social media is their relatively open access. It means that anyone (or any group or organisation) wishing to support and/or influence others has the opportunity to try. The potential sources of identity influences grow beyond number.

These new sources are different from their predecessors:

- Their choice of target can be random.
- They do not need to have any previous contact with their target.
- They do not need to have any obligation towards their target.
- They can be anonymous if they choose.

- They can fake their own identity at will.
- Their location or origins can be untraceable.
- They can act in concert without their collusion being manifest. In fact, it can be masked in order to enhance their effectiveness by appearing to provide independent verification of claims.
- They can target individuals in a personalised way, but at the same time launch a general campaign that targets many people.
- They can incorporate third-party affirmation for their messages by associating themselves with people of significance to the target or people who have general celebrity or status in novel ways, because the choice of endorsement can be linked to an individual target's own habits, attitudes, and preferences.
- They can control the way the target interacts with them (i.e., shaping the flows and format of information exchange). They are effectively setting the rules of the game to be played. This can be a game without any assumption of mutuality.
- They can bring together information about the target from many other sources (e.g., databases on shopping behaviour) and use it to shape what they say, and the inducements of engagement or life changes they offer.
- They exist in a place that makes them simultaneously close to the individual they target (sitting there in their bedroom on their screen) and distant from that individual (present only in bites of information in their laptop).

There are probably other differences that could be added to this list. Some of these attributes may have been associated with earlier sources of social influence (e.g., the use of celebrity endorsement in advertisements or the use of personalised messages in political campaigns). It is the concatenation of all these possible options that makes the metaverse so novel for social support and influence.

The characteristics that make these sources potentially significant manipulators of identity construction and maintenance also make them likely to be limited in their impact on certain people. There is something disconcerting about interacting with sources that are literally insubstantial, without past or assumed future, that can make people suspicious and wary of compliance. People with higher levels of identity resilience are less likely to be open to social media influence. This may be because social media sources have less to offer them in terms of enhancement of the four identity principles. It may be because they are less likely to trust sources with whom they have no established relationship or who they feel owe them no obligation or commitment.

Social media removes some of the disadvantages of apparent randomness, fakery, lack of mutuality, and anonymity when the source becomes established as recognisable in their own right. This is the foundation for the existence of 'social media influencers' (SMIs). A social media influencer typically is someone who has established credibility in a specific industry, has access to a huge audience, and can persuade others to act based on their recommendations. In 2022, the top eight most famous SMIs on Instagram were each reported to have over 23 million followers. Even lesser players had more than 10 million followers. This is a business that relies on SMIs, mostly through letting followers know that they like something or someone, to change the commercial behaviour of large numbers of people. SMIs may not be thinking about their impact on the identities of their followers, but indirectly they do shape those identities by supporting people to change their attitudes and behaviour towards particular things or people. SMIs also have a more direct impact on identity by becoming role models. Followers emulate the SMI, assimilate new identity components copied from the SMI, and adopt evaluation standards evidenced in the behaviour of the SMI.

Celebrity SMIs are one phenomenon of the metaverse. But anyone can have a go. There are now training schedules for amateurs who want to learn how to use social media to build influence. The techniques advised include the following:

- Build connections online with like-minded people.
- Collaborate and engage with your audience so as to make a strong network with your community.
- Give due credit and acknowledgement to other people.
- Share information strategically, in a timely way, and make what you say valuable to the people who see it (this can include offering something that they wish to pass on to others, or things which give them some early taste of things to come).
- Work to a plan in what you post.
- Give feeds to your other messaging routes (e.g., blogs).
- Be persistent in messaging.
- Be consistent.
- Be authentic.

Obviously, most of these are slightly revamped versions of the standard advice on putting together messaging that is persuasive or influential. However, this is now a medium available for use for these purposes by almost anyone, anywhere, anytime. Social media are great levellers.

With regard to identity processes, social media create opportunities for others to influence an individual's identity in many ways. Some of these can be regarded as positive (e.g., when the social media community champions an individual's decisions on identity choice, such as in relation to gender identification or sexual orientation). Some of these can be regarded as negative (e.g., when the social media community chastises and condemns someone for a decision to leave a relationship or abandon support of a sports team). Some can be thought incoherent or meaningless by an outsider but may have an inordinate impact on the target (e.g., a post involving a line quoted from a song). The social media influence channel allows either an individual or a number of individuals acting in concert deliberately or coincidentally or accidentally to influence identity processes of one or more others.

Simultaneously, social media give the individual freedom to express their identity. Identity-expression through social media is not without its risks. The typical limitations (via social norms) on attacking, demeaning, or challenging someone's identity are less effective on social media. Nevertheless, it does mean that the individual has the opportunity to give expression to his or her identity, and this may be an important way to test how people will react to any change that is being considered before revealing it in other ways. Retreat from the expression of identity online is probably easier than in the flesh for most people. Also, social media probably offers more diversity of response than might be found in smaller, tight-knit, local, real-world networks.

Social support and identity processes in context

This chapter started by stating that social support is a fuzzy concept. Having unpacked some of the questions surrounding the concept, it seems sensible to treat social support as a particular manifestation of social influence processes, one that has positive effects on the construction and maintenance of the identity structure over the entire lifespan. However, social support influencing takes place in a complex context. Any specific instance of social support is given meaning for the individual concerned by a series of interacting factors, including:

- the material circumstances in which it takes place;
- the extent to which support is an answer to established need;
- the characteristics of its source and the motivation of that source;
- the cognitive, affective, and conative states of the individual involved at the time that social support is proffered – cognitive capacity is a particular factor of importance in early and later life;
- the existing identity structure of the individual and the degree to which it satisfies the motives for achieving and maintaining self-esteem, self-efficacy, positive distinctiveness, and continuity;
- the past relationship history of the individual and the source of social support;
- the social context (e.g., the social hierarchy, the cultural expectations, the ideological system) in which the support is offered.

The meaning that the individual gives to any act of social support will determine the possibility that it will have the capacity to change the identity structure through the processes of assimilation-accommodation and evaluation. Depending on the meaning attributed to it by the individual, social support will influence identity in different ways and to varying degrees. It can result in changes at the level of individual components of the identity. It can also result in significant reorganisation of the way components are fitted together and major changes in the value placed on components or on identity as a whole. Such reorganisations and re-evaluations are most likely to occur if the identity is facing some crisis or is under attack. The next chapter examines what happens under such circumstances.

5

THE ASSESSMENT OF THREAT TO IDENTITY

Be firm on principle but flexible on method.
Zig Ziglar (2013)

Issues addressed in this chapter

This chapter briefly describes the origins of threat to identity. It focuses upon presenting and critiquing some methods that can be used to assess the form and effects of threat to identity.

Origins of threat to identity

Threats to identity are manifested in many forms. Many types of experiences can act as threats. Some will be selective, affecting individuals with specific social or psychological profiles (e.g., being blacklisted by a professional association for not espousing its values). Others will be indiscriminate, affecting multitudes, perhaps simultaneously (e.g., being forced to flee one's homeland when it is invaded by a foreign army).

Threat cannot be adequately characterised merely in terms of its form. The definition of a threat must be derived from its implications for identity. Many types of experiences can act as threats, and they may share very little in common in their outward form. Their commonality lies in the structure of the predicament that they pose for identity. Identity Process Theory posits that *a threat to identity occurs when the processes of identity (assimilation-accommodation and evaluation) are, for some reason, unable to comply with the identity principles of continuity, distinctiveness, self-efficacy, and self-esteem that habitually guide their action*. The reason for this disruption of the identity processes constitutes the threat.

The proximate (or immediate) origin of the threat can be perceived to be either internal or external to the individual who feels threatened. A threat can be thought to originate internally when the individual chooses to initiate some change in one of the components of identity. This choice may be motivated by one identity principle, but then is found to conflict with one or more of the others. For instance, motivated by a desire to prove her distinctiveness and self-efficacy, a teenager might drop her old 'best friends' to gain new friends but then find that, in doing so, she was putting her sense of continuity and self-esteem at risk when the new friends fail to live up to expectations. Such a threat has a proximate origin that is internal in so far as the individual initiates the change in her interpersonal network. The less immediate origin of the threat will lie in the social influences that led her to feel she wanted different friends. Even threats that appear to have an internal origin can usually be traced back to some external influences associated with changes in the social or physical environment.

Sometimes, the proximate origin of the threat is also external to the individual and is in no way mediated by his or her own choices. For instance, a global pandemic results in governments imposing international travel restrictions that prevent someone from a poor family who has won a scholarship place at an elite university in another country taking up her place for a year, in that year her mother and father die from the virus, and she, being the eldest of seven children, is expected to stay and be responsible for their care. She believes that she has no possibility of ever pursuing her academic aspirations. In this case, the changes are thrust upon this young woman. Many components of her identity may be changed because her circumstances have changed so radically.

Differentiating position threat and perceived threat

There may be little doubt that the pandemic, and the implications it had for living conditions and social life, represented a proximate, external threat to identity in the case described above. However, it points to an important distinction that must be made between being in an identity threatening position and subjectively experiencing identity threat. Looking at it from the outside, it sometimes seems obvious that a person should feel identity threat in the situation that they are in. When they are asked about it, they may say that they do not believe or feel that their identity is threatened. The young woman might not experience identity threat if she is capable of assimilating-accommodating to the changes in her circumstances and can evaluate her changed identity content highly. You might then ask: is she is not experiencing identity threat because she has already deployed coping strategies to ameliorate it? Is denial of the existence of the threat one of the strategies used in protecting the identity structure? Has the operation of the identity processes assuaged identity threat to such a degree that it is not experienced? This is possible.

Certainly, some studies of people dealing with identity change in threatening positions show that as they successfully evolve new identity structures, they are clear that they are not experiencing threat. Singh et al. (2014), in a study of young trans-sexual people, found that this happened. Others cope by reinterpreting the threat as less significant for identity. This can be done, for instance, by projecting the threat onto others and, thus, reducing its personal salience. For examples, Bennett and Holmes (1975) conducted an experiment with 112 female undergraduates. Subjects in a threat condition were informed that they had failed an important test, while subjects in a non-threat condition were not told that they had failed. To manipulate the use and timing of coping strategies for dealing with threat, subjects were told to (a) redefine the nature and importance of the test before receiving feedback, or (b) redefine the nature and importance of the test after feedback, or (c) estimate the performance of their friends on the test (i.e., projection) after receiving feedback. Repeated measures of subjective anxiety and pulse rate indicated that the threat manipulation was effective in increasing stress, and that redefinition occurring after the onset of threat was ineffective in reducing stress, but projection onto friends reduced the report of subjective anxiety.

How quickly these adjustments happen is very much a function of the severity of the threat (indexed, for instance, in the type, amount, or speed of identity change undergone) and the resources available to the individual to renovate the identity structure (e.g., initial identity resilience and social support). For instance, Zare et al. (2017), based on an interview study with a small number of Iranian women divorcees, report that divorce for Iranian women represents a significant identity threat. They argue that the patriarchal cultural norms and anti-divorce attitudes in Iranian society and the critical importance of marital status for Iranian women make divorce a threat to identity that is hard to resolve. The women reported feelings of discrimination, rejection, social stigma, humiliation, shame, worthlessness, and dishonour. Such identity threat is embedded in an ongoing revision of social status. It might be anticipated that the identity processes set in motion by the divorce itself are hampered in achieving a stable, positive restructuring for the identity structure by the additional, long-term life changes that divorce initiates in this culture.

After finding many examples of the schism between occupying a threatening position and perceiving oneself to be threatened, IPT has reiterated that what counts in predicting the consequences of being in a threatening position is how the individual involved construes it. Since how it is construed can change, sometimes quickly, there are implications for anyone doing empirical research on threatened identities. It is important to examine separately what can be called 'position threat' and 'perceived threat'. Given that perceived threat can be modified or even erased by the normal work of the identity processes (sometimes quickly), capturing it empirically is a difficult task. This is made more problematic because the speed with which modification or erasure takes place varies enormously and, depending on the nature of the threat, may be unpredictable.

It calls for a very systematic approach to the empirical capture of both position threat and perceived threat. Deciding which parameters to examine is the first task. Deciding the method to be used is the second task.

Position threat assessment

Establishing the substance of position threat can be done from the perspective of an independent observer or it can be done from the perspective of the individual who is involved (or both). Either way, the following are the parameters that might be considered for examination:

1. What happened?
2. Did it involve a potential threat to identity?
3. What type of potential identity threat was involved?
4. What events represented the threat?
5. What was the sequence of those events?
6. What was the length of time involved in individual events in the sequence or in the overall sequence?
7. What people were involved in each of those events?
8. What was the variety of immediate consequences for the individual who was potentially threatened?

The methods for accessing responses from any independent observer(s) may include the use of archival records (e.g., histories, media reports, diaries, police reports or medical records, video recordings, or contemporary social media interactions). They may include structured or in-depth free-form interviews. They can be compilations of information sought immediately after the events or retrospectively (in some cases this could be a considerable time later, even years).

The methods for accessing responses to these questions from the individual potentially threatened could include any objective evidence (e.g., photographs, videos, documents, third-party corroboration) that they have for their recollections and reports of the events in question.

However, in the absence of corroborating evidence, self-reports (whether questionnaires or interviews, and whether structured, semi-structured, or free-form) are regularly used.

The answers the individual provides to the questions that are focused on whether there was a threat to identity (questions 2, 3, 4, and 8) are clearly subject to the after-effects of any coping strategies that have been deployed to protect identity. They would need to be interpreted with caution. It may be that asking these questions is inadvisable if the individual is to be subsequently asked about their perceived threat. Answers to these questions on threat could frame the interpretation of later questions and bias answers to them.

The methods used to examine position threat cut across the qualitative/quantitative dichotomy in data collection and analysis approaches. This seems to be necessary if we are to understand the complexities and subtleties of the social processes that create identity threat positions. It is important to start with thorough, meticulous descriptions of the circumstances in which threats arise, whenever possible. Moving on to measurement in its various forms before that is achieved can result in being misled. It is important to measure the relevant parameter in the appropriate way.

The methods described above assume that the putative threat is naturally occurring. There is a possibility that the dynamics of position threat could be explored experimentally by placing someone in a situation *a priori* objectively defined as likely to threaten. Whether it is ethical to do such an experiment is questionable. However, various paradigms have been developed that essentially have the potential to establish position threat. They include the following:

- False feedback: Under controlled conditions that allow a comparison of an experimental and control group, this simply entails offering inaccurate (usually negative) feedback about their performance on a task or on the implications of choices that they make (e.g., Finkelstein et al., 2019). The effects of such feedback vary according to the personality traits of the individual and the tasks involved (e.g., Swift & Peterson, 2018). However, false feedback on important components of identity structure (e.g., on masculinity; see Braly et al., 2018) are consistently effective in modifying behaviour or attitudes expressed. False feedback can be used to create a position threat explicitly designed to challenge the status of any of the four identity principles. For instance, level of self-esteem can be put in a threatened position if the feedback undermined specific bases for claims of self-esteem (e.g., excellence in sports, or sexual attractiveness). It should be emphasised that false feedback of this sort is not threatening the self-esteem principle itself as a motivation force for assimilation-accommodation and evaluation of identity structure. If it has an effect, it affects the level of self-esteem, not the motivation to achieve it. The distinction between the identity principle as a state of identity structure and as a motivator of identity processes should always be remembered.
- False feedback studies should only be conducted if thorough debriefing of participants in the experiment is provided (i.e., offering an explanation of the experiment's objectives, the falsehood involved, and follow-up support). False feedback studies are only valuable if the feedback given is believed. Producing credible feedback that deviates from that which a participant would expect based on their knowledge of their previous performance is very difficult. It is more difficult to achieve credibility if the feedback involves something of great importance to the individual or the feedback

deviates greatly from what the individual would expect. Furthermore, false feedback studies often entail very artificial situations because they require the maintenance of complete comparability of the experience of the participants in the experimental and control conditions. Consequently, generalising the threat effect of feedback is problematic.

- Structured recollection: This (sometimes called evoked recall) involves participants in the experiment (or quasi-experiment) being asked to recall an event that happened to them which might, on an *a priori* basis, be regarded as likely to have entailed a position threat. The objective is to ascertain whether reliving the event through memory results in the participant perceiving in retrospect that the event was a threat to identity at the time it happened. When faced with such a task, typically people are able to recognise that a recollected event was a threat to their identity at the time it occurred. They may be able to do this even though they had coped with the threat, and even though it may not have resulted in any change in identity structure that they acknowledge (e.g., see Breakwell & Jaspal, 2022). Structured recollection is a useful tool, but it has drawbacks. First and foremost, asking a person to recall a significant, potentially threatening, event may cause them distress and it can be unethical to put them at such risk. Assuming that you have informed consent and relevant ethics committee clearance, there are practical matters to consider: (a) How do you know that the individual has experienced the type of position threat that interests you? You may think that this is simple. For instance, you could sample people on the basis that they satisfy certain criteria that suggest it is likely that they will have experienced such a threat event. On that basis, it would still be possible that they had not. So, as an alternative, you may sample by asking people who have experienced such a threat event to contact you. This is likely to introduce biases into the sample. For instance, people for whom the threat event was particularly significant may either be more likely not to come forward (if they found it too threatening to deal with) or more likely to come forward (if they coped well with the threat). (b) How do you know that the recalled memory is accurate? The malleability of memory is becoming increasingly clear. Many influences can cause memories to change or even be created anew, including our imaginations and the leading questions or different recollections of others (Loftus, 2003). Indeed, for several decades, Loftus engaged in manufacturing memories in unsuspecting minds (see Loftus, 2020). Sometimes she used techniques to change details of events that someone actually experienced. Other times, the techniques create entire memories of events that never happened: they create 'rich false memories'. Collectively, this work shows that people can be led to believe they did things that would have been rather implausible. They can be led to falsely believe they had experiences that would have been emotional or traumatic had they actually happened. False memories, like true ones, also have consequences for people – affecting their later thoughts, feelings, and behaviours. For the researcher who wants to examine previous position threats to identity, the malleability of memory poses great difficulties. At one level, it suggests that the individual believed to have experienced the threat may be a totally unreliable witness about it. At another level, it suggests that the mere act of inviting the person to think about their memory of a particular set of events may modify the memory (perhaps resulting in its threat capacity being elevated or diminished).

- Can we tell true memories from false ones? Probably not reliably. In several studies, Loftus created false memories in the minds of people, compared them to true memories, and discovered that once planted, those false memories look very much like true memories: they have similar behavioural characteristics, emotionality, and neural signatures.
- Considered as a whole, these findings on 'false' memories raise important questions and not just about the methods that can be used in studying identity threat. There is the question of what pseudo-memories say about the nature of memory itself. Since IPT emphasises the role of memory as the repository of the identity structure, its malleability itself becomes a threat to identity. In fact, the malleability of memory may compound the impact of other threats on the identity structure. This may be particularly significant in public crises or personal attacks that intrinsically involve attempts to plant false memories or invalidate authentic memories. Given the use of memory manipulation on a large scale in all major conflicts, there is also a question about how it can be controlled or neutralised. We return to this later in relation to crises.
- Evidently, there are fundamental problems in relying on the individual to give anything but a biased assessment of position threat. It is biased by the contemporary operation of the same identity principles and identity processes that have previously responded to whatever threat the events presented. This suggests that assessment of position threat solely based on memories from the person who has possibly been threatened is unwise. Such assessments lie more on the perceived threat side of the equation.

Perceived threat assessment

Establishing the substance of perceived threat can be done only from the perspective of the individual who is, or has possibly been, threatened. Following are the parameters that might be considered for examination:

1. What identity component or components are perceived to be targeted by the threat?
2. What change in a component or in relationships between identity components is perceived to be required by the threat?
3. What change in a component or in relationships between identity components is perceived to have occurred in response to the threat, either immediately or over specified time periods?
4. What change is the threat perceived to have brought about in the levels of self-esteem, self-efficacy, positive distinctiveness, or continuity? Have these changes varied over specified time periods?
5. What change is the threat perceived to have brought about in the levels of motivation to achieve self-esteem, self-efficacy, positive distinctiveness, or continuity? Have these changes been modified over specified time periods?
6. What change is the threat perceived to have stimulated in the relative importance of the four identity principles in motivating thought, feeling, or actions? Have these changes been modified over specified time periods?

It is notable that these parameters are not actually concerned specifically with how the threat itself is perceived; they are primarily concerned with the targets that the threat affects and the effects it is perceived to create. It is the perception of threat in terms of its consequences.

These parameters of the perceived threat should be seen alongside the parameters of the position threat. The methods for assessing the parameters of perceived threat, like those used for position threat, will cut across the qualitative/quantitative dichotomy in data collection and analysis approaches. The mixed-method approach advocated by Breakwell et al. (2020) is valuable in this context. Bringing together data from different levels of analysis (intra-psychic, interpersonal, intra-group and intergroup) and with different data collection methods (e.g., observation, questionnaire survey, quasi-experiments, and interviewing) creates a more comprehensive appreciation of how threats are perceived.

Inevitably, understanding that a threat has been perceived to exist relies heavily on self-report from the individual who has experienced position threat. This has been the primary means of gathering data on perceived threat. It will probably remain so. However, other approaches are possible. The individual's reactions to an identity threat can be monitored independently of what that person consciously reports about it. Changes in behaviour following the threat, for instance, can be observed; brain imaging can reveal changes in neurological functioning associated with threatened identity components; or the effects of threat to identity on emotional lability can be assayed using biomarkers. These approaches may tell us something about the effects of a threat that the individual has experienced. They can suggest that the individual has perceived that a threat exists or has been present. They cannot tell us much for certain about what the threat means for identity without an accompanying explanation from the individual concerned. Of course, as soon as we turn to the individual for an account of their perceived threat, we pass beyond what can be verified empirically.

When assessing perceived threat, it is not good enough to say simply: what matters is what the individual says they had perceived. The malleability of memory makes that untenable. Any account that the individual gives of the perceived threat's effects must be assumed to be, to some unknown degree, a product of the operation of the identity processes that respond to threat. This is why using a mixed-method approach is so important. The corroboration of the individual's account from other sources of data provides a semblance of verification. Nevertheless, it is still vital to acknowledge that what really matters in determining the ultimate effects of identity threat is that the individual actually does perceive it during the time that it is present. Conscious self-awareness, which is at the heart of identity processes, has to recognise that a threat exists for changes in the identity structure to be motivated.

Viewed over time, the status of the perception of threat becomes more of a conundrum. If a threat position emerges and the individual perceived it as a threat, then a threat exists for identity. If the individual does not perceive it as a threat, then no threat exists for identity. What, then, happens when the threat position persists over time? It is unlikely to remain the same. The threat position may be compounded and become more significant for identity as the individual's or societal circumstances change. Alternatively, it may recede in importance for the individual following such changes. The individual's awareness and perception of the threat over time will wax and wane with variations in the personal, societal, and environmental context.

There is some scope for the assessment both of the perceived threat and of the ongoing effects of the threat over time using an experimental approach. For example, Breakwell and Jaspal (2022) conducted a between-participants experimental study of 333 gay men in the UK in 2020, who were allocated randomly to one of two groups and asked to recall either a coming out experience that they felt had resulted in a negative change when it happened or one that had resulted in things staying the same. Participants wrote two to three sentences on what they recalled. Then, immediately after, having been asked to think carefully about the experience they had described, they rated how distressed they felt by recalling the experience and also rated its impact on their levels of self-esteem, self-efficacy, positive distinctiveness, and continuity. This contemporaneous measure of identity change initiated by the recollection was very direct. On a five-point scale, they were asked how far they agreed with four statements: it undermines my sense of self-worth; it makes me feel less competent; I feel that my identity has changed; it makes me feel less unique as a person. Participants in the negative recollection condition reported higher levels of identity change. Feeling distressed by the recollection increased the level of contemporaneous identity change. As was mentioned in Chapter 3, baseline level of identity resilience was also measured in this study using the Identity Resilience Index (Breakwell, Fino, & Jaspal, 2022). Identity resilience moderated the negative identity change effect of recollecting a negative coming out experience. This study did not attempt to capture the perceptions of identity threat during coming out. Instead, it says something about the effects on current identity if erstwhile position threat is reawakened. The position threat explored here is historical, vested in memory. The study did not attempt to examine the accuracy of the memory. The significance of the study is that the memory of what the participant felt to be a negative experience was enough to trigger perceivable identity change in the present. Further experimental work on this would seem to be worthwhile. The more imaginative use of experimental approaches to the assessment of identity threat and identity change is desirable.

Social influences on the perceived threat

In concluding this chapter, that perception is an ongoing, dynamic process has to be reiterated. Perceiving a situation, or a set of events, as embodying a threat to identity should not be regarded as a binary yes/no or once-and-for-all decision that is made. The perception of threat can vary in stability and in clarity over time. One of the key features of the process of perceiving that a threat is present is the uncertainty and doubts that accompany it. In fact, the uncertainty that surrounds the perception of position threat is a form of meta-threat for identity. We will return to the role of uncertainty in perceptions of identity threat in Chapter 8. Uncertainty is itself a prime outcome of position threat, especially in public crises or when individuals are targeted for attack.

While the individual's perception of a position threat is what turns it into something that identity processes must address, in concluding this chapter it is necessary to emphasise that the individual's perception of a position threat is subject to social influence. The social meaning attributed within a culture or community to the set of events that pose a putative threat to identity will significantly affect whether the individual involved perceives them as an actual threat. Social influence processes are major factors in shaping the individual's initial awareness of the position threat and subsequent interpretation of its possible implications for identity. Indeed, these social influence processes are not infrequently the stimuli for the events that are identified as threatening. For instance, the importance of ideological and value systems for threat definition and perception is evident when the example used earlier of the implications of divorce for women's identities in different cultures is recalled.

6

IDENTITY IN PUBLIC CRISES AND WHEN UNDER ATTACK

Within crisis, are the seeds of opportunity.
Often attributed to Marilyn Monroe

Issues addressed in this chapter

This chapter examines how public crises act as threats to identity. One way is that crises trigger cognitive and emotional reactions that challenge the identity principles and influence the way the assimilation-accommodation and evaluation processes operate. Another is that crises occasion the manufacture of new, or restructuring of existing, social representations, and, consequently, modify the social milieu from which identity components and values are derived. This chapter will examine these effects of crises. While crises can threaten identity, the threat may not be purposeful or individualised. However, some threats to identity are deliberate and targeted. When this happens, identity can be said to be under attack. This chapter explores the coping strategies that are deployed to defray the effects of attacks upon identity.

Characterising public crises

In examining identity reactions to crises, it is useful to differentiate public from private crises. We will focus here on public crises. Generally, a crisis is defined as a time of intense difficulty or danger. A public crisis is one that affects many people, where they share some risk of failure, disadvantage, or harm. The actual level of risk they face will vary. Also, not everyone who shares the same level of risk will actually suffer the same level of harm during a crisis. The nature of the sharedness in a public crisis is always complicated. Individuals are differentiated when situated in a crisis by many factors, particularly by the nature of their immediate involvement in the crisis, the relevance of their past experiences, their social standing, and the established uniqueness of their identity structure.

Public crises range in scale, from the global (e.g., economic depression, climate change, or pandemic) to the local (e.g., hospital closures, redundancies, storm flood damage, or criminal activity). They also vary in their longevity. They tend to be characterised by:

- having a complex and/or uncertain aetiology;
- being out of immediate control;
- being irremediable by single or small collections of individuals;
- having consequences that are unforeseen initially;
- having the power to initiate or exaggerate social conflicts;
- being unequal in their impact on the individuals involved;
- causing the erosion of trust in, and blaming of, authorities.

As a consequence, public crises typically arouse rampant social representation processes. These prove to be particularly important for the forms of, and reactions to, identity threats evoked by public crises.

Social representation processes in times of public crisis

Breakwell (2020b) argued that any particular uncertainty will be seen against the backdrop of the overall levels of uncertainty that prevail in that society at the time. For instance, uncertainties about climate change and those about disease control impact on each other in diverse ways in the public narratives of societal risks. Societal uncertainty is itself the product of active, continual interpretation of events through the agency of individuals and many other social actors (e.g., activists, media, governments, and professions). Societal uncertainty is many-faceted and reconstituted continually.

Moscovici (2001), in the theory of social representations, described some of the processes that do this reconstruction work. He studied how people give meaning to novel social realities, objects, and situations that they have not seen before. They do this through communication with others, negotiating through their interactions shared understandings. Moscovici described how these 'anchoring' and 'objectification' processes come into play when a community is facing something novel or unexplained. Both processes contextualise the novel, and by doing so make it part of an intelligible set of meanings: anchoring ascribes meaning to a new phenomenon by linking it to pre-extant understandings or explanations; objectification gives it substance by associating it with exemplars that the audience has experienced, directly or indirectly.

New or changed uncertainties thus become manageable by being reconceptualised, normalised, or identified within the pre-existing system of societal uncertainty – often by reference to existing social representations of comparable events. In relation to public health crises, Barnett and Breakwell (2003) described how 'hazard sequences' and 'hazard templates' develop. They examined the history of oral contraceptive health scares, showing that the way that the public is notified about a health risk over time builds representations of the hazard. These hazard templates are part of the fabric of shared social representations of uncertainties associated with a crisis.

Another example is the way that the uncertainties surrounding the emergence of the COVID-19 virus (2019–2020) were articulated by policy makers and the media relied on understandings, or at least awareness, of other infectious fatal diseases (notably the 1918 influenza pandemic, H1N1, MERS-CoV, SARS, Ebola, measles, smallpox, and tuberculosis). The threat of the new coronavirus was anchored and objectified by reference to past experience of health crises that shared some of its features. The object was to make the levels of uncertainty concerning the consequences of the new viral threat more intelligible to the general public by grounding the explanations in commonly available (if not comprehensive) understandings of what had happened before and so what might happen in the future. In this case, the social representational processes deliberately served to lead the public to expect uncertainty to continue. Solutions (treatments, cures, vaccinations, containment) would be sought, but when they would be found was left uncertain. Acknowledging uncertainty has been found in some contexts to enhance trust in the risk communication. But the effect on perceived trustworthiness of persistently acknowledging uncertainty is not known.

Responses to the COVID-19 crisis particularly illustrate the significance of the societal pervasiveness of uncertainty. The uncertainties posed by such a global pandemic encompass all aspects of human existence – including not just physical and psychological well-being but also economic and political security. It is barely possible to conceptualise the range and complexities of the social representation processes that would be needed to objectify and anchor these uncertainties. Such processes are inevitably iterative and often apparently chaotic. They are also open to contestation. Conflicting social representations will emerge (e.g., conspiracy theories claiming that the COVID-19 virus was deliberately manufactured).

Moscovici acknowledged in the earliest formulations of his theory that there are different types of social representations and that subcultures shape the representations that they develop to serve their self-interests. Fischer et al. (2012) provide an example of this in their study of representations of climate change. They used qualitative interviews, across five European countries, to explore how people conceptualised climate change within a wider context of energy use and sustainability. Their work showed that people construct multifaceted representations, reflecting a variety of prevalent and contradictory discourses, about climate change. They emphasised that representations have cognitive, normative, and affective components and these contend with each other. This may mean that an individual's behaviour is not predictable on the basis of the social representation that they espouse.

Moscovici (1988) notes the scope for groups to use social representations strategically and identifies three types of representation:

- Hegemonic representations: These are shared by all members of a highly structured group without them having been produced by the group; they are uniform and coercive. For example, the system of beliefs that characterise a 'Doomsday' cult that prophesies the end of the world might constitute such a representation.
- Emancipated representations: These are the outgrowth of the circulation of knowledge and ideas belonging to sub-groups that are in more or less close contact – each sub-group creates and shares its own version. These representations are freed in the sense that the sub-group is at liberty to elaborate and shape them based on the access that they have to sources of information. For a single issue, there can be a number of emancipated representations – take, for example, the way different sub-groups will interpret a news report that migrants are attempting to enter the country illegally. The social representations generated may have many dimensions and each sub-group is at liberty to select or emphasise different dimensions (see, for example, de Rosa et al., 2021).
- Polemical representations: These are generated in the course of social conflict or controversy, and society as a whole does not share them; they are determined by the existence of antagonism between sub-groups and are intended to be mutually exclusive. The clash between climate change 'nay-sayers' and those who attribute global warming to human action is an example.

Social representations of a specific crisis are likely to include all three types at some point. However, the type of social representation that is prevalent at any one time is a significant determiner of how people will respond to the crisis. Where the social representation of the crisis is hegemonic, it is not a product of a subculture but substantially shared by everyone. Such consensus can be a powerful motivator for common reactions to the crisis. Where the social representations of the crisis are polemical, individuals will face contradictory pressures on their reactions. Competition between alternative social representations, often targeting different aspects of a complex crisis, against a background of general societal uncertainty, will be unlikely to result in a coherent, common understanding of the crisis or predictable patterns of reaction to the crisis.

Social representation processes can also transform events or phenomena into public crises (or, indeed, prevent them from becoming one). For instance, the way that an increase in the price of oil is presented to the public by the mass media, talked about in wine bars in New York, London, or Shanghai, criticised on social media, or debated by politicians will have a part to play in determining whether it becomes a public crisis. Gossip and rumour, whether malicious or otherwise, can convert a minor inflationary pressure into a serious economic crisis because it can change behaviour as well as perception. In the case of oil prices, consumption patterns may change, or stockpiling might occur, or energy companies' share values might swing erratically. The reactions to the social representation may themselves precipitate the crisis. A parallel with the warning of the Second World War propaganda campaign in Britain that 'careless talk costs lives' springs to mind. Something similar should capture the dangers of social representation processes during crises. Perhaps 'rogue representations ravage rationality' might do.

This echoes the idea that risk can be socially amplified or attenuated. Kasperson and others (see Pidgeon et al., 2003) proposed the Social Amplification of Risk Framework (SARF) in 1988 at roughly the same time that Moscovici developed Social Representations Theory (SRT). The SARF specifically focuses upon the dynamic social processes that underlie risk perception and decisions. It highlights that certain events or hazards, which experts would state are relatively low in risk, can nevertheless become a focus of societal concern (risk amplification), whereas other hazards, which experts judge as more serious, attract less public attention (risk attenuation). In the UK, an example of amplification would be the elaboration of scare stories about the MMR vaccination and consequent refusal by some people to let their children be vaccinated. An example of attenuation would be the reaction to naturally occurring sources of radiation, such as radon gas, which is much less than might be predicted on the basis of the scientific estimates of health risks.

The SARF proposes that risks (or risk events, which can be either real or hypothesised) will have an impact not only through their primary physical effects, but also, and often more importantly, through the way people communicate them to others. The act of communication requires that the risk is translated into various 'risk signals' (images, symbols, and signs) that will interact with a variety of psychological, social, institutional, or cultural processes, and this will result in the intensification or dampening of the perceptions of the risk and its manageability. The SARF indicates that the risk, or risk event, is given meaning through a complex and iterative process of interactions between different actors in the social structure (e.g., activist groups, mass media, commercial organisations, or policy makers, etc.).

The meaning it is given will then determine the secondary, tertiary, and subsequent effects that the risk can have on different social entities (e.g., a local community or a company). It will also constrain the nature of the actions taken in response (e.g., legislative, organisational, and economic). The ripple effects can spread far beyond the originating risk event. This diffusion of impact points out that there are many potential transmitters that can contribute to the amplification or attenuation process. This suggests that the risk event will have no ultimate or consolidated interpretation. It will change over time as each element in the ripple system is brought into play. For some risks, the timescale for interpretation and reinterpretation may be very extended (i.e., over centuries, as is the case of climate change or nuclear emission effects). It is therefore possible that delayed or intermittent reinterpretations will stimulate different cycles of impact and will change the targets impacted (for an analysis of the social amplification ripples around a terrorist plot to bomb an aircraft in August 2006, see Breakwell, 2007, pp. 227–237).

The SARF, like SRT, emphasises that the interpretation of a hazard or a crisis does not reside in some purely objective universe. It depends on what are fundamentally self-interested judgements, choices, and pronouncements that individuals, groups, governments, and international organisations make. Inevitably, this raises the question of how their decisions are determined. There are many social psychological theories that can be applied to that question. However, the task here is to examine how the social representation and amplification of risk processes in crises affect identity threat.

Identity processes and social representations

Social representations of a public crisis can act to erect, or simply refine, the threat to identity that materialises from that crisis. They can do this explicitly or implicitly. So, in a public crisis there will be changes in the material conditions that can threaten the identity structures of certain individuals; there will be the manner in which social representations amplify or attenuate the import of those conditions for identity; and there will be the extent to which social representations specify who is likely to be most affected by those conditions and how far they explain how they will be affected.

For example, typically in a major economic depression (such as the Great Depression of 1929 in the US) unemployment rises, homelessness increases, people cannot pay their debts, housing prices plummet, international trade collapses, and deflation soars. Social representations will identify the social categories most at risk in such a crisis and will predict the likely consequences of vulnerability and poverty on their lifestyles, their families, and their future social status. Social representations of the victims of a crisis can be relatively generalised and broad-brush. They can also be individualised and customised to the point where people that become aware of the social representation believe that they are the victims that are being described. This is particularly likely if they have already experienced one of the changes in circumstances that the depression precipitates (e.g., being made redundant). Such individuals can be seen to be triply threatened: the crisis is personally affecting them; social representations say there are other dire changes that they should expect; and they also say they fit the prototype of someone who will be a victim. The triple threat package is not uncommon in public crises.

It is important to emphasise here that the individual is not a passive recipient of influence from social representations. Breakwell (2010a, 2015b) described how individuals can be agentic in their dealings with social representations. She distinguishes between the social representation and the personal representation that the individual holds of the social representation.

She suggested the individual's relationship to any social representation can be described along a number of dimensions:

1. Awareness: Individuals will differ in their awareness of the social representation. Exposure to, and thus awareness of, a social representation will be affected by social category memberships and past experience. But awareness will also be determined by the significance of the object of the representation.
2. Understanding: Individuals will differ in the extent to which they actually understand the social representations of which they are aware. There is ample evidence that individuals are capable of reproducing all or part of a social representation even though they cannot explain how or why its elements fit together, and, if challenged, they cannot justify it. Such individuals can be said to 'know' the social representation. This is different from saying that they can understand it. In the same way, a person can know a plane can fly, but that does not mean that they understand the aerodynamics that explain its flight.
3. Acceptance: Individuals will differ in the extent to which they believe or accept a social representation even if they are fully aware of it and understand it. Typically, people can say: this is what is generally believed but, nevertheless, this is what I believe. The importance of being able to resist wholesale acceptance of the social representation so that it appears individualised should not be underestimated. While seeking identification with others through communality of understandings and interpretations at one level, people also simultaneously seek distinctiveness and differentiation through rejection of the social representation. The personalising of social representations within personal representations is part of a process of establishing and protecting an identity – a type of coping strategy.
4. Assimilation: Any aspect of a social representation that is accepted will be assimilated to pre-existent systems of personal representation. Since these differ across individuals, the way in which new social representations are assimilated will be different across individuals. Just as social processes ensure that the new social representation is anchored in prior social representations or in material evidence, at the individual level, cognitive and emotional processes ensure that it is anchored in prior personal representations and experiences. In fact, there must be an intimate connection between the social processes of anchoring and objectification and their parallel individual processes. It is individuals using prior knowledge mediated through cognitive and conative (i.e., affective) networks that generate the social communication which ensures that novel events and ideas are interpreted in terms of existing systems of meaning to ensure the anchoring of a social representation. Social exchange can produce understandings that no single participant in the interaction might be able to create, but at some level even these emergent representations are limited in some ways by the ability of the individuals involved to contribute to anchoring and objectification.
5. Salience: The salience (i.e., prominence) of a social representation will differ across people and for the same person across time and contexts. The salience of the social representation, for instance, may increase if the community that generates it is

> important to the individual. Similarly, it may increase if the social representation becomes relevant to the individual's ongoing activity. At the level of the community, if the object for social representation is non-salient, it is likely that the social representation will be difficult to elicit if it is simple, undifferentiated, and relatively unconnected with other components of the community's belief system. At the level of the individual, the salience of the social representation will be likely to influence how accurately and completely the personal representation mirrors it. There is, however, no empirical evidence on this yet.

It is notable that some of the dimensions that shape the personal representation are potentially non-volitional (e.g., awareness and understanding), and others are possibly volitional (e.g., acceptance). However, this distinction may rightly be regarded as arbitrary. Even those which appear volitional are largely predisposed by prior social experiences and constrained by identity considerations.

Therefore, even individuals who share the same general social representational environment in a crisis may differ from each other in their exposure to a specific social representation, and in their acceptance of it or willingness to communicate it to others. Groups are particularly influential in filtering how a member is exposed to social representations and channelling the way that members might use them. The individual is also likely to try to resist the influence of a social representation if accepting it would compromise self-esteem, self-efficacy, positive distinctiveness, or continuity. The success of resistance will depend on many factors, and some of these are examined later.

It seems reasonable to suppose that in some situations, individuals do have scope for selectivity in their adoption of social representations. The range of social representations is complex and dynamic. Moscovici, in moving away from Durkheim's notion of collective consciousness, emphasised the multiplicity of social representations that exist in modern societies and their capacity for change. It would seem reasonable to assume that, in this complex world of different and changing social representations, any one individual would rarely have access to all of the social representations that are operating and might not have access even to a single social representation in its entirety. Individuals will have different roles in the social process of construction, elaboration, and sharing of the representation. Essentially, this is to suggest that each individual is uniquely positioned in relation to the process of social representation and the products of social representation. This forms the platform for their personalisation of representations and even their resistance to the influence of social representations. It is one of the elements that make coping with identity threat possible.

How do public crises pose threats to identity?

Public crises come in many guises, from the anthropogenic to the natural, the global to the local, the short-lived to the open-ended. Irrespective of their specific substantive form, they have the potential to pose threats to the identity of the people that live through them. The most common threats centre on certain key aspects of the person's life, these include:

- Expression of identity: They change the ways that the person can exhibit in thought, feeling or action the components of their identity that make them unique (e.g., the emergency can intensify discrimination against marginalised groups and make expressing that group membership dangerous).
- Management of risk: They change the profile of hazards that the individual faces (e.g., in finances, health, relationships, physical safety). By doing this, they increase the person's likelihood of harm and possibilities of failure.
- Self-determination of goals: They change the level of control the individual has over decisions (e.g., where, when, and with whom they interact).
- Future-planning: They change levels of certainty about what will happen next and trust in others.
- Emotional stability: They change emotional states (notably associated with fear and anxiety).
- Social support: They change the availability and activities of support networks (e.g., family separation).

These are some of the changes typically caused by a public crisis that initiate threats to identity. The substance of these changes will differ across individuals. The embodiment of threats will vary. Consequently, between people the perceived threat levels will also differ. However, they still share, in the crisis, a common ultimate source of their threat. This is important in determining exactly how individuals will react to the identity threat that they personally experience. Merely knowing that one is not alone in facing identity threat can change the meaning of that threat and the coping strategies it evokes.

Psychological consequences of public crises and emergencies

There is a large literature of the psychological consequences of public crises and emergencies (particularly humanitarian crises). Basically, findings point to considerable effects on mental health. The World Health Organization (2022) reports that almost all people affected by such emergencies will experience psychological distress, which for most people will improve over time. It indicates that among people who have experienced war or other conflict in the previous 10 years, 9% will have depression, anxiety, post-traumatic stress disorder, bipolar disorder, or schizophrenia. People with pre-existing severe mental disorders are especially vulnerable during crises. Additionally, emergency-induced mental health problems may include grief, acute stress reactions (e.g., breathing problems, panic attacks, and sleep pattern disturbance), or harmful use of alcohol and drugs.

Such data emphasise that public crises entail enormous personal costs. The changes in mental health during a crisis point to the great threat that a crisis poses to identity. The partial or substantial recovery of the majority from these mental health consequences, once the immediate crisis is over, indicates that people have considerable resilience. The question then becomes: how do people cope with this sort of threat to identity? Some mental health problems in the midst of a crisis may themselves be the symptoms of the changes to the identity structure that the threat position brings about. They may also indicate that identity processes are failing to cope with the threats that the crisis poses.

Coping with identity threat in public crises

It is difficult to protect identity against threat in public crises because some of the strategies commonly used to cope with threat are precluded by the nature of the crisis itself. For instance, a coping strategy that depends on social support networks might be unusable if the support network is removed by the crisis. IPT defines a successful coping strategy as 'any thought or action which succeeds in eliminating or ameliorating threat ... whether it is consciously recognised as intentional or not' (Breakwell, 2015a, p. 79).

Coping strategies can have any or all of the following targets:

- removal of aspects of the social context, material or ideological, that generate threat;
- movement of the individual into a new social position that is less threatening;
- revision of the identity structure, on the content or value dimensions, that enables satisfactory levels of self-esteem, self-efficacy, positive distinctiveness, and continuity to be regained.

Strategies can reside at different levels: intra-psychic, interpersonal, and group or intergroup. Coping activity at one level will usually affect the options for coping at the others. For instance, the action of one person who is trying to deal with the threat a crisis poses for herself (e.g., breaching quarantine rules in a pandemic) may result in her rejection by her interpersonal network (e.g., because she is seen to be selfishly putting others at risk of infection) and the loss of it as a source of support.

Intra-psychic coping strategies

These can rely on modifications in assimilation-accommodation or evaluation (and sometimes a combination of both). The assimilation-accommodation processes will use deflection or acceptance strategies. There are many sorts of deflection tactics:

- Denial: This is a well-documented response to stress. The distressing reality is denied (the facts are denied, then their relevance, then their urgency, then the need to act, then the emotions aroused, and then the importance of these emotions). In relation to threat to identity, four layers of denial are possible: denial of being in the threatening position; denial that the position is threatening; denial of the need to change the identity structure despite recognising the position is threatening; and, after changing the identity structure in response to threat, denial that a change in its evaluation or emotional meaning is needed. Such denial does not change the existence of the threat. It is basically a tactic that can buy a psychological time-out before again facing the unpleasant reality. Denial, if used habitually, can be very destructive of mental health.
  In some types of public crisis, denial strategies can be used by some parts of the populace affected. Refusal to accept that the crisis applies to oneself is not uncommon, but denying that it has negative personal consequences is more common. In the

COVID-19 pandemic in 2020, people in lower risk categories for morbidity from the disease (e.g., young adults) were particularly likely to minimise its threat and reject measures meant to control infection spread. Illusions of one's own unique invulnerability in the context of risk are a component of denial.

- Real and unreal selves: Turner (1976) argued that people distinguish between their real enduring self and their unreal or inauthentic selves. Circumstances that precipitate thought, feelings, or action that is not in keeping with an established identity structure result in the individual refusing to acknowledge that any change has been made to the real identity. It has affected the unreal self, and can be discounted.
  As a deflection tactic, this might seem far-fetched. Yet there are instances of people, once a crisis has passed, who talk about their 'crisis self' as some separate entity whose activities have little bearing on their ongoing identity. The crisis represented a time when the usual social rules or expectations about behaviour were in obeyance. They could behave differently, and they did. But they do not feel impelled to assimilate those experiences into their identity structure. That was a different self, which passed with the end of the crisis. In retrospect, people may see the way they behaved in the crisis as so atypical for themselves that it is unbelievable and should not affect ongoing identity structure. For instance, people can show great courage during a crisis, fearlessly dealing with danger, but not recognise this as part of what they think themselves to be and will not accept plaudits for their actions. The heroes, as well as the villains, that emerge in crises can want to preserve their erstwhile identities.
- Fantasy: Fantasising can also be deployed to block a threat to identity. A fantasy can be constructed in which the threat is not present. Such fantasies are not delusions, they are a conscious creation. Fantasising in the face of threat can be thought of as a displacement activity rather than tackling the stark realities of the crisis.
  In public crises, people will often fantasise about the better times that will come when the crisis ends. In the middle of an enemy air raid, as they crouch in a damp cellar, refugees will fantasise about their lives after liberation and peace. Fantasy is a salve rather than a solution to the identity threat that surrounds them in that cellar. There is a question as to whether fantasising does actually deflect identity threat; it may be merely a short-lived distraction from the threat.
- Reconstrual and reattribution: These involve either reinterpretation of what position one is in, or a redefinition of the reasons that one is in that position. Reinterpretation of the properties of the position may involve ignoring or downgrading the importance of some aspects of the situation, introducing information from the wider context which modifies the meaning of the position, or inventing properties for the position which previously did not exist. Reattribution of the reason for being in the position may involve denying responsibility for being there.
- In public crises, people may find reconstrual of the nature of their position and reattribution of the reason for being in it relatively attractive. Since so many people are caught up in the crisis, their personal responsibility may be a moot point.
  The individual can then claim that the consequences for the identity structure of being caught in the crisis cannot be regarded as their responsibility. Any corollary implications for aspects of identity can be deflected. Since the crisis is complex, opportunities for reinterpretation of its properties are endless and the individual's

position within them can be reconstrued to offer a better outcome for identity structure maintenance. An illustration of how this might work in a financial crisis would be the case of the financier who loses a lot of client money as the markets bomb. His identity components derived from being a hot-shot trader are threatened. But he deploys reconstrual and reattribution: he could not control a global crash (not his fault); he finds ways to interpret his performances as better than those of other traders. He does not recognise the need to change his identity.

Threat can result in acceptance rather than deflection. Such acceptance strategies represent creative adaptations. They may also be based on using some redefinition and reattribution deflection tactics as a foundation. Acceptance strategies operating through assimilation-accommodation may involve the following:

- Anticipatory restructuring: Making changes before the threat becomes acute. Typically, this can provide more room for manoeuvre. This is effective only if the identity changes demanded by the threat are accurately predicted and if the changes made reduce the level of damage that would otherwise have been done to the identity principles. This may be possible if the changes to identity are perceived as volitional rather than imposed.
  The problem with anticipatory restructuring in the context of a public crisis is that predictability levels are low, and the identity changes required are typically not easy to reconstrue as volitional. Anticipatory restructuring is not a coping strategy much used in crises – except in those that have a long lead time. Climate change would fall into this category. Those parts of an individual's identity that are linked to international air travel, fast diesel cars, and eating meat could be due for earlier rather than later renovation.
- Compartmentalism: Crises can change the content dimension of identity. A pandemic may introduce to the identity of many people over 70 years of age the 'vulnerable' component (assuming that they did not have it before). Compartmentalism simply involves drawing a strict boundary around the dissatisfying addition to the identity structure. In effect, in so far as it is feasible, assimilation of the new component occurs without accommodation across the identity structure. Thus, compartmentalisation could make being 'vulnerable' a psychological irrelevance or trivial (a bit like having to renew your driving licence every three years in the UK after you are 70 years old). Compartmentalism only works to allow the rest of the identity structure to grow and flourish as long as the boundaries retain the unwanted component of identity incommunicado.
- Compromise changes: This involves making a change compatible with the threat but not the one initially expected in response to the threat. The individual that recognises the climate change crisis may not become a vegan but may pay for 10 acres of trees to be planted. Chosen carefully, the compromise change can serve the identity principles well.
- Fundamental changes: This involves making the changes to the identity structure required to permit the individual to continue to function without perceiving any threat. This is a coping strategy in so far as it may eliminate the stress of

> being threatened. However, it may have a negative effect on the identity principles. It may need to be linked to other coping tactics if it is to be deemed acceptable by the individual concerned. This could use a coping strategy that entailed revising the relative salience of the identity principles themselves. A change to the identity structure that lowered self-esteem might be accepted if less significance could be placed upon self-esteem and if that reduction could be compensated for raising the salience of the other identity principles. Such trade-offs that rationalise or justify certain identity changes are needed to maintain the dynamism of the identity structure in response to change in circumstances.

Public crises require compromise and fundamental changes in content dimension of the identity structure, and they will result in transient or long-lived changes in the salience of the identity principles. By their very nature, public crises create demands for identity changes that cannot be managed through deflection or countered by anticipatory restructuring.

Public crises also require changes in the evaluation dimension of the identity structure. Such crises can very significantly change societal values. Crises can change the value society places upon individual freedom, loyalty, expertise, altruism, education, nationalism, and many other concepts (such as specific social categories or religious or ideological beliefs). In doing this, they automatically reset the evaluation of a particular identity structure. So, in crises, individuals will need to reassess the value they place on existing identity components, but also set the value they will allot to new or prospective identity components. In doing this, they can attempt to minimise any negative effect on the identity principles. They can employ coping strategies that ameliorate the worst effects on their identity evaluation of changing societal value systems. These largely centre on varying the criteria that they use when judging the value of an identity component or challenging the legitimacy of any evaluation that lowers their personal worth. For instance, an identity component might be devalued during a crisis in one's own country (e.g., being bilingual during a conflict where speaking the language of the enemy is seen as a sign of treachery). Rather than accept this revised evaluation of identity, the individual who is multilingual may focus on it less as a source of self-esteem; she may look to other countries and find that they are more positive about the value of being multilingual; and she might join together with other linguists to challenge the attempts to undermine the value of multilingualism. Crises will proliferate uncertainties in the evaluation of identity components, but this will be met with rebuttals because people will fight to keep their sense of personal worth.

Interpersonal coping strategies

Interpersonal coping strategies are also needed in crises. They rely on changing relationships with others in order to cope with threat. One significant aspect of interpersonal strategies, social support, was discussed in an earlier chapter and we will not return to it here. Here we focus more on the individual's role in interpersonal engagements. In dealing with crisis-induced identity threat, the individual may seek to minimise the impact of the threat by isolating from other people and thus reducing opportunities for discrimination or stigmatisation.

For instance, having escaped persecution, a refugee who has gained asylum in a new country may find that limiting interpersonal contacts to those who understand something of the many identity threats that she has encountered is preferrable. The key thing here is the value to identity processes of having some degree of control over which interpersonal contacts are made. Such control may be difficult to find in a crisis or its aftermath, but total isolation is not the objective since some shared self-disclosure of the threats faced in a non-judgemental relationship has been repeatedly shown to be valuable for mental health.

Negativism is another coping strategy but is rather unusual. It entails acting against the requirements or pressures from others. Negativism is an important foundation for the identity principles because they rely on an ability to resist the pressure of social influences that generate threat. In interpersonal relationships, negativism is one base for establishing individualism and independence. In older age groups, negativism is sometimes evident in what is sometimes called 'cantankerousness', marked by being argumentative, bad-tempered, and uncooperative. In a crisis, negativism can be a resource that resists conformity or compromise.

Negativism is not an easy strategy to learn or deploy because it is alien to the norms that socialisation in most cultures implants. It can also backfire badly in crises, or it can be a route to escape. On the downside, the people sharing the threat position may justifiably consider negativism unreasonable and destructive of the cohesiveness that they see as necessary for surviving the crisis. Negativism can be misperceived as selfishness. However, it can also be the basis for differential survival in a crisis. In crises, it can be the preferred strategy of people with high identity resilience. Essentially, they are more willing to back their own instincts and decisions about dealing with the crisis because they have higher self-esteem and self-efficacy, but also because they already think of themselves as different from others.

Sometimes, in crises, people will hide some important and threatened component of their identity from others and instead present an alternative. This form of coping strategy has been labelled 'passing' (Watson, 1970). Passing entails representing oneself as having an identity component that is not present in the identity structure. Passing normally refers to the process of gaining identification with a group or social category (e.g., gender, sexuality, racial, religious, political, or economic) by camouflaging one's actual origin. Often this process is a long-term identity project, requiring many incremental stages of gaining social acceptance of the projected alternative identity component. There has been much research on people (of all genders and across the LGBTQ+ spectrum) 'passing' as heterosexual (e.g., see Ingraham, 2022; Johnson, 2002) that illustrates how passing has complex implications and is not a simple strategy to use for coping with identity threat. Jaspal (2019) provides a broader examination of the social psychology of identity processes in gay men.

Passing is essentially a social process, relying on deceiving others. Whether it inevitably involves intra-psychic concomitants, such as denial and compartmentalisation, is unclear. Nor are the long-term implications for identity structure established. In some circumstances, for instance where the passing is successful in transitioning the individual into a desired new social position, it might be expected that assimilation-accommodation will attempt to squeeze the 'passing' component (and the experiences that it gives rise to) into the identity structure. Whether or not it can probably depends on the significance of the established components that have to be accommodating and on whether any of these components need to be seriously modified or eradicated. For some types of pass, incorporation into the existing identity structure will be unproblematic (e.g., passing as a novice pianist). For other types of passes, for instance where passing involves one's race or religion, there may be a disjuncture between the pre-passing identity structure and that which would be expected post-passing. The individual may never find a way to bridge the chasm. Some have argued that the process of passing is not based on a rejection of stigmatised or threatened identity, but is situationally employed to resist social oppression (Kanuha, 1999). Where this occurs, the effects of successful passing for ongoing identity structure are likely to be totally different. Indeed, the pre-passing identity may become more resilient. It suggests that the impact of passing on the individual will depend on whether it is construed as an act of capitulation or rebellion.

The final interpersonal coping strategy that should be mentioned is 'role play'. This entails the threatened person living up to the expectations associated with being in the threat position. The object of the strategy is to reduce the negative consequences of appearing to challenge a social hierarchy or by deviating from its social norms. The threatened person seeks to gain social approval by compliance with what is expected. This may look like 'passing' but is very different. Role play is also a manipulative strategy, but it does not change the position of the threatened person. Rather, it is aimed at changing the consequences of being in that position. In thinking about the likely psychological consequences of role play when under threat, it is probably useful to remember the distinction between compliance that is designed to achieve some advantage and capitulation, which is a recognition of defeat and where no further advantage is sought. Compliance can also be selective, for instance targeted at gaining credibility or favour.

In crises, passing and role play can be vital tools. In crises, resources are often distributed unequally. For instance, in an environmentally precipitated humanitarian crisis, involving drought, food shortages, and mass displacements of populations, where persecution and violence are commonplace, there will be unfathomable threats to the identities of the people involved. In addition, there will be limitations on the material aid available. Some categories of people will be prioritised for support. Passing successfully as someone belonging to a prioritised category yields many benefits. Similarly, a person playing the role of the 'worthy' victim, living up to the expectations of aid workers, may be being compliant with a view to gaining an 'edge' over others that are competing for support. People in these situations are seeking survival not just of their unique identity but of their lives. In fact, identity may be a secondary concern.

Intra-psychic and interpersonal coping strategies are used in conjunction with others at the group and intergroup levels. We will return to the intergroup coping strategies in the next chapter.

Deliberate individualised identity attack

While public crises can threaten identity, the threat is not usually purposeful or individualised. It emerges as a consequence of the concatenation of many events. However, many threats to identity are deliberate and personalised. When this happens, identity can be said to be under attack. The individual may become the target as a result of having a specific identity component (e.g., a physical disability) or a particular constellation of identity components (e.g., being a woman, a teenager, an anorexic, and a lover of art). The important thing is that the attack occurs because an individual has this identity configuration; the attack is not a coincidence or a collateral effect of other aggression against the individual. Of course, sometimes identity attacks are spin-offs from other forms of attack (e.g., in a street mugging, the physical assault may be accompanied by abuse that is meant to shame or taunt the victim about their strength, ethnicity, or occupation). However, here we are focused on the attack that is primarily targeted against some identity component.

Anyone is fair game for this sort of attack. Anyone can mount such an attack. We learn how to attack the identity of others at the same time as we become self-aware and realise that we have our own unique identity. Children in playgrounds can be heard practising their attack. One says to another 'you can't play with us, you're too small'. The attack has two parts. It asserts something about the other (being smaller) and says that this is not good (because it means exclusion from the game). Even the most complex deliberate attacks on identity intrinsically have these two parts: singling out the identity component and the devaluation of it. If the identity component already has a negative connotation in a particular culture or group, then this fact can be highlighted or exaggerated.

If it is an identity component that the victim would prefer to remain unnoticed or invisible, in spotlighting it, the attacker is already issuing a meta-threat to the way the victim would prefer to express their identity. The attack is a threat both to a current expression of identity and to the ongoing ability of the person to control his or her expression of identity. The revelation does not need to involve an identity component that has social opprobrium attached, it can be something that is quite acceptable or even lauded. The threat arises because the victim wishes it to be a secret. Sometimes people do wish very worthy components of their identity to be kept private. For instance, some people resist public awareness of their bravery record, their charity work, or their high intellectual ability. Even revelation of such identity components can undermine the individual's confidence in their ability to manage how their identity is expressed.

The attacker is not restricted to making truthful statements about the other's identity. The attacker can try to attribute components that are completely absent or inflate the significance of ones that are present. All the attacker ideally has to do is achieve two things: the victim has to be aware of the attack and to be conscious of how it is likely to affect other people's evaluation of her or him; and other people need to be alerted that the victim may have this identity component. The second of these two objectives is nice to have but not essential. For the attack to threaten identity, it is enough that the victim is anxious about the reactions that others might have.

The reasons for deliberate identity attacks largely cluster around two motives:

- Attackers see their victims as not like themselves. They are different and they do not belong. So, they are motivated to exclude or segregate their victims.
- Attackers perceive their victims as competitors and thus dangerous. So, they are motivated to devalue their victims or remove their capacity for self-defence or reprisal.

These motives have a common root in self-interest. The attacker who is successful is likely to move on with enhanced self-esteem, self-efficacy, positive distinctiveness, and continuity. This is in addition to any material gain that is achieved.

The description above, which started with the illustration in the playground, may suggest that identity attacks are all about the actions of one person against another. They are not. In fact, identity attacks based on these motives can be mounted by people acting in concert (organised via many different types of networks or groupings). In addition, the attack can be launched simultaneously against any number of victims.

Identity attacks made in cyberspace are particularly flexible. They can be highly customised and targeted at a single person. They can also be very generalised and indiscriminate. From the attacker's point of view, cyberspace can be the ideal arena for an assault. It permits detailed dissection of the victims' identities. Attributions or accusations can be made without evidence or justification and with limited opportunity for rebuttal. Attacks can be repeated and elaborated over long time periods. The attacker's claims can be broadcast to selected, varied, and potentially receptive audiences. The chances of reprisals from the victim are small. The attacker can remain anonymous. So, cyber identity attacks have grown exponentially. Cyberspace also clearly creates other forms of identity threat. For instance, identity theft or cloning. Cyberspace is the perfect growing medium for identity threat of all types. However, as was described earlier in this chapter, it also offers opportunities for coping strategies that have not previously been available. Individuals can use cyberspace to reassert and gain support for their identity.

Identity attacks, irrespective of the participants involved, are rarely totally purpose-built. They capitalise on existing societal mechanisms for discrimination, segregation, and devaluation. In formulating an attack, the dominant social representations within the culture involved will be important in shaping the choice of negative attribution that is made. For instance, an attack on the identities of migrants who gain entry to a country illegally or through people trafficking might make use of the many critical mass media images of the 'economic migrant'. In using available social representations, attackers will have an arsenal of stereotypes and prejudices to weave into the narrative that they deploy. Even social media trolling that is designed to attack a victim's identity will often use memes that are trending as a platform for the assault. For example, memes about the religion (Aguilar et al., 2017) or the appearance of targets can be used to justify or substantiate slurs against them (Morrissey & Yell, 2016). The link to the meme has an additional advantage in enhancing the likelihood that the attack will be communicated and repeated more widely.

The implications of threats to identity that originate in deliberate attacks are not so very different from those beginning in public crises. If the attack is perceived to threaten self-esteem, self-efficacy, positive distinctiveness, or continuity, or to have already eroded the level of any one or combination of these four, the individual will deploy coping strategies. The same battery of coping strategies that are available against threat derived from public crises can be considered for use in a deliberate and personalised attack. Some or all of intra-psychic deflection and acceptance strategies and interpersonal coping strategies using negativism, role play, and passing may be viable options. Group and intergroup coping strategies can also be used depending on the nature of the identity component under attack. If it is linked to a group membership, defence against the attack might involve seeking group support or group action.

Very deliberate personalised identity attacks are likely to be experienced differently from those that emerge during public crises. The victim feels singled out and often alone.

The social support systems available differ from those in a crisis (for good or ill). The threat itself is not diffuse. It tends to be explicit and immediate. The coping strategies that could be called upon will have different efficacy in these circumstances than they would if used in response to identity threat in a crisis. Intra-psychic strategies may be more likely than the others to be used in an identity attack. However, negativism and resistance have an important role in handling identity attacks. Actively refusing to be silenced, asserting the positive value of the identity component under attack, and publicly rejecting misrepresentations of one's identity may be hard to do. Failure to try may have other negative consequences for identity value. We will return to this in the chapter on identity failure.

The remoulding of identity during crises and when under attack

From this chapter on identities within crises and when under attack, it seems that several conclusions should be drawn. Threat to identity can arouse a complex array of coping processes that may resist change in the identity structure or minimise damage to it, but they are most likely also to initiate identity process action that results in the modification of the identity structure to varying degrees. The idea that some identities might be so resilient that they would evade all change is unsupportable. Coping strategies inevitably result in some identity remoulding and some of this may be change for the better. The effects of identity resilience may be less characterised by inertia in the identity structure and more by adaptive and creative change in it. The way individuals respond to the threats to identity that arise from crises and attacks is fundamentally influenced by contemporary social representations and the individual's awareness, acceptance, and use of them. Social representations, and the social influence processes associated with them, are the terrain within which coping strategies are chosen and identity structure is remoulded in response to threats.

7

IDENTITY AND GROUP DYNAMICS

I don't want to be a member of any club that will accept me as a member. Groucho Marx, Letter of resignation to the Friars Club

Issues addressed in this chapter

Individuals' identity structures will influence how they behave with regard to groups or social categories. This chapter examines how having a group or social category membership as an identity component can affect thought, feelings, and action, particularly in the context of intergroup competition or conflict. It discusses how the membership of several distinct groups or categories can become a problem or a solution for identity maintenance.

Positioning group membership in the identity structure

Identity Process Theory has always asserted that membership of a group or social category can be perceived by an individual as a component of their identity structure. However, there are many different forms of social unit that can be labelled groups or social categories. The terms can be used to encompass some very different entities, ranged along a series of dimensions. At one end of the stack of dimensions would sit the group/category that is characterised by being a mere transient and arbitrary aggregation of individuals, who are without past associations or connections, without common purpose or beliefs, and without interdependent or shared actions or fate. Many of the 'groups' used in social psychology experiments on group dynamics would fit this identikit image. At the other end of the stack of dimensions would sit the group/category with a long or established history and clear, even if debated, reasons for its existence, in which the members have ongoing associations and connections with each other, who share goals, values, and patterns of behaviour, and on whom their future life course is heavily dependent. Some organisations sit at this end of the stack of dimensions. For instance, professional groups in medicine, the law, or the armed forces might fit here. More often, groups will not sit at one or the other end of the layered stack of dimensions. For instance, they may have a long history, but their contemporary members do not share a belief system or face a common fate. This position might represent where nationality as a social category sits. Where the group or category sits in relation to these dimensions will be important in determining the meaning that membership has for the individual's identity structure.

The status of any particular membership in the individual's identity structure will depend upon several factors:

- *Terms of the membership*

Memberships vary on a series of continua. These include their source (ranging from involuntary/imposed/ascribed to self-determined/chosen) and their permanence (ranging from fixed and unchangeable to variable and open).

- *Costs–benefits ratio of membership*

The costs and benefits involved can be material (e.g., wealth, power, or social standing) or subjective (e.g., a sense of belonging or beliefs to adopt). Memberships differ in the extent to which they involve either costs or benefits. They also differ in the ratio between the costs and benefits associated with them. Sometimes, low cost involves low benefits, but they can be either positively or negatively correlated, and even uncorrelated. The ratio, and its changes over time, is a significant influence on the role that the memberships will play in the identity structure.

The costs and benefits of membership will be intimately connected to the position and social representations of the group or social category in society as a whole. Additionally, the individual will be agentic in evaluating the costs and benefits of any membership, in the same way that any identity component is subject to evaluation.

- *The call membership makes upon members*

Memberships differ in the extent to which they require an individual to perform in specific ways in thought, feelings, or actions. Some are onerous in their performance expectations, but, at the other end of the spectrum, some expect nothing. In the latter, membership would seem to be in name alone. Interestingly, there is no direct correlation between the demands made by a membership and its importance to the identity structure. For instance, some memberships are honorific, requiring no future activity (e.g., being made an alumnus of a university through the award of an honorary degree). They may still play an important part in the identity structure.

- *The residual effects of past memberships*

The identity structure may retain traces of memberships that have ended (e.g., an ex-soldier may no longer be a member of her regiment but having been a member remains a way in which she defines herself). The traces of ex-memberships will vary largely according to the significance that they had held for identity while they were current and the manner in which they came to an end. The lifetime of ex-memberships as influential forces in the identity structure needs to be studied.

- *The constellation of memberships operating at any one time*

Inevitably, individuals have more than one membership. In IPT, each membership is not treated as a different identity. IPT does not treat multiple memberships as multiple identities (which has been said frequently already in this book!). A membership can be one component of the wholistic identity. The position that any one of them will occupy in the identity is dependent on the way the others are positioned. The significance of multiple group membership cannot be ignored. We return specifically to the issue of multiple memberships at a number of points below. The existence in the wholistic identity of what could be components derived from memberships of groups that are in conflict or competition is the basis for trouble.

Each of these factors, and probably others, will affect the way assimilation-accommodation and evaluation processing modifies the positioning of the identity component derived from each membership within the wholistic identity structure.

Membership belonging and resistance; insecurity and uncertainty

In recent developments in IPT, there has been increasing emphasis on the importance of examining the substance of the specific membership when considering the impact that being part of a group or social category will have on identity and behaviour. In addition to the factors listed above that influence how memberships affect identity structure, there is the question of the status of the membership itself. The ability of any membership to influence behaviour is dependent on the extent to which the individual believes or feels that they 'belong'.

Belonging

Belonging is an awkward concept to capture. It covers feeling a strong, deep-rooted positive regard for the membership, being comfortable with it, and feeling secure in it. It is this sense of belonging that Social Identity Theory (SIT) (Abrams & Hogg, 1990b; Tajfel, 1978) and later Self Categorisation Theory (SCT) (Hornsey, 2008; Turner, 2010) call 'social identification' or 'self-categorisation'. Social identification is associated with adoption of beliefs and attitudes that characterise other members, and with conformity with the social norms of behaviour prevalent in members. Social identification entails 'belonging' to the group or category. This reflects the other commonplace meaning of 'belonging' as being owned by, or the property of, someone or something. Once having socially identified with the group or category, the individual is hypothesised to be under pressure to comply with the expectations of membership and be motivated to further the interests of the group or category.

Social identification is argued in SIT and SCT to be a necessary precursor to membership motivating involvement in intra-group and intergroup activity. Social categorisation or membership *per se* are insufficient conditions for the generation of intergroup differentiation and intra-group cohesion, and this appears to be mediated by social identification. IPT treats social identification as the point at which the group or category membership is assimilated into the identity structure and when other accommodations within the structure have begun, though may not be completed.

IPT does not conceptualise social identification as a one-off decision, that once taken is irretrievable. Satisfaction with belonging may reduce (e.g., due to the group or category changing, or to other more attractive but mutually exclusive options opening up, or because other modifications in the individual's life result in alternative priorities) and, with it, social identification. It may not be possible for the individual to exit the group or category, but social identification with it may wane significantly or be lost. Changes to the wholistic identity structure would follow, along with changes in patterns of group-related action, thought, and feelings.

Social identification with, or belonging to, one group is relatively simple to conceptualise, even when it is acknowledged to encompass a number of complex dimensions that cut across beliefs, values, feelings, and action. It becomes more difficult to build a picture of social identification when tracking it across multiple group memberships that may intersect and could involve groups that are in conflict. How do social identifications interact with each other? IPT proposes that social identifications will be developed in ways motivated by the identity principles. So, for instance, a group membership will not develop into a fully fledged social identification unless it contributes to one or more of the major objectives of the identity processes – self-esteem, self-efficacy, positive distinctiveness, or continuity. As memberships multiply, the relative contribution that social identification with each of them can make towards these objectives will be changed. Choices about which social identifications to start, retain, or reject will be made against the backdrop of this complex matrix of evaluations of their value to the wholistic identity structure.

Speaking of 'choices' might make this sound like a self-conscious process. In fact, it is more like a programme that functions autonomously unless it spots some incongruity in an incoming data stream. If that happens, then processing is raised to the central processor, more commonly called consciousness. Social identifications that are significant to the identity structure or are under attack will be salient in self-consciousness. It is reasonable to assume that higher levels of multiple group memberships (with their attendant social identifications) will not only increase the number of points where threat to identity may occur, they will also increase the complexity of those threats.

Research on multiple group memberships has been flourishing recently but it has a long history. For instance, Killian (1952) showed how community disasters created public crises that made the latent conflict between ordinarily non-conflicting group loyalties apparent. Conflicts were found to arise between the family and secondary groups, 'heroic' roles and prosaic occupational roles, 'the company' and fellow workers, and the community and extra-community groups. More recently, the benefits of multiple group memberships have been emphasised. Having multiple group identifications has been shown to be associated with enhanced well-being (Haslam et al., 2014) and has been proposed to offer a 'social cure' when facing problems (Jetten et al., 2012). This seems reasonable if the memberships are benign and interact positively. In groups that experience high levels of discrimination or that have very limited resources, the benefit returns are unlikely to be so clear-cut (see Johnstone et al., 2015, for a study of the homeless).

Resistance

An important corollary of the significance of belonging and social identification in identity processes is the motivation for resistance, rejection, and rebellion. Not all group memberships are voluntary (many social category memberships involve ascription from birth). Not all group memberships ultimately prove satisfying materially (e.g., regarding physical safety or wealth). Most importantly, some group memberships ultimately prove dissatisfying for one or more of the four identity principles. Unwilling or dissatisfied group members may perceive themselves to be in a position that threatens their identity. They may respond with a variety of coping strategies, and some of these are described later in the chapter. Some involve 'de-identification' from the group. De-identification is a process that occurs primarily while the individual is still a member of the group. It is one way the individual has to reduce the threat that group membership is creating.

De-identification can be manifest in various ways:

- Psychological distancing – for instance, revising down the importance of the group membership in identity evaluations; the internalisation of negative stereotypes of the group (an example of this would be how some gay people internalise homonegativity; see Berg et al., 2016); and the reduction of emotional investment in or adherence to group beliefs, norms, or customs.
- Interpersonal distancing – this is not a simple matter of physical distancing, although this can be involved. It includes, for example, dissociation from communication with other group members; sharing criticisms of the group with others inside and outside the group; and selectively seeking new contacts outside the group.
- Intra-group withdrawal – this involves failing to participate in group activities or avoidance of incorporation into the hierarchy of the group (e.g., refusing any recognised status in the group, such as spokesperson or representative).
- Referencing other group memberships – where the individual belongs to multiple groups, exaggerating or emphasising the importance of these other memberships can be used to lower the salience of the group targeted for de-identification. This represents another benefit that multiple group memberships can provide.

De-identification does not necessarily lead the individual to exit the group, even when exit is possible. Sometimes, de-identification itself produces sufficient benefits for the individual to stay a member. Also, the material or psychological costs of exiting the group might outweigh the costs of remaining. So, the individual stays but the nature and quality of the membership is changed. A common example of this appears in people who find they are working in a group that has lost its purpose or moral compass and no longer satisfies their identity principles. They may de-identify from the work group but stay there because they need the job.

De-identification can also occur in retrospect, after the individual does actually exit the group. This can be considered a form of rationalisation or dissonance reduction. The group left behind is basically recast in a way that explains and justifies exit. Often this involves a form of personalised historical revisionism (Krasner, 2019). In Chapter 5, the malleability of memory was described. It is a foundation for revising the meaning of past social identifications and the legitimacy of de-identification.

Insecurity and uncertainty

Memberships can vary in what might be termed their security. Memberships that can be withdrawn against the individual's will or are liable to end without warning or explanation can be considered insecure. Membership can also vary in its certainty. Uncertainty can develop if the legitimacy of the claim to membership is challenged by someone else or by something that has happened that marginalises or alienates the individual. Uncertainty can also arise when an individual begins to doubt their 'belonging' because they no longer feel that they can fulfil the obligations or expectations of membership. It can also emerge when an individual begins to believe that the group no longer satisfies their own needs or motivations. In the latter case, uncertainty can be the precursor to resistance.

Membership insecurity or uncertainty on occasion may be more a product of the constitution and position of the group or category itself than of the position of the individual in it. Entitativity is defined as the extent to which a group or collective is considered by others to be a real entity having unity, coherence, and structure. Groups whose members share a common fate, are similar to one another, and are located close together are more likely to be considered a high-entitativity group. Low-entitativity groups are more likely to engender membership insecurity or uncertainty.

Membership insecurity and uncertainty can be powerful motivations for changes in thought, feelings, or action related to the intra-group and intergroup context. Hogg (2000, 2007) developed what he called uncertainty–identity theory, which is a further development of the motivational aspect of SIT. It proposes that feelings of uncertainty, particularly about or related to self, motivate people to identify with social groups and to choose new groups with, or configure existing groups to have, certain properties that are most likely to reduce, control, or protect them from feelings of uncertainty. Hogg considers uncertainty reduction is a motivation for human behaviour. He has shown that people who feel uncertain are more likely to identify with groups and for their identification to be stronger. He has found in various empirical studies that extreme uncertainty may encourage extreme identification (e.g., zealotry, fanaticism). He suggests that high-entitativity groups are best equipped to reduce uncertainty through identification.

Hogg's theory would suggest that group membership insecurity or uncertainty would be a strong motive for changing group allegiances where exiting the group is possible. If objective intergroup mobility (i.e., exit) is impossible or very unlikely, membership insecurity or uncertainty is likely to result in significant efforts either to improve the entitativity of the group or to alter the position of the individual in the group structure (these efforts may entail various coping strategies that are described later in this chapter). Having multiple group memberships may also provide the individual with a means of damage limitation against instability and uncertainty by allowing them to gain stability and certainty from other memberships. Resistance, rejection, and rebellion are motives that will also come into play in mobilising these coping strategies.

Emotional and identity consequences

The emotional consequences of de-identification and of membership insecurity and uncertainty should be recognised and are different. Fear, anxiety, distress, and anger are common where memberships are perceived to be insecure or uncertain. Disturbances in the emotional attachment to the group can have broader implications for emotional expression (e.g., depression) and mental health (e.g., suicidal tendencies and neuroses). The emotional effects of de-identification without leaving the group are more varied. Some are positive (e.g., relief or hope) but some are negative (e.g., doubt or anxiety). Emotional correlates of retrospective de-identification, subsequent to disengagement from the group and particularly 'role exit', have been studied (e.g., Dziewanski, 2020; Ebaugh & Ebaugh, 1988). In keeping with the dissonance reduction and rationalisation role of de-identification in this situation, the emotional effects seem largely positive.

The identity consequences of de-identification without membership ending are also important. De-identification may be initiated as a coping strategy for dealing with identity threat derived from a group membership. However, it may then emerge as an identity threat in its own right unless accompanied by other coping tactics. The individual is having to manage the identity implications of inconsistencies between an identity component (a group or category membership) and identity-expression (e.g., when de-identification dictates that expected membership-related behaviours are muted or omitted).

One very important way to deal with this is for the individual to focus on the difference between psychological belonging and social belonging in the group. The individual who de-identifies is withdrawing psychological belonging. The external trappings of the social belonging remain but, for the identity structure, their meaning is radically redefined and re-evaluated. This separation process is reflected in many of the narratives of people who de-identify with their biological sex but have not undergone gender reassignment (Cooper et al., 2020). This process may reduce the consequences of de-identification for the identity principles and lower perceived identity threat levels. However, it is questionable whether it represents a long-term solution. The 'dual belonging' strategy is fraught with having to maintain an identity component in two contradictory states simultaneously within the identity structure. We return in the next chapter to how strategies that are meant to enable coping can result in subsequent problems for the identity.

Dilemma for the group

De-identification is a form of resistance for the individual who remains a member or who is not yet disengaged. It is embodied in deviations from the behaviour and beliefs that a group seeks from members. Although it may precipitate it, it is not synonymous with outright rejection of membership or explicit insurgence. Membership insecurity or uncertainty are also often motives for exit from a group or antipathy towards it, and possibly some sort of action against it.

The group has to manage these dynamics. While the problem at one level can be regarded as located in the individual, it also has widespread implications for the group (or social category) as an entity in its own right. The group, as an entity, is put at risk because deviant perceptions or behaviours on the part of one individual can spread to others. If members question the meaning or the value of the attributes (e.g., beliefs, objectives, attitudes) that have been said to define the group, the continued existence of the group may be uncertain. The identity of the group itself can be put at risk. A group's identity is determined by a series of interacting attributes:

- its history;
- its position relative to other groups – including comparative coercive power;
- its purposes or objectives;
- its material characteristics – including size, geographical distribution, and wealth;
- the behaviour of its members;
- the beliefs of its members.

In parallel, a group's identity depends upon how these attributes are perceived and socially represented, both by its own members and by those outside the group. A group's identity is a product of the interaction of its attributes (which change over time) and the social representations generated internally and externally of those attributes (which can change over time). Since to varying degrees through any deviation in expected beliefs or behaviour it will put at risk the internal representation of these attributes, de-identification by individuals can threaten the identity of the group.

The dilemma for the group, as an entity with an identity of its own, is to remove the deviant's potential influence without alienating its general constituency. The prime problem facing the group is that de-identification, insecurity, and uncertainty are liable to be contagious within the membership, particularly if the initial carrier is influential within the group. Moreover, the emotional consequences of these experiences (such as fear, distress, anxiety, depression, and anger) are also likely to spread within the group. Parkinson (2020) calls this phenomenon intra-group emotion convergence. Under such circumstances, maintaining identification and affiliation levels becomes vital for the group. The group is motivated to set in motion a complex battery of measures to re-introduce identification, security, and certainty, and thus bolster its own entitativity and identity.

History offers many illustrations of groups acting to control those of their members who de-identify or who resist group power in other ways (who can be called non-conformists). The strategies available to a group in order to protect its own identity depend most on two factors: how much control they have over material resources and how much control they have over the social influence processes that can change the social representations of the identity of their group. These factors will determine which of the possible techniques they can actually use. The techniques used against non-conformists have included:

- expulsion from the group (e.g., exile, withdrawal of citizenship, or revocation of membership rights such as the right to practise a profession);
- isolation outside the group (e.g., the use of external detention centres or transportation);
- quarantining inside the group (e.g., involving imprisonment or house detention);
- marginalisation inside the group (e.g., assigning them to roles which limit their contacts with other members, or which undermine their status, influence, and personal worth in the group);
- conversion (e.g., compulsory re-education or thought-transformation camps);
- persuasion (e.g., targeted propaganda aimed at changing the individual's perceptions of their membership, often involving third-party endorsement of the persuasive arguments from people valued by the target);
- revision of incentives (e.g., offering material or social rewards for conformity and re-identification);
- basic operant reinforcement methods built into the everyday operations of the group (e.g., differential reward/punishment structures associated with exhibition of the desired group conformity, including the use of intermittent reinforcement).

The first four techniques (expulsion, isolation, quarantining, and marginalisation) typically are used to effect three things: punishment for non-conformity (i.e., retribution); setting an example (i.e., showing other members what will happen if they do not conform, in order to encourage their conformity); and sending a signal to outsiders (i.e., signalling the power of the group over their members). The second four techniques (conversion, persuasion, incentivisation, and operant reinforcement) are typically used to achieve compliance from the non-conformist without the apparent presence of coercion or of ongoing restrictions or constraints. The advantage of these techniques, if successful in producing compliance, is that the erstwhile deviant is resurrected as a member in good standing and can be offered as a role model for others who might be insecure or uncertain in their membership. Although someone's 'conversion' may have this effect on other members, external evidence of the convert's compliance cannot be inevitably equated with a genuine renewed identification with the group. Such methods have variable effects upon the individual's own sense of belonging in the group. There can remain big differences between what people say and do, and what they think and feel regarding the group (Taylor, 2006).

Other techniques that groups can deploy when tackling de-identification, especially when the problem is not just focused on a very small number of members, involve more emphasis on changing the nature of the group and its activities in order to improve social identification and reduce the insecurity or uncertainty more generically. These include many of the intra-group and intergroup coping strategies outlined in the next section. Under certain conditions, embarking on or inciting a conflict with another group can be thought by the group as a particularly important way to raise identification levels within a group.

A cautionary note seems appropriate before moving on to intergroup coping strategies. The discussion above of the group's dilemma may have implied that groups 'think'. In effect, this is just shorthand for saying that groups engage in data collection, recording, collation, and interpretation; communicate internally about these data; and use these data to inform choices needed in order to achieve the group's objectives. These processes are achieved through the activity of the membership, organised often with hierarchical decision-making authority. The processes generate decisions that are shared and accepted to varying degrees by the members of the group. There are strong motives within cohesive groups to accept the decisions or beliefs that emerge from these processes (the phenomenon sometimes called 'groupthink' after the original work of Irving Janis; see Turner & Pratkanis, 1998).

Identity processes influencing the individual in the group

Group dynamics are a frequent source of threats to an individual member's identity. The group's own identity and its efforts to secure that identity will have many threatening implications for the identities of individual members. These threats may be collateral damage rather than the objective of what the group does. Most often, they are not specifically aimed at one individual member (though they can be, as in the case of the non-conformist), but rather at the membership in general. Sometimes the threat generated is not directly to the individual's identification with the group that gives rise to it, but to other components of the identity structure. For instance, in intergroup conflict, members may be asked to engage in activity that contradicts previous beliefs and possibly seriously damages, or removes, previous family or friendship networks. Threats to identity that originate in a group membership are, however, most frequently a product of the interaction between the effects of the position of the group within an intergroup matrix (e.g., in terms of material resources, social stigma, or social influence processes) and the group's efforts to optimise that position. For example, a member of a group that is subordinate in an intergroup matrix may perceive a threat to self-esteem or positive distinctiveness. The group's efforts to climb out of this subordinate position and to gain comparative value, by showing or negotiating its similarity to another more highly valued group, may, for a member, reduce the threat to self-esteem while enhancing the threat to positive distinctiveness.

Once it is a part of the identity structure, an identity component that reflects a group membership is a potent source and channel for identity threat because so many forces impact on:

- the status of group membership that the individual has (i.e., extent of belonging);
- the positivity of the individual's position in the group (i.e., role);
- the structure of the whole group membership (e.g., hierarchies or number);
- the effectiveness of the social influence and social representation capacities of the group;
- the relative positivity of the position of the group in the intergroup matrix.

The meaning of the group-based identity component in terms of both its content and its value will change as these forces come to bear and an identity threat can be erected. Equally, because the intra- and intergroup dynamic are so complex, they can become a very important route to coping with identity threat.

Group-based coping strategies

Group-based coping strategies can operate at several levels. Breakwell (1986, 2015a) identified three levels, some aspects of which have been mentioned in earlier chapters:

- *Membership of multiple groups*

We saw in Chapter 6 that the individual can use multiple group membership to support intra-psychic or interpersonal coping strategies. It is also important as an intra-group or intergroup strategy. Multiple group membership, when used as a coping strategy, can involve gaining an entirely new membership that offers benefits to personal worth and/or continuity. When done in this way, it becomes another form of social mobility. The new group membership can be used as a counterbalance to the negative value for the identity structure generated by other memberships, even though they are retained.

A carefully blended mixture of group memberships can operate to nullify or ameliorate the threat to identity derived from any single membership. This may happen because the stigma associated with one membership can be modified by having other memberships. For instance, a person may experience discrimination due to her ethnicity or her gender, but if she is a member of a highly educated profession she may find that the level of discrimination that she experiences is lower than it might otherwise be. Early work on intergroup discrimination (e.g., Harding & Hogrefe, 1952; Minard, 1952) showed that it can be fine-tuned to take into account the range of group memberships an individual possessed. People are discriminating about the way they use discrimination. The whole package of memberships that an individual has can be factored into what is considered the appropriate level of discrimination to use against them.

Multiple group memberships are interesting because they create the possibility of what Doise (1978) called 'crossed categorisation'. This occurs where people share one categorisation but not another. The positivity of the shared membership seems to override the tendency to discriminate or differentiate on the basis of the non-shared membership. There has been a great deal of research on crossed categorisation (sometimes called cross categorisation) since the 1970s (e.g., Brewer, 2000; Crisp et al., 2006). Much of this research has entailed minimal group experiments. It seems that cross category membership may reduce discrimination based on the non-shared membership. There has been speculation that this may occur because the shared membership results in the non-shared membership having less significance in the evaluation of the other person or in the determination of behaviour towards them. It is hard to know how crossed-categorisation effects actually operate in real-life groups, especially where the non-shared group is in conflict with other groups to which the discriminator has allegiances. In the real world, multiple group memberships have costs as well as benefits. Maintaining group memberships so that they remain valuable for identity typically takes investment of both psychological and material resources. This suggests that a successful multiple group membership coping strategy will probably involve a very small number of carefully selected groups.

Indiscriminate accumulation of memberships is counterproductive. However, it is tempting in an era of cyberspace and with the advent of the metaverse to think that having many group or category memberships is a simple, low-cost adventure. This is to ignore how processes of social influence and control have migrated to cyberspace and are as virulent, or more virulent, there than anywhere else. Stigmatisation, bullying, and threat enjoy cyberspace (Lee et al., 2021; Nam, 2021; Piccoli et al., 2020).

- *Group support*

Individuals experiencing threat to their identities can choose to use coping strategies that involve gaining group support. It is notable that such strategies need not be restricted to groups where the individual already holds membership. Indeed, they can be groups that the individual helps to create in order that they can be used against identity threat.

The formation of a group aimed at people sharing the same type of threat is sometimes used as a coping strategy. Not all members will have experienced the type of threat that inspires the group to be formed. Some people will participate in the group because they wish to help or empathise with those who are threatened. Such groups are self-defining and range from the informal, spasmodic gathering of individuals over short or limited time periods, to

those with an established organisation, name, structured communication channels, a
purposes.

At the less formal end of the spectrum, membership may be transient but serve to provide individuals with a 'safe' environment in which to express the way they are thinking and feeling about the threat they perceive they share with others in the group. Such groups can grow up inside larger group structures. For example, within large organisations or institutions, individuals that feel discriminated against or stigmatised due to some aspect of their identity (e.g., being migrant workers, educational background, or physical characteristic) can come together informally to share experiences and information.

The value of these informal groups, whether inside a larger organisation or free-standing, in tackling identity threat can be threefold. Membership reduces the individual's isolation and allows other interpersonal social support to be sought. Membership entails limited levels of commitment, allowing the individual to remain independent and to select when and how to engage in order to optimise threat reduction. Membership provides access to information that may be otherwise unavailable, and which can be used in managing the threat.

Groups that start as informal can evolve into something quite different. They can mature into groups that have set purposes and membership entry requirements. They can become formally recognised self-help or consciousness-raising groups. Self-help groups tend to offer direct emotional or practical help to the threatened, rather than just information. Probably the most obvious self-help groups are those set up to help people with physical or mental illnesses. People with phobias linked to panic attacks can find their condition particularly threatens their self-esteem and self-efficacy. Membership of a self-help group is one of the support options recommended by the National Health Service in the UK. Such groups are considered to provide environments where uncertainties and emotions can be expressed to others who share the condition, and who may be able to explain how they have dealt with the problems. This sort of sharing of the problem, learning that others have faced the threat and survived, and being part of the group, can be enough to instil greater optimism and persistence. This would be predicted from the 'social cure' model of the effects of group identification (Jetten et al., 2012).

Consciousness-raising groups offer a different type of support. Philpott (1982), writing about the early days of the women's liberation movement in the US, described how it started with small groups of women meeting regularly to talk about their experiences as well as to take other forms of action. The label 'consciousness raising' was coined to describe what the feminist movement was doing in the late 1960s. Consciousness raising is also a process of social influence, and a group dedicated to it becomes a medium of personal and, thereby, social change. Consciousness raising can radically alter the way the individual experiences their threatened identity and may suggest ways the threat position itself may be changed, or even removed.

However, consciousness raising, as ultimately conceived by the women's liberation movement, was not just about changing the awareness of the women inside the movement, it was aimed at changing the societal attitudes towards and status of all women. To some extent, consciousness raising is an intrinsic part of social movements. The series of anti-government, pro-democracy protests, uprisings, and armed rebellions against regimes that spread across much of the Arab world (including Bahrain, Libya, North Africa, Syria, and Tunisia) between 2010 and 2013, labelled the 'Arab Spring', illustrate the importance of widespread consciousness raising to the efficacy of social movements. Galvanising support involved raising awareness of the inherent injustices of the regimes, the harm done to individuals, the possibility of bringing about change, and the evidence that change had been wrought. This process probably could not have happened without the use of social media and input from the mass media. Instantaneous, mass communication was a foundation of consciousness raising inside the Arab world and outside it. In fact, the example highlights that outgroups are often porous to the consciousness-raising activities of a group or movement. The messages of the Arab Spring rippled across the rest of the world. Once social support translates into social influence, a new set of group-based coping strategies come into play. These involve group action.

- *Group action: direct and indirect*

These strategies involve group action in the intergroup context that has the effect of changing the level of threat individuals experience. Direct action in favour of the threatened tends to hail from pressure groups or social movements. Group action that indirectly favours or disadvantages the threatened can occur as a result of the wider dynamics of intergroup relations.

Pressure groups try to influence public policy in the interests of a particular cause by changing public opinion and the position of policy makers (e.g., through lobbying, advocacy, electioneering, and propagandising). A pressure group can coalesce around any type of cause (e.g., the survival of endangered species; the banning of food additives; the prevention of corporal punishment; the drilling of a new oil well in a rural village, etc.). The types of causes that merit a pressure group at any period in history is revealing of the moral values and economic climate of that era.

Typically, pressure groups operate within the existing social and legal order and use methods mostly accepted as legitimate, although some protest activities may lie outside the law. Such groups sometimes coalesce around a constituency of threatened people (as in the case of the pressure group Mind for the mentally ill or Action for Children for vulnerable children). Such groups can be highly centralised, bureaucratised, and expert organisations, and may gain charitable status. They are likely to be managed by people who have sympathy with their cause of the threatened but are not themselves experiencing the threat.

Pressure groups offer support for the individuals coping with a threat to identity at two levels: by trying to change the conditions (in terms of both social representations and legal or environmental frameworks) in which they live, and by providing an activist community with which they can communicate or identify. Importantly, threatened individuals can benefit from a pressure group without ever being part of it.

Social movements are not totally dissimilar from pressure groups. Social movements come in many shapes and sizes, with varying lifespans and differing success rates. A social movement is an effort by a large number of people to solve collectively problems they feel that they share. Social movements, like pressure groups, want to bring about change but they tend to be more diffuse in specification of the changes required and do not restrict themselves to using methods that are considered legal (e.g., they will use violent protests, terrorism, and even self-mortification). Pressure groups work within the system to achieve small, incremental changes; social movements act to bring about more radical, immediate, and large-scale changes from outside the system.

As forms of direct group action, pressure groups and social movements have a common underlying purpose: to serve the interests of the people that they represent; to wrest greater power or social influence for their constituency; and to attain self-determination and independence. They therefore pursue a series of objectives that serve this overall purpose:

1. They will seek to change the value attributed to the qualities deemed characteristic of the people they represent.
2. They will seek to change the characteristics associated with the social category to which the people they represent belong.
3. They will seek to shift decision-making powers into their own hands. This will entail reconfiguring the aspects of the intergroup hierarchy and establishing new social representational or ideological systems.

Sometimes they will achieve one or more of these objectives. When they do, they may greatly alter the life course of the people they represent. It is notable that the threatened individual is not controlling how direct group action operates as a coping strategy. If the individual is a member of the pressure group or a part of the social movement, it is possible that they will have some say in the group's decisions. Yet it is the intra-group and intergroup dynamics that will determine whether or how the individual benefits.

Independently of pressure groups or social movements, group action that is embedded in the wider dynamics of intergroup relations can favour or disadvantage the threatened. A group may act without any intention of influencing the position of the threatened or, indeed, without any awareness that it is influencing them. This sort of collateral effect of group action on the threatened is referred to here as indirect group action. Many of the influences on identity threat originate in this way, as by-products of intergroup dynamics. These effects are difficult to examine systematically because they involve interactions of complex networks. But they can be seen every day in commonplace political or economic struggles.

Take a purely hypothetical illustration. One country invades, and makes war on, another country. No one is quite sure why. However, the invading forces decimate the capacity of their victims to harvest or transport their grain to their normal markets in other countries around the world. In a developing country, thousands of miles away, which is dependent upon these grain exports, food shortages ensue, driving up food prices, pushing people into poverty, and destabilising entire regions. Families there, who were already in poverty, find it difficult to feed their children. The threat to identity that economic destabilisation and poverty represents is intensified, without those families having any say in the matter. This illustration ignores the enormous complexities of such a conflict and its consequences globally. Its purpose is to show how, indirectly, the action of one group can impact on threat at the individual level even for those remote from the action itself. A more positive illustration can be found in the way a commercial organisation, a pharmaceutical company, acting solely in order to undermine its business competitors, can make a life-saving product available at cut price in certain countries, and those suffering with the disease in those countries find their lives transformed. Indirect group action is something that impacts on the threatened, affecting their level of threat, but certainly does not involve a strategic decision by threatened individuals. Nevertheless, they can be serious winners or losers. The indirect impact of intergroup dynamics on identity threat levels should be researched more systematically.

Effects of identity principles on intra-group and intergroup processes

This chapter has focused primarily on the effects that a group has on its members. It has looked at how de-identification from the group creates a dilemma for the group and the consequences for its treatment of individual members. But it has not considered the effects that the individual's motivation to achieve self-esteem, self-efficacy, positive distinctiveness, and continuity has on intra-group or intergroup processes. In concluding this chapter, these will be examined briefly.

There is the interesting question of how far the behaviour of groups is driven by the effects of its members' desire to build an identity structure that is concordant with the identity principles. In the preface to the collection summarising Henri Tajfel's work (Tajfel, 1981), published just before his death, Jerome Bruner (pp. xi–xii) comments that there is a 'profoundly puzzling relation that exists between individual, human psychological functioning on the one hand and the large-scale social processes and events which shape this functioning and are shaped by it on the other'. Bruner indicates that Tajfel recognised the constant interaction between the more structural 'superorganic' forces that animate the wider society and the individual reactions that appear superficially to impel human behaviour. Tajfel chose to study this interaction in the phenomena of group prejudice and intergroup differentiation (Tajfel, 1978). Tajfel rejected the notion that prejudice and intergroup differentiation are only aggregate expressions of individual self-interest. They are products of large-scale societal processes that channel individual behaviour and, indeed, establish what the individual perceives to be self-interest and how it can be served most effectively.

Nevertheless, as Social Identity Theory was developed, the 'self-esteem hypothesis' (Abrams & Hogg, 1990a; Rubin & Hewstone, 1998) emerged in an attempt to explain why people will discriminate against and stigmatise members of outgroups (i.e., groups to which they do not belong) even when no material gain can be achieved from doing so. The basic idea is that differentiating their own group from other groups in positive ways (i.e., being prejudiced against the outgroup) results in individuals being able to claim greater self-esteem for their own social identity (i.e., in IPT terms, that component of their identity derived from that group membership). This suggests that group prejudice or intergroup conflict may be partly explained by individuals using them as opportunities for identity gains. The self-esteem hypothesis has been argued by some to muddy the distinction between social identity and personal identity. From an IPT perspective, this is obviously not a problem since it does not distinguish between the social and personal identities. However, it is important to consistently differentiate between a specific group identification and the wholistic identity structure.

In addition to intergroup differentiation aimed at denigrating the outgroup as a means of improving the self-esteem, Tajfel originally emphasised additionally the importance of 'exit' and 'voice', following the seminal work of Hirschman (1974). Essentially, an individual who is dissatisfied with the contribution that a group membership is making to his or her sense of personal worth may choose to exit the group (assuming exit is feasible, and sometimes it is not) or to stay and try to change the group through using 'voice' (which Hirschman said could be graduated, all the way from faint grumbling to violent protest). Voice is the social action response to group discontent (such as involvement in a social movement or pressure group like those described earlier in this chapter). Hirschman included a third option in his model: loyalty. This reflected the option of staying on without voicing discontent, ranging from enthusiastic support to passive acceptance or even submissive silence. This definition of loyalty is important because it allows for the individual to feel discontent while taking no action to express it, acting in some cases in ways meant to mask it. It may be considered the sort of loyalty that outweighs discontent for the individual or the sort that is feigned in order to avoid the consequences of discontent. It may be akin to de-identification while remaining a member.

Hirschman originally modelled these options as mutually exclusive: the more available the exit option, the lower the likelihood of voice, with loyalty (of whichever variety) basically seen as delaying both exit and voice. However, many economists and political scientists who applied the model concluded that all three options could be deployed by an individual, if not simultaneously, in quick succession, and sometimes iteratively in respect to loyalty and voice (e.g., Hoffman, 2010). It is notable that exit does not preclude subsequent voice. Exiles may be very active in propaganda against their erstwhile group or social category.

Take up of any of these options has implications for the group. Any of them may impact on intra-group behaviour or on intergroup interactions. For instance, exit may be a good solution for the individual but a bad thing for the group, especially if exit is used by a significant number of members or merely a prelude to attacks (voice) by the exile from outside the group. In any particular case, the actual cost–benefit analysis for both the individual and the group will be highly dependent on the contemporaneous 'superorganic' forces at work. Voice also has complex implications for the group. Broadly speaking, voice tactics (which involve many forms of social action, including terrorism or rebellion) can be used for or against the group's interests. They typically involve seeking to change the group's characteristics (e.g., norms, values, objectives, methods of decision-making, power hierarchy, symbols, and self-representations, etc.) and/or relationships with other groups. Group members acting in unison using these tactics can destabilise or remodel the group's existing identity and may displace it completely. Even a minority that is vocal in unison (acting as a choir) can have substantial effects on the group (cf., the effects of pressure groups on tobacco smokers). Inevitably, minorities that start to be successful rarely remain minorities.

Intergroup differentiation can be seen as a form of voice. Manoeuvring the intergroup position of one's own group through expressions of outgroup deprecation might have limited immediate material impact on the positivity of one's own group's position, but the change it can achieve in the wider social representations of the outgroup may have a longer-term effect on the material opportunities for the ingroup. Voice, in the intergroup context, does not necessarily have to be linked directly to the deprecation of the outgroup. It may be more focused on achieving a better standing for the ingroup through emphasising its positive achievements, through being creative in identifying new achievements or aspirations, or by negotiating a reinterpretation of the value of attributes of the group. Voice can be used to 'big up' the ingroup without overt mention of outgroups, but its position in the intergroup matrix is changed nevertheless. Even by ignoring the outgroup, intergroup differentiation can be achieved through voice.

All of this suggests that what individuals do inside their group, motivated by the level of their contentment with it, will have serious implications for the group and its intergroup context. However, taking into account the nature of the processes involved, it will rarely be the activities of a single individual, unless they occupy a position of great power within the group, that produce these effects for the group. Exit, voice, and loyalty tactics normally have consequences for a group if used in the same way by more than one individual at the same time. However, such effects can be achieved by a minority acting in concert within the group.

If people within a group are discontented about what it offers for them in terms of self-esteem, self-efficacy, positive distinctiveness, or continuity, IPT would also predict that they will deploy a range of intra-psychic, interpersonal, or group coping strategies, which have been described earlier, that may significantly change the character or position of their group. The probability of the change occurring, or being significant, depends crucially upon the initial character or position of the group and on the number of individuals who adopt a common battery of coping strategies over the same time period. The changes brought about can result in heightened differentiation, competition, or conflict between groups, but this is not inevitable and, where it happens, not necessarily intended. But the bottom line has to be that threats to an individual's levels of the identity principles can form part of the chain of events that result in intergroup conflict. They are not 'the' reason for the conflict. They are more likely than not to have been caused themselves by the other 'superorganic forces' that are the foundations of the conflict (e.g., opportunities for material gain, unjust power differentials, historic injustices, or discriminatory social representations and ideologies).

Group membership in identity processes; identity principles in the group dynamics

In examining the effects of group membership on identity processes, and of identity principles on group dynamics, this chapter has suggested the fundamental importance of these interactions. While IPT states that a group membership comprises just one component of a complex wholistic identity structure, it is important to note that a group membership is a particular type of identity component. Unlike many other identity components, one based on a significant group membership may have great power to situate the whole of the individual's identity structure in the social structure and in the social influence and ideological milieu. Since it can do this, it contributes probably disproportionately to the determination of the resources (material, social, and psychological) that the individual has available when attempting to optimise the identity structure in terms of self-esteem, self-efficacy, positive distinctiveness, and continuity.

Clearly, not all memberships have this level of impact, but the fact that some do means that it is important to understand what belonging in and identification with a group mean and how membership insecurity, uncertainty, and de-identification or resistance influence not only the individual's emotions and behaviour but also the group's treatment of the individual. The importance of group memberships also means that we need to understand the effects of holding multiple memberships. Identity processes influence more than just prejudice or intergroup discrimination; they are crucial to most aspects of social change and some aspects of social inertia.

8

IDENTITY PROCESS LIMITS

Life is a whim of several billion cells to be you for a while. Groucho Marx

Memories are the architecture of our identity. Brian Solis

Issues addressed in this chapter

The successful construction and maintenance of the identity structure depends on the processes of assimilation-accommodation and evaluation. This chapter describes the influences that limit the operation of identity processes and indicates the complex interactions between them. It reviews the impact that cognitive or emotional impairment resulting from organic sources (e.g., dementia) or severe trauma (e.g., dissociative identity disorder) can have on identity dynamics. It describes some of the physical and social influences affecting identity processes. It also examines some of the limitations on identity processes resulting from cognitive styles. It explores how the success of identity processes is influenced by the nature of the contextual changes that are occurring and to which a response is necessary, the current identity structure, and the existing status of the identity principles. The complex relationships between the identity principles are also considered. It discusses what happens when identity processes are not successful. It concludes with some comments on identity process resilience.

Limitations on identity processes

Identity processes do not always work to plan. Assimilation-accommodation is entirely dependent on other systems. It depends on the effective operation of a host of neurological and physiological processes that underpin consciousness and memory, and the other cognitive and emotional activity that these in turn make possible. Any malfunction in those very complex systems can disrupt or even prevent the assimilation-accommodation process from operating or from acting in accordance with the identity principles. Such organic problems and their cognitive correlates or effects on emotion regulation can also affect the evaluation process.

Organic problems influencing identity processes: dementia

Dementia is probably the most common illness that affects identity processes. Dementia is not a disease in itself. It is a collection of symptoms caused by damage to the brain by different diseases. It primarily entails the loss of cognitive functioning (NHS, 2022). It affects thinking, remembering, and reasoning, and, in some people, results in reduced emotional control. It is more common in older age groups. Sometimes the symptoms are mild and may get worse only very gradually. If the symptoms are not severe enough to be diagnosed as dementia, it is often identified as 'mild cognitive impairment'.

A range of medical conditions can contribute to the development of dementia. There are various forms of dementia. Some appear to be caused by abnormal build ups of proteins in the brain (e.g., Alzheimer's). Vascular dementia is caused by medical conditions that damage blood vessels in the brain or interrupt the flow of blood and oxygen to the brain. Neurodegenerative disorders, such as dementia, result in a progressive and irreversible loss of neurons and brain functioning.

The symptoms of dementia can vary and can include memory loss, poor judgement, and confusion; difficulty in expressing thoughts and finding the right word; difficulty in carrying out familiar daily tasks; acting impulsively and mood changes; ignoring the feelings of others; and hallucination, delusions, or paranoia. Becoming withdrawn or anxious is also common in sufferers of dementia. Dementia is not alone in initiating such symptoms. Other medical conditions that involve brain disease or trauma (e.g., Creutzfeldt-Jakob disease, Huntington's disease, or repeated brain injury) can result in similar symptoms.

It is not hard to see why such radical changes in the operation of the brain and neurophysiological system will disrupt the identity processes. In the early stages of dementia, the symptoms are themselves a direct threat to self-esteem, self-efficacy, positive distinctiveness, and continuity. Dementia begins to threaten the personal intellectual and communication skills that are the foundation of goal-attainment and social competence. At that stage, the identity processes do set about coping with the threat. Intra-psychic strategies are used, such as denial, often involving 'explaining away' functional deficits (e.g., rationalising memory loss in terms of overload or stress or even 'normal ageing'). These may be accompanied by using 'safety netting' so that forgetfulness is less likely or less visible (e.g., the use of 'to do' lists or checklists). Interpersonal strategies are also used: reaching out for support from family and friends can reduce the likelihood of depression or anxiety that is linked to finding oneself less capable of living as usual. Identity processes can set in train these and other coping strategies to protect the status of the identity principles in the short run. In the longer run, as degeneration progresses, such adaptations become ineffective. Two things happen. The first thing is that the deficits in self-esteem, self-efficacy, positive distinctiveness, and continuity become so marked that the identity processes have no means of repairing them. This is made more likely by the fact that typically it is all four identity principles that are simultaneously attacked by dementia in one way or another. The second thing is that the neurophysiological foundation of the identity processes themselves is also being undermined. As memory ceases to function, the identity structure that resides in it itself cannot be maintained.

There is a hard question that emerges at this point. In the latest stages of dementia, do the identity principles still motivate the individual even when the previous complex identity structure no longer has a psychological reality? If the identity principles are still there, do the identity processes continue to strive to develop an identity structure? Research on late-stage dementia has begun to suggest that while many competences are lost, others remain and may substitute for those that are lost (e.g., non-verbal for verbal communication; Clare et al., 2020). Much more research on the expression of identity in late-stage dementia is needed. However, there seems to be no doubt that the way that the identity processes operate will need to change if they continue into late-stage dementia.

Indeed, the identity principles themselves may change. Given how long-term memory and short-term memory deficits differ in their patterns of response over the course of dementia (Jahn, 2022), it could be that the continuity identity principle does continue, as least for some time, to motivate identity maintenance. It would be interesting to establish whether the absence of identity change (that would be needed were short-term memory still feeding continuously updated information) focuses the identity processes on maintaining an earlier incarnation of the identity structure.

Variation in types of memory and memory loss and the phenomena of memory malleability are really crucial to the ways identity processes work. If identity processes do continue to operate even after a considerable degradation of memory has occurred as a consequence of neurophysiological change, it will be important to establish how that can be empirically evidenced. Organic problems are not the only basis for identity processes failing to operate as expected. Severe psychological trauma may also disturb their operation.

Psychological conditions influencing identity processes: severe trauma

Many psychological illnesses involve some disruption of the individual's sense of identity. For instance, 'identity disturbance' is one of the criteria in DSM-5 (American Psychiatric Association, 2013) for borderline personality disorder (BPD). Wilkinson-Ryan and Weston (2000) investigated the symptomatology of identity disturbance. Four identity disturbance factors were identified: role absorption (in which patients tend to define themselves in terms of a single role or cause, and feel that they are always playing a role), painful incoherence (a subjective sense of lack of coherence), inconsistency (an objective incoherence in thought, feeling, and behaviour), and lack of commitment (e.g., to jobs or values). Zandersen and Parnas (2019) suggested that identity disturbance is also frequently found in schizophrenia and schizotypal personality disorder.

Dissociative Identity Disorder (DID, also in the past called Multiple Personality Disorder or Split-personality Disorder) is another exemplar of the psychiatric conditions focused on identity dysfunction. People with DID are said to have two or more separate identities. These identities are thought to control their behaviour at different times. Each identity manifests as having its own personal history, traits, likes, and dislikes. DID is one of several dissociative disorders. These disorders affect a person's ability to connect with reality. Other dissociative disorders include depersonalised or derealisation disorder (which causes a feeling of detachment from actions) and dissociative amnesia, or problems remembering information about the self. DID is very rare. The disorder affects between 0.01 and 1% of the population. It can occur at any age. Women are more likely than men to have DID. DID is thought usually to be the result of sexual or physical abuse during childhood. Sometimes it develops in response to a natural disaster or other traumatic events (e.g., experiences in combat). The disorder is believed to be a way for someone to distance or detach themselves from trauma. However, some of the symptoms can be a product of head injuries or brain tumours.

The symptoms of DID include gaps in memory, hallucinations, delusions, disorientation, depression, anxiety, drug or alcohol abuse, suicidal thoughts, and actual self-harm. However, the crucial symptom is that the person presents with two or more distinct identities: the core (or base self) and the 'alters' (after the notion of alter egos). Some people with DID have up to 100 alters. Alters tend to be very different from one another. These identities might have different genders, ethnicities, interests, and ways of interacting with their environments. DID usually is not diagnosed until adulthood. When symptoms occur earlier, they may be confused with other behavioural or learning difficulties prevalent in childhood (e.g., attention deficit hyperactivity disorder).

Therapy for DID and for identity disturbance in BPD often focuses on identifying and working through the past trauma, abuse, or neglect that are thought to be the cause of the problems. This may involve recovering memories that have been suppressed earlier. Additionally, there are attempts to help the sufferer manage the sudden behavioural and emotional changes that characterise the conditions. In the case of DID, an emphasis may be placed on measures aimed at merging separate identities into a single identity, and on avoidance of the circumstances that trigger the appearance of alters (e.g., stress or drugs and alcohol). Reducing the frequency of different alters taking control of the individual's behaviour can aid identity re-integration. People can develop greater control over their behaviour as a result of therapy and ongoing social support from family and friends. The struggle by sufferers to manage their identities is likely to be long term.

On examining the evidence for BPD and DID, it could be argued that they are both in part products of identity process failure rather than precursors to it. Looking at BPD identity disturbance, we see single role or cause absorption, subjective incoherence and inconsistency, and a failure of commitment. Each element seems either to reflect the absence of assimilation and accommodation of appropriate identity components into the identity structure or to indicate that the evaluation of identity components is inappropriate. DID symptoms can also result from identity processing errors. The existence of multiple 'alter' identities rather than an integrated identity structure certainly indicates assimilation and accommodation has failed. It suggests that coping strategies, such as denial or compartmentalisation, deployed in childhood to deal with trauma were insufficiently fine-tuned or inadequate in the circumstances that surrounded the child.

It is not unreasonable to assume that the identity processes have had a hand in the genesis of these psychiatric conditions. However, once they are in existence, these conditions influence how the identity processes can subsequently work. This is most marked in the case of DID where the fragmentation of the identity structure into a core self and other 'alter' selves means ongoing identity change has to occur amid great uncertainty. For instance, which self gets updated to accommodate the new identity components? If someone with DID gets in a fight and the opponent is killed, which self is the killer? Are the identity processes always biased to protect the 'core' self from identity principle losses? Or is it more likely that it will all depend on the specific circumstances? In any case, the idea that the identity processes can go on as normal to comply with the identity principles is not tenable.

An identity structure that is already insecure and uncertain makes appropriate identity adaptation in response to external changes enormously difficult. The task of optimising assimilation-accommodation and evaluation may be so complex and intractable a problem that it results in the equivalent of a system shut down. New experiences and potential new identity components are not processed. Alternatively, they are processed but without adequate quality assurance. Inconsistencies and incongruities between the new and earlier identity components become evident. This is when the limitations of the identity processes become most obviously a risk to psychological well-being. The subjective loss of control over one's own identity and the inadequacy of the identity's responsiveness to reality trigger hopelessness, fear, anger, depression, or asocial or antisocial behaviour. Effectively, when the identity processes fail in their jobs because they are operating in the midst of an ongoing psychiatric condition, more symptoms of poor psychological well-being can appear. It becomes a vicious circle that the individual alone cannot escape.

Physical and social influences on identity processes: material resources

Identity processes are limited in their operation by the organic and psychological state of the individual. They are also circumscribed by the physical, social, and environmental conditions that surround and enfold the individual. If those conditions are aversive, representing a significant and immediate risk to the life or physical health of the individual, identity processes have to respond with speed but caution. Consider a hypothetical vignette:

A man (let's call him John) in his early 80s is walking down the street of a small town in broad daylight. It is a fine day, he is happy, he has no symptoms of dementia, he has a set of supportive friends but they are not with him, he has just had coffee in his favoured café, and is going to the library to get a newly published book on forensic science. Out of the blue, he hears his new mobile phone ring. He doesn't get many calls and he doesn't want to miss this one. He gets his phone out and, as he does, vaguely notices a group of young men loitering across the road, leaning against their bicycles. He opens his phone and, as he does, he is suddenly aware that the lads have mounted their bikes and are charging down on him. Before he knows it, one has grabbed his phone, another has pushed him over, and a third is kicking him. Then they are gone. The whole thing takes less than two minutes.

It turns out that he was not too badly hurt – a very sore rib, and a few other bruises and scrapes. His best trousers were ripped. The police were called by a passer-by, but the lads got clean away. The way John reacts to this experience may well affect him for the rest of his life. How do identity processes come into play in such an event? John has to deal with what this means to his self-esteem (does it make people think he is weak?), his self-efficacy (does it signal he is defenceless, incapable of seeing and avoiding a threat?), his positive distinctiveness (will he only be remembered now as the old man who got robbed?), and his continuity (will this mean freedom to walk around town is at an end?). The task for the identity processes is to pick up the pieces and, in this case, marshal resources to substantiate an interpretation of the events that provides the answer 'no' to each of the questions posed in brackets. So, it is possible that John accumulates a series of material resources that say 'no' loud and clear. The medic that checked him in the hospital says he is remarkably fit for his age and that his instinct to roll into a ball as he fell saved his ribs from serious damage. The police say these lads have robbed a few people during the day, and no one had realised what they were about to do. They also say that all the others had been in their teens and early 20s. His friends tell him that such events are rare, and he should not let bullies rule his life, and, in any case, they would go visit the library with him any time. The evidence that these sources provide offers the resource needed for identity processes to assimilate-accommodate to the event and to evaluate it appropriately. On its basis, John's identity structure might not be weakened; it might even have been reinforced.

In this version of the vignette, John's identity processes successfully satisfy the identity principles because they had some useful material resources. But it might have been very different if the fragments of evidence that John collected, and which contextualised the event, had answered 'yes' (rather than 'no') to the questions posed in brackets above. Identity processes, if they are to create the desired identity effect, need the right material resources to work with. To some extent material resources can always be redefined, reinterpreted, or simply invented. But for identity processes to consistently function effectively, it is best if the material resources required are available and real. The more the material resources constrain identity processes, the less effective those processes will be.

Cognitive style limitations on identity processes

The operation of identity processes is limited by the way the individual's established cognitive processes work. Normal psychological functioning, where no psychiatric condition is involved, entails the use of what could be called cognitive 'shortcuts' or biases. These biases seem often to be attempts to simplify information processing, allow rapid assessment of a situation, and speed up decision-making. Cognitive biases can be functional but can also result in mistakes because pieces of information or counterfactuals are ignored or misinterpreted. People often develop habits of cognitive bias. These are usually called cognitive styles.

Cognitive biases affect self-governance (Sali et al., 2018). Cognitive styles also affect identity processes. For instance, differences in habitual attribution biases are important. Self-serving biases in attribution (i.e., in which we attribute positive events and successes to ourselves but blame negative results to external factors unrelated to us; see Sedikides & Alicke, 2019), which may themselves be influenced by identity principles (e.g., the desire for self-esteem), may also affect how realistic or optimal adjustments in identity structure actually are. There is also a complex interaction between the perception of identity threat and the direction and extent of the self-serving bias (Campbell & Sedikides, 1999) – essentially, threat magnifies the self-serving bias. Attributional cognitive styles may also have an indirect effect on identity processes. Individuals not characterised by a self-serving bias, but rather by the reverse (a self-critical bias), when they fail at a task, are liable to become depressed or feel helpless. Helplessness is associated with cognitive deficits, passivity, lowered self-esteem, sadness, anxiety, hostility but reduced overt aggression, and norepinephrine depletion. Helplessness influences identity processes directly but also through its impact on cognitive functions and emotional state.

There is an irony lurking in the interaction of these processes. Cognitive biases are developed in order to support adaptation to demanding environments where speed of response is valuable, and 'rules of thumb' may be right more often than not. When they get enmeshed in identity processes, self-serving biases are fairly inevitable. The problem is that they generate unrealistic and unstable representations of events and the meaning of those events for the identity structure. Identity processes affected by cognitive biases are liable to produce identity structure changes that cannot be sustained. They may offer temporary fixes. But, if they are not flushed out of the identity structure, they may result in further self-misrepresentation and build the path towards dissociation from social reality. The irony, of course, lies in the fact that identity processes will have inculcated the self-serving bias in cognition in the interests of the identity principles. Both too much and too little of the bias represent limitations on the subsequent operation of the identity processes. Self-awareness of such biases is much to be desired.

Factors determining the success of identity processes

Identity processes are responsible for adjusting the identity structure in response to any psychological, social, or physical change. They do not only respond to threats. They respond, guided by the identity principles, to any form of change. They are limited in their operation, as described above, by certain characteristics of the individual. Psychological health (particularly mental illness); cognitive styles, habits, and biases; and organic (particularly neuro-physiological) factors play a part in determining how identity processes operate. The success of the responses to change that identity processes make will also depend upon three other sorts of factors:

- the nature of the changes that are occurring and to which a response is necessary;
- the current identity structure;
- the existing status of the identity principles.

Before considering them, it is worth examining what is meant by 'success' for the identity processes. One indicator might be the improvement achieved in the levels of the four identity principles. This improvement might not only be indexed simply in terms of their absolute levels, but also in terms of their relative levels and the stability of this configuration. However, measuring identity process success is not simple. Accessing levels of self-esteem, self-efficacy, positive distinctiveness, and continuity in any objective way poses a fundamental dilemma. It is not sensible to rely on self-perceptions reflected in self-report assessments. These can be influenced by the operation of the very identity processes that are the object of study. Also, it is not sensible to rely solely on independent observer assessments of the individual's identity principle levels. For one thing, it is hard to know whether they can be said to have the necessary access to relevant data; for another, it is difficult to determine that they are truly neutral in their judgements.

Some combination of self-report and external assessment may seem a viable compromise approach. However, the success of identity processes probably needs to be seen not just in response to a single change, but over a period of time where several changes occur. The overall value of any single adaptation of the identity structure can only be understood in its psychosocial context and over time. It is possible to imagine an assimilation-accommodation or evaluation adaptation made in the identity structure immediately following a change in circumstances might seem productive for one or more identity principles initially, but later it may be seen to be very counterproductive. It seems likely that any systematic measure of identity process success will need to include monitoring the effectiveness of any modification of the identity structure over time. Success in this context is not static. It is contextualised and conditional.

Nature of the situational changes that are occurring

Changes in circumstances might be classified on a number of dimensions likely to influence the success of the identity processes:

- To what extent is the change desired or regretted by the individual?
- Magnitude – how big a change is it?
- Does it occur without warning or is it expected?
- Is it permanent or temporary?

- Who does it affect? Does it affect only the individual or many other people? How many? Who are they? How are they related to the individual?
- To which components of the identity structure does it seem relevant?

A superordinate question that identity processes must address in answering each of these is: does this change have substantive, potential consequences for the identity structure? Many psychological, social, and physical changes do not necessitate any significant modification of the identity structure. They are an expected part of the status quo. Accurately differentiating change that requires a response from anything else is key to the success of identity processes. Both false positives and false negatives will lead to inappropriate action.

The answers to each of the bullet point questions will affect the likelihood that identity processes can achieve a satisfactory identity structure adjustment. There will be interactions between these features of the change, and these will also impact on the likelihood that identity processes can find adaptations that are effective.

Taking account of these dimensions of the change that initiates the response is essential in modelling what adaptations to the identity structure are likely to be attempted and how likely they are to be effective. This suggests that research on identity structure adaptation will need to pay due attention to the characteristics of the situational changes that instigate any modification. Finding ways to measure or describe these situational changes to which the identity processes are responding is important. The measurements need to be independent of any measurement of the subsequent modifications in the identity itself. This implies that retrospective self-report concerning the stimuli for identity change should be used with great caution. It points to the usefulness of more experimental methods.

The current identity structure

Features of the current identity structure also have a bearing upon the potential efficacy of the reaction of the identity processes to a situational change. These features include:

- the developmental stage in the life course (which may affect malleability of the structure as well as, at both ends of the age spectrum, the cognitive competencies that can be brought into play);
- the specifics of the current configuration of identity components (including the current coherence of the configuration within the identity structure, i.e., extent of being logically or consistently linked together, forming a unified whole);
- the prior history of the stability/instability of the connections between identity components;
- the nature of each of the specific, current identity components (e.g., including values, beliefs, group memberships, and personality traits).

The existing organisational structure and content of identity constrain the options that are available to identity processes in dealing with any situational change. All adaptations possibly have ripple effects across the entire identity structure. They can have unanticipatable consequences. A mature, coherent, stable identity structure increases the odds that the consequences of the adaptation will be those that are anticipated and targeted. However, even then, the specific nature of each of the identity components can play a part in shaping success. For instance, individuals who have personality profiles favouring higher tolerance of ambiguity (Furnham & Ribchester, 1995) may be more able to benefit from adaptations resulting in reduced coherence in the configuration of identity without loss of self-efficacy. The actual success of identity processes in any particular change scenario will hang upon the interaction of the nature of the situational change and the character of the existing identity structure. Research is still needed in order to pinpoint the patterns of these interactions.

Since the initial chain of change-adaptation (i.e., the situational change identity adaptation > further change > more adaptation > next change > etc.) can be fleeting and simultaneously linked to other chains, the success of identity processes might be best assessed not in regard to single interventions but in relation to profiles of identity structure modification over longer time periods. Understanding them will probably require cohort-sequential, longitudinal research designs using fine-grained multiple measurements.

The existing status of the identity principles

The existing status of identity principles influences the chances of the identity processes adaptations being regarded as successful by the individual concerned. The status of the identity principles reflects the levels of satisfaction that the individual feels with each of them. IPT treats these levels as independent, while recognising that they can be correlated. When looking at responses to identity threat in Chapter 3, identity resilience was defined in terms of having what the individual perceives to be optimally high levels of satisfaction across the four principles.

Features of the status of the identity principles that may have a bearing on the success of the identity processes in responding to any change include:

- the existing actual absolute levels of perceived self-esteem, self-efficacy, positive distinctiveness, and continuity;
- the relative levels across the four identity principles;
- the extent of motivation to achieve higher levels in each of the four principles;
- the relative motivation to raise levels across the four principles.

Each of the identity principles will affect the response of identity processes but their relative impact will depend on their relevance to the change event. Essentially, the existing profile of self-esteem, self-efficacy, positive distinctiveness, and continuity will set the direction and intensity of motivation for identity structure change. They also provide the criteria against which changes produced by identity processes in the identity structure are judged to be acceptable. Following a situational change, identity processes can be thought to be succeeding or failing in the adaptations they make as a result of how the new profile of self-esteem, self-efficacy, positive distinctiveness, and continuity compares with its predecessor. Irrespective of the complexities and difficulties of the changed circumstances with which they had to cope, they can be deemed to have failed if the new profile is worse than that before.

However, this is less likely to happen when the levels of the identity principles are mostly initially high. The higher baseline levels result in changes in circumstances being less likely to be perceived as requiring identity structure adjustment. This is more likely to happen when baseline levels are low since the initial motive to improve levels of one or more of the identity principles is likely to be high. Adaptations will be seen to be necessary and any that fail to raise levels will be seen as identity process failures. Once this happens, it can initiate a vicious cycle of seeking identity structure adjustment but failing, which then motivates further adjustment, and so on. Escape depends on changes occurring in the resources (material, social, or psychological) available to identity processes. Individuals can seek to elicit such changes in resource. Indeed, identity processes will often set in train coping strategies that do garner such resources (e.g., the access to social support or the acquisition of new skills). The baseline profile of identity principle levels does not have fatalistic control over responses to change. It cannot have such control because of the inherent complexities in the relationships between the identity principles over time.

This discussion of the factors that influence the success of the identity processes emphasises the extraordinary complexity of the interaction between the nature of the changes that are occurring and that need a response, the current identity structure, and the existing status of the identity principles. Things get even more complex if the relationships between the identity principles are factored in.

The complexities of identity principles

The identity principles reflect four different motivations – for self-esteem, self-efficacy, positive distinctiveness, and continuity. They affect not only the operation of the identity processes, but also other aspects of the individual's psychological and behavioural activities that are not necessarily mediated by the identity processes. For instance, self-esteem motivation can shape the individual's behaviour directly (e.g., encouraging competitiveness or attempts to gain social status). This may then trigger responses from the identity processes in order to deal with the success or failure in the effort to increase self-esteem. This illustrates the first complexity of the identity principles – they influence identity processes both directly (by setting the objectives for them) and indirectly (by motivating changes in individual behaviours that necessitate identity adjustments).

The second area of complexity lies in the fact that these four motives do not always require the individual to think, feel, or do the same things. The motives, not infrequently, require different changes in behaviour or in the identity structure. When they do, two variants of complexity can emerge. Either the changes are compatible with each other but cannot all be achieved at the same time, or the changes are incompatible and cannot all be achieved ever. Obviously, there can be degrees of incompatibility, so, in practice, the complexities are more variegated.

The most frequent incompatibilities in expression of identity principles arise between continuity and the other three. Self-esteem, self-efficacy, and positive distinctiveness (i.e., the 'identity worth' principles) tend to motivate compatible types of changes. Continuity tends to motivate conservation rather than change objectives. The differences between the identity principles are most evident when the individual is faced with significant hazards.

These differences have been shown in relation to responses to the COVID-19 pandemic. Breakwell, Jaspal, and Wright (in press) investigated whether identity worth and identity continuity differentially predict variance in COVID-19 fear and risk, science mistrust, vaccine positivity, and vaccination likelihood. Data were collected online from 643 UK and 485 Portuguese adults during March 2021. They found that, while the UK and Portuguese samples did not differ on vaccination likelihood or identity measures, UK respondents reported less science mistrust, COVID-19 risk, and fear, but higher vaccine positivity. Structural equation modelling indicated identity worth and identity continuity were linked to science mistrust, COVID-19 fear, COVID-19 risk, vaccine positivity and vaccination likelihood to different extents and mostly in opposite directions. Identity worth was associated with science trust, less COVID-19 fear, and less perceived COVID-19 risk. Identity continuity was associated with science mistrust, more fear, more perceived risk, and greater vaccine positivity. This evidence that these two constructs can behave differently in the face of the same stressor is important. Greater identity continuity is associated with higher perceived risk, more fear, greater mistrust of science, and directly with greater vaccine positivity. It seems to be acting as a counterbalance to the effects of higher identity worth, which are more optimistic, and, thus, possibly encouraging greater risk-taking with regard to vaccination. In fact, in the UK sample, identity worth is directly associated with lower vaccination likelihood.

In the research study described above, the extant levels of identity worth and identity continuity were measured. The degree of motivation to enhance those levels was not measured. When there are incompatibilities between the responses to hazards that the identity principles require, it is possible that variations in the strength of the motivation will determine the actual response chosen. However, this has not been established. A lot more empirical research is needed on the effects of the identity principles motivating different and incompatible objectives. Such incompatibilities are inevitably going to make success for the identity processes more problematic. It is possible to imagine the sort of compromises and iterating changes to the identity structure that might be needed. Identity processes are, after all, remarkably persistent.

When identity processes do not succeed

They may be persistent, but identity processes sometimes do face insurmountable problems in finding ways to construct and maintain the desired identity structure. The outline in this chapter of some of the limitations that surround them suggests that identity processes will not always succeed. What happens then? Of course, we can assume that what the individual considers to be the full complement of coping strategies (intra-psychic, interpersonal, and group levels) has been deployed without the desired effect. So, the impact is very likely to be undesirable. Just how undesirable will depend on which and how many components of the identity structure are affected, their importance, and the amount of change required of them.

The individual's physical, psychological, and social resources may have been seriously depleted by the effort to resist the situational change or by their attempts to make acceptable adaptations to it. As a result, the failure of the identity processes may compound the negative effects of any threat to identity. In effect, the failure of identity processes crystallises or 'realises' the threat. It moves from representing a possibility of harm to reflecting the reality of actual harm.

Having failed to execute adaptive coping, the identity processes may continue to operate but only by using more extreme responses and consequently increasing the risk to the individual's psychological or physical health. Some of the psychiatric conditions described earlier (e.g., BPD and DID) may follow episodes of ineffective coping and, as we saw, may precipitate such failure. Unsuccessful coping is also highly correlated with hopelessness, anxiety, and depression. These are, in turn, likely to reduce the chances of later, more effective coping unless the individual can gain therapeutic or broader social support that will change or redirect the coping strategies used.

Self-harming is also associated with failed coping efforts. Remember, the motivation to achieve self-esteem, self-efficacy, positive distinctiveness, and continuity most often continues even when coping strategies are failing. So, to satisfy these motives, maladaptive behaviours may occur. For instance, anorexia sometimes evolves from the desire to achieve greater self-esteem with regard to body image (Brockmeyer et al., 2013; Hartmann et al., 2014). The absence of effective self-regulation mechanisms (i.e., via identity processes) means that no matter how thin the sufferer is, they are never thin enough to satisfy the self-esteem motive – probably because the image of the perfect self changes to preclude success.

Other types of self-harm may also follow failures in coping that can arise from having to face complex multifaceted threats to the identity principles. Taliaferro et al. (2019) studied the factors distinguishing transgender/gender non-conforming (GNC) adolescents across three groups: no self-harm, non-suicidal self-injury (NSSI) only, and NSSI and suicide attempt (NSSI + SA). Data were collected in 2016 from 1,635 transgender/GNC students. Over half (51.6%) of transgender/GNC adolescents reported past-year self-harm behaviour. Factors that consistently distinguished transgender/GNC youth who reported self-harm from those who reported no self-harm included reports of a mental health problem, depression, running away from home, and substance use (alcohol or marijuana use). Factors that distinguished the NSSI + SA group from the NSSI only group were reports of a mental health problem, physical or sexual abuse, relationship violence, bullying victimisation, less parent connectedness, lower grades, lower levels of perceived school safety, and running away from home. This study illustrates vividly how identity processes may have to deal with multiple, complex threats to self-esteem, self-efficacy, positive distinctiveness, and continuity simultaneously. The more intense this concatenation of threat becomes, the more likely it seems that adaptive coping will succumb to physical self-harm as an outcome.

There is another potential outcome of identity process failure. The individual who cannot satisfy identity principle motives through socially accepted means may seek to do so by asocial or anti-social behaviour. Once established, this may become the individual's preferred route rather than using other more conventional methods. It could be argued that identity processes often skirt the edges of rule-breaking when engaged in creative reinterpretations of where boundaries of propriety rest. Indeed, there is a spectrum from completely prosocial to totally anti-social behaviour that can be involved in coping strategies. Anti-social approaches to satisfying identity motivation may be used because:

- other options are blocked or have been tried and were unproductive;
- anti-social behaviour is expected of members in the groups to which the individual aspires;
- they represent relatively easy routes for achieving positive distinctiveness rapidly (i.e., regarded positively in the groups that matter to the individual);
- they offer intrinsic rewards (e.g., criminal gains);
- they are an outlet for emotions (e.g., anger, hatred, envy) expressed in violence or vandalism targeted at people who are thwarting their identity objectives (e.g., competitors or oppressors).

Anti-social and asocial responses to the motivation that the identity principles initiate are more frequent than might be expected. Minimalist or minor rebellion against established protocols occur regularly in the process of creating and maintaining a unique identity. Resistance is a path to the individuation that underpins the unique identity. Not all anti-social behaviour that is used in the interests of the identity structure is predicated on failures in the earlier operation of the identity processes. Identity processes are broad-minded in the coping strategies that they employ. The success of anti-social or asocial coping approaches ultimately depends on the individual being persuaded that the changes they produce in the identity structure are valuable. This is most likely to occur if the change is badged as socially approved by a group or social category with whom the individual wants to identify. However, some individuals do dispense with seeking such approval, and reconcile themselves to being outside such systems. Such perceived independence from societal norms and sense of personal invulnerability is more likely in those who either have a lot to gain or little to lose.

Prior levels of the four identity principles also seem to have an effect on willingness to use rule breaking to achieve one's ends. For instance, higher levels of self-efficacy have been found to reduce inhibitions and increase dishonesty when it offers significant advantages (Baran & Jonason, 2020). Higher self-esteem, in contrast, reduces the likelihood of anti-social and other unacceptable behaviours (Orth & Robins, 2022). Greater positive distinctiveness, when associated with extreme feelings of pride, can stimulate aggression and anti-social behaviour (Bonaiuto et al., 2019). Higher continuity will increase the chances of anti-social behaviour continuing once it has been started.

When identity processes do not succeed, it is quite clear that it is not the end of the story. Many consequences follow their failure. One interesting thing to note is that the variety of responses include some very extreme changes in behaviour evidenced in psychiatric conditions, self-harming, and anti-social activities. Except in a few very extreme psychiatric conditions (e.g., schizoaffective disorder), there is no strong evidence to suggest that the identity processes simply cease to operate after coping strategies are unsuccessful, even when they are serially or regularly suboptimal in results. So, it is worth concluding this chapter by considering the resilience of identity processes.

The resilience of identity processes

People vary in how successful their identity processes are in constructing and maintaining their identities. This is not surprising since people, across their lifetime, will be exposed to different extents to the various factors that limit the effectiveness of identity processes. Individuals who have been exposed in their past to repeated experiences where their identity processes have coped with changes in circumstance inadequately are more likely to find that they will be unsuccessful in tackling change or threat in the future. Clearly, this 'success breeds success' prediction is relative and probabilistic. It will not apply universally.

However, there are three reasons why this is the favoured prediction. The most important reason is that past successes have been likely to produce an identity structure that is characterised by relatively high levels of self-esteem, self-efficacy, positive distinctiveness, and continuity. The fact that they are high gives the identity processes more cognitive and emotional resources (e.g., lower emotional lability, less helplessness, greater concentration, more self-confidence) to work with when developing coping strategies for a new threat. Additionally, when they are all high, they also tend to be more resilient in the face of change, and they are less likely to be motivating incompatible directions for identity structure adaptations. The second reason why identity processes with a history of success may continue to be successful is that, unless the individual's circumstances have changed radically, they will still have the social resources that helped coping in the past available to them (e.g., family or friends, social status, group memberships). In fact, the success of past coping strategies may actually mean that the social resources are still intact. The third reason that past success predicts future success is that the cognitive capacities and styles that supported early coping are probably still intact.

The 'success breeds success' prediction naturally hits some limitations when the individual's social resources or cognitive competences are significantly modified. Major societal changes (e.g., international conflicts, environmental disasters, or economic depressions) or severe physical trauma could certainly challenge the prediction. However, all other things being equal, the prediction would still persist in suggesting that people with past identity processes success would fare better, even in such dire circumstances.

It is important to avoid the error of assuming that because 'success breeds success', 'failure breeds failure' in identity processes. In most cases of failed responses to identity threat, there is limited evidence that identity processes persevere with maladaptive coping strategies. The strength of the motivations to achieve self-esteem, self-efficacy, positive distinctiveness, and continuity tend to result in the use of alternative coping options. As an illustration of this sort of serial coping strategy, one can consider what someone might do when she discovers that her self-esteem is being damaged by being identified with a particular group. First, she tries to change the social image of the group (perhaps by broadcasting the benefits of the group on social media), but this fails and actually stimulates more slurs and diatribes about the group in response. Second, she calls on other group members to campaign to establish the value of the group, but this fails because other members don't see the need. Third, she tells herself that if other members don't see a problem, it really does not represent a threat to her self-esteem, but this fails because she knows she does not agree with other members and, in any case, she thinks membership is lowering her positive distinctiveness as well as her self-esteem. Finally, she exits the group and joins another that offers her greater self-esteem, and this does not fail. Apart from the fact that she should have done the fourth thing first (since she had the ability to leave the group), this illustrates how coping generally works in practice. Identity processes run though successive approximations to a solution. What this means is that failed coping experiences can lead to later success. It also means that failure can provide good learning opportunities so that the number of successive approximations to the solution can be fewer the next time around. As individuals mature, through failure (as well as success) they learn the shortcuts to the most effective coping approaches, given their own identity structure, identity principle levels, and circumstances.

Thus, the simple 'failure leads to failure' prediction fails. However, there are conditions where it might be relevant. Where the identity structure is already weakened by low self-esteem, self-efficacy, positive distinctiveness, and continuity, and by a long series of failed coping sequences (i.e., ones which have not resulted ultimately in any form of success), then it is fair to assume that the identity processes will be less resilient. There is less evidence of attempts at coping. There is less evidence of being motivated to cope. Some clinical conditions that are associated with lowered self-esteem, self-efficacy, positive distinctiveness, and continuity are also linked to low coping motivation and efforts. For instance, this is seen in clinical depression.

Under some circumstances, the resilience of identity processes will wane. However, in general, despite the limitations that enmesh them, the identity processes are remarkably strong and will bounce back to revitalise the identity structure that remains after a threat is 'realised'. Identity processes will continue to go on in the background while other psychological functions do their work. They are analogous to the autonomic nervous system, which is not under conscious control particularly closely, but it ensures that other bodily functions are delivered. Identity processes are the essential underpinning of many aspects of the individual's psychological and social functioning. It is therefore important to have more empirical research on identity processes. It is particularly needed on how coping can be reinvigorated most effectively after severe coping failures. Understanding more about why identity processes may be limited or fail is one avenue to finding ways to support people in learning how to cope better with both everyday change and threatening change.

9

USING IDENTITY THEORIES

Practice without theory is like the sailor who
boards ship without a rudder and compass.
Leonardo Da Vinci

Issues addressed in this chapter

This chapter examines how theories in social psychology find their way into practice. It describes the value of being intuitively plausible. It discusses the advantages and drawbacks for a theory of being popularised, using models of groupthink and cognitive dissonance as examples. After discussing the sequence of stages that a theory can go through in coming to be seen to have practical value, it describes the ways that identity theories have become useful, focusing on their function in explanation and prediction linked to interventions. It concludes by outlining some of the ways that Identity Process Theory has been used.

Practical, expected, and popularised

Kurt Lewin (1943, p. 118), one of the great early social psychologists, is often attributed with the quote 'there is nothing so practical as a good theory'. This is not such a strange idea if you take a definition of 'theory' from science. Typically, in science, a theory is a system of ideas intended to explain something, particularly one based on general principles independent of the thing to be explained. It is an even more obvious idea if you include Lewin's assertion that it has to be a 'good' theory. Getting people to think that social psychology is providing 'good' theory, and therefore something useful, has met with mixed success.

One problem was very clearly identified by Michael Argyle, another of the great early social psychologists, best known for his work on non-verbal communication and social skills. In his own experience of conversations over dinner at high tables in Oxford colleges in the 1970s, senior academics from other disciplines would react to the latest findings from social psychological research with a shrug and a simple statement that 'everyone already knows that'. The problem with social psychology is that, in general, once you state a theorem, people think it is obvious. Argyle, ever the empiricist, decided to test whether people really did 'know it already'. He told friends about an elegant experiment in which he presented his participants with either the accurate results of a social psychological experiment or a false result diametrically opposed to the actual findings. They were then asked to rate whether they would have expected the result. Participants in both conditions were equally likely to say that they expected the result. Argyle does not appear to have published these findings.

People may be disinclined to accept that social psychology has something new to say. That can have its disadvantages around a high table in Oxford, yet it bodes well for the absorption of social psychology into common usage. There are a couple of very notable examples that illustrate something about the way this absorption occurs: Janis's theory of groupthink and Festinger's theory of cognitive dissonance.

Groupthink

Janis (1982) studied decision-making in threatening contexts and conditions that give rise to irrational complacency, apathy, hopelessness, rigidity, and panic. One aspect of this work was on what he called 'groupthink'. Janis was very clear that this was most likely to happen if certain antecedent conditions were present: when a group is highly cohesive, insulated from experts, performs limited search and appraisal of information, operates under directed leadership, and experiences conditions of high stress with low self-esteem and little hope of finding a better solution to a pressing problem than that favoured by the leader or influential members. When present, these antecedent conditions are hypothesised to foster the extreme consensus-seeking characteristic of groupthink. This in turn is predicted to lead to two categories of undesirable decision-making processes. The first category, traditionally labelled symptoms of groupthink, includes an illusion of invulnerability, collective rationalisation, stereotyping of outgroups, self-censorship, 'mindguards', and belief in the inherent morality of the group. The second category, typically identified as symptoms of defective decision-making, involves the incomplete survey of alternatives and objectives, poor information search, failure to appraise the risks of the preferred solution, and selective information processing. Combined, these forces are predicted to result in extremely defective decision-making by the group.

Groupthink theory has had vast multidisciplinary impact and pervasive appeal to the broader public. It caught the imagination of the mass media because it provided a comprehensible explanation of some major fiascos, current and historical. Thus, it has been used retrospectively to explain such varied errors as the decision to market the drug thalidomide, NASA's decision to launch the *Challenger* space shuttle, and the Carter Administration's decision to use military measures to rescue hostages in Iran.

Despite its popularity, groupthink, in the first 20 years or so of its existence, was subjected to only a small number of empirical investigations. Turner and Pratkanis (1998) explained this in terms of the difficulties in doing well-founded experimental work on a theory that involves a large number of independent and dependent variables and which has theoretical specifications that are quite ambiguous (e.g., are all the antecedents necessary before groupthink occurs, or does it become increasingly more likely or pronounced as the number of antecedents in play increases, or does it all depend on the unique situation created by the antecedents?). They argue that the theory is unclear about how its construct should be operationalised or coded in archival data. Few of those experimental studies that were conducted provided unequivocal evidence of the existence of 'groupthink' impaired decision-making.

By the late 1990s, the phenomenon of groupthink was being reinterpreted and analysed within other theoretical frameworks (e.g., social identity maintenance, collective optimism/avoidance, and risk choice shifts). However, by then, 'groupthink' was well established in the vocabulary and texts of virtually every applied social science domain. It is still current in the shorthand of media reports on major public decisions that are open to question. It even now appears as a clue in newspaper crosswords. Like many theories that are popularised, the initial complex model has been simplified. Few people who refer to groupthink now take into account the very significant batch of antecedent conditions that Janis stated were necessary for groupthink to occur.

Constructs like groupthink have a life independent of the strictures of their original theoretical formulation or evidence base. People (including the public, the media, practitioners, and academics) were willing to accept it and claim it as something they had suspected all along. Resonating with people's need for explanations of some very strange, high-profile decisions and with their *post hoc* expectations, it survives. Indeed, it was used earlier in this book. There is no question that groupthink is a construct that provides a new way of thinking about errors in decision-making. Once articulated, it seemed intuitively to make sense – confirming something that people could say that they already suspected to be happening. This is the basis for its rapid absorption into the popular consciousness. It is what has made it a useful theory. Being popular makes it even easier for a good theory to be practical. Sadly, it does not mean its use in practice is always appropriate.

Widespread dissemination and usage of a social science theory has an additional effect that changes its usefulness. Once people know about groupthink, especially about the simplified or non-caveated versions of it, it is possible for them to see it everywhere. It is certainly tempting to attribute decisions made by outgroups that you dislike to groupthink. The mere presence of the theory in prevalent social representations also changes the group dynamics it has described. For instance, knowing about mindguards and how they influence group behaviour can change how people behave in groups (e.g., identifying, 'naming', and undermining the mindguard). The key perennial question is: can social psychological theories like groupthink retain their predictive or explanatory power after their own practical application? Social science theorists have to be alert to the possibility and monitor the practical impact that their model has. Social psychological models that are used to inform practice and shape interventions, if they are any good, are going to change the very phenomena they were meant to explain. The theory, to remain useful, has to evolve.

Cognitive dissonance

The second example of a highly influential social psychology theory was formulated by Leon Festinger. Festinger (1957) introduced cognitive dissonance theory, based on two basic hypotheses: the existence of dissonance (or inconsistency) is psychologically uncomfortable and so will motivate the person to try to reduce the dissonance and to achieve consonance (consistency); and when dissonance is present, besides trying to reduce it, the person will actively avoid situations and information likely to increase it. Dissonance reduction is hypothesised to be achieved by changing cognition, by changing actions, by selectively acquiring new information or opinions, or by some combination of these three. Basically, dissonance is quelled by changing the cognitions or behaviour that are the source of inconsistency or by changing the way the inconsistency between them is interpreted such that no, or less, inconsistency is perceived.

People introduced to the notion of cognitive dissonance, after a moment or two of introspection, typically have no hesitation in saying it sounds plausible. It explains some of their responses to inconsistencies in their own cognitions. It rings true to their observations of others. This is despite the fact that when it was first described, it represented a significant rejection of the predictions made by learning theorists. Like groupthink, cognitive dissonance is now embedded in a wide range of applied social science models and explanations of thought, feelings, and behaviour. Unlike groupthink, cognitive dissonance has been subjected to much experimental examination and has received substantial support (Cooper, 2019). It has also been extended to encompass the effects dissonance has on how people behave in groups. It is strange to note how what were originally non-obvious predictions based on the theory are now popular axioms, such as the following examples:

- People come to like what they suffer to attain – and the more they suffer, the more they like it.
- Children devalue a precious toy if they are warned not to play with it, and, the milder the warning, the greater the devaluation.
- Having made a choice between two products, with all other things remaining constant, people raise their evaluation of the item they chose and lower their evaluation of the item they rejected. The more reason they had to like the rejected alternative before the choice, the more they devalue it after the choice.
- People so abhor inconsistency that they may prefer to fail rather than succeed at a task if their prior experience led them to have expectations of failure.

Both groupthink and cognitive dissonance illustrate ways that social psychological theories can become perceived to have practical value, whether or not they can be defined as 'good' by classical scientific standards. These include, probably in temporal sequence:

- focusing on a 'relevant problem' – in the case of groupthink, this entailed high-profile cases of errors in governmental or commercial decision-making; in the case of cognitive dissonance, it was concerned with the everyday inconsistencies of individual behaviour;
- providing for previously unexplained phenomena, an explanatory model that could be regarded in retrospect as expected (or 'just commonsense') and thus is unthreatening;
- over time, being used, and thus accredited, by a growing number of varied groups of social scientists, practitioners, and policy makers – this would be linked to having some vociferous and well-placed advocates in the mass media as well as academia;
- becoming increasingly accessible over time – i.e., through the process of popularisation, becoming simplified in terms of exposition, and less caveated (original technicalities are lost during transmission);
- achieving a place in the public's everyday lexicon, and thus becoming part of social representations that attribute meaning to broader societal processes;
- by being well-known and generally used, starting to run the risk of changing the phenomena that it was designed to explain and beginning to evolve in response.

Social psychological theories do not achieve this sort of social status overnight. Being used in earnest to explain or predict social phenomena will often cause a theory to be developed beyond its initial premises. It will also mean that the theory will pass into the hands of people other than its creators, who will influence its development further for their own purposes. All this takes time. In trying to understand how a theory should be used, it is helpful to consider where it is in its life cycle. A butterfly has four distinct life stages: egg, larva (caterpillar), pupa (chrysalis), and adult. It is pointless to expect the caterpillar to fly. Similarly, it is pointless to expect an early-stage theory to be as useful as it can be once it has its wings.

What practical use do identity theories typically have?

Some theories of identity have certainly developed to the point where they have wings. Erikson's theory of identity development, which was described in some detail in Chapter 4, is one of those. Erikson's classification of the dynamics of the eight stages of identity development has been instrumental in establishing approaches to child-rearing, educational provision, and teaching practice, and across a range of therapeutic interventions and organisational systems. Similarly, ways of using Social Identity Theory (SIT) have been proposed. These include using SIT in the analysis of intergroup relations (Hogg, 2016), in respect of organisational behaviour (Turner & Haslam, 2001), in optimising leadership behaviours (Hogg et al., 2012), and in predicting conformity or compliance (Bradford et al., 2015). At this point, SIT should be differentiated from Identity Theory (Hogg et al., 1995; Stryker & Burke, 2000). The latter uses a micro-sociological approach and focuses upon the linkages between social structure and identity and on the processes of self-verification that create and sustain social structures. Both SIT and Identity Theory are trying to model the self in social context, as all theories of identity do to some degree.

In the various contexts where they are used, what practical use do theories of identity actually have? Their practical uses include the following:

- *Explanation* – providing an explanation or interpretation of how people think, feel, and behave at different times in their lives or in different social contexts.

Each of the identity theories shows how the superficial randomness or chaos of a person's life can be explained, interpreted, and given meaning within a conceptual framework. These frameworks show how individuals who, on the surface, appear so unique actually share some common psychological characteristics or patterns. The constructs that comprise this framework are the skeleton of the theory and represent the tools that can be used to systematically describe how people think, feel, and act. Although the constructs used by different identity theories look very similar, they may differ in the way they are specified and do differ in the way they are fitted together to erect the explanatory framework. As a consequence, theories of 'identity' do not necessarily mean the same thing when they refer to identity. This is most evident in the differences between personal identity, social identity, and wholistic identity theories. Nevertheless, as long as a user of an identity theory is very clear about the specification of the framework that is being used, and fully aware of the limitations of its applicability, it has practical value because it explains how people react.

Simply having an explanation that makes sense of what is happening helps you, in practice, to respond appropriately to what is happening. Consider a not infrequent scenario: a middle-aged man walks past you in the supermarket car park, clearly muttering quietly and berating someone; the young lad collecting shopping trolleys says to you 'take no notice of him, he is always around here talking to himself'; a middle-aged woman opening her car door next to you smiles and says 'he was on his mobile, I overheard part of what he said'; and, as you unload your own shopping into your car, the man returns, heading back to the shop, he nods to you, and says 'I'd forget my head if it was loose, left my shopping list in the car, I saw that you thought it was odd that I was cursing myself. Sorry!'. Each of the three explanations in turn seems feasible. Each would suggest a different way of thinking about the man. They probably also suggest a different way that you might deal with him if you ever come across him again. The explanations that we have available have practical implications. Of course, if an explanation is correct, it can be useful in shaping decisions that are helpful and appropriate. If it is erroneous but is believed, an explanation can be equally powerful in producing bad decisions.

Erikson's theory of identity represents a quintessential explanatory framework. It offers generic descriptions and explanations of how people change through eight stages in their life cycle. The theoretical construct underlying the specific nature of each developmental stage is the psychosocial crisis that must be resolved at that age (and the age range linked to each stage is specified in the theory). Each crisis has its own sort of challenge: these are, in sequence, achieving hope, will, purpose, competence, fidelity, love, care, and wisdom. Success or failure in resolving each crisis shapes the psychosocial resources that the individual acquires which can be used in the future. Such an explanatory theory of identity has practical value. It allows us to make sense of how individuals change as they grow older. In turn, this allows us to adjust our treatment of them, taking into account the 'crises' that they are managing.

Much of the criticism of Erikson's theory has revolved around whether it is an accurate generic description of lifelong development and whether it is merely a description of identity growth in one era, one culture, and, possibly, for only one gender. Questions are raised about the sequencing of the stages and their linkage to particular age ranges and culture-dependent value sets. Erikson is also criticised for not going into detail about what causes the particular stages in development that he identifies, for not explaining how resolution of the conflicts that they involve is achieved, and for failing to show how the transition from one stage to the next occurs. The criticisms point to a common feature of many plausible explanatory frameworks. They do not include an unambiguous specification of the predictions that they would make about what happens next.

Erikson gets closest to offering testable predictions when describing how adolescent development links to activities in early adulthood. In adolescence, a person has to reconcile who they are with what society expects them to be. This is the core of the adolescent identity crisis. Erikson postulates that resolving this crisis is the basis for success in later crises. For instance, it is a precursor to loving, intimate, committed relationships in early adulthood as opposed to isolation and attendant negativity to self and others. However, even in indicating this linkage between stages, Erikson is not tying his prediction down to detailed, testable hypotheses. Often where the theory has been used to inform practical development in psycho-therapeutic or educational settings, predictions from it have been inferred or assumed and these are then used. Such use is itself perfectly predictable and is one viable basis for developing a 'good practical theory'.

Descriptive or explanatory theories of identity typically have some practical value even when they do not offer specific predictions. However, this can be magnified when they are interpreted and elaborated by new people who see ways in which they might be used. Often, what happens is that an existing theory is used as the skeleton for explanations of more diverse phenomena and for specific predictions about what will happen if interventions occur. This is what might be called 'retrofit prediction'.

- *Prediction linked to intervention*

The second practical use for a theory of identity is to provide a framework that allows prediction of future thoughts, feelings, or actions. Prediction is a step beyond description and explanation because it is associated with being able not only to understand what is happening, but also to anticipate what will happen next. The great 'practical' theories will link this first level of prediction to a higher-order level of prediction that encompasses what will happen if certain conditions are changed as a consequence of a specified deliberate intervention.

Most often, identity theories start life with first-level predictions and grow into providing higher-order predictions. For instance, Social Identity Theory, as first formulated by Tajfel (1978) (see also Tajfel, 1974; Tajfel et al., 1971), postulated that individuals are intrinsically motivated to achieve self-esteem. One way in which they do this is by seeking to positively differentiate themselves from other people, and they will use their group memberships where possible in order to gain such distinctiveness. This leads to the prediction that individuals will be biased to positively differentiate their own group from other groups.

The early research on Tajfel's model, using so-called 'minimal group' experiments (Brewer, 1979; Turner, 1978), found that randomly ascribed membership to a notional group (i.e., one defined solely for the purposes of the research) would stimulate discriminatory behaviour against a notional outgroup. The question these experiments addressed reflects a focus on the roots of prejudice and intergroup conflict that was a key concern for Tajfel. However, the theory not only predicted differentiation through acts of negative discrimination, it also predicted that people would seek differentiation through enhancement of their own group without associated deprecation of other groups. This second part of the prediction has gained more attention in recent years.

Tajfel's basic model is intuitively attractive. It is what Oxford high tables might have called 'obvious'. The intriguing thing about his early experimental work was that people would show such a tendency to differentiate in favour of groups that had such a minimal existence, in which their membership had no prior meaning for them. The studies attracted great interest partly because the finding was so unexpected in such artificial, contrived circumstances (even though they might have been quite expected in relation to real groups and memberships). The other reason that they attracted attention is that the findings could be interpreted as indicating that people operated in accordance with a norm of outgroup discrimination. If true, this would have great practical and policy significance. Most obviously, it might suggest that interventions aimed at reducing intergroup discrimination and conflict would be harder even than had been imagined before. Almost equally obviously, it suggests that measures (e.g., telling a person that her attitudes and values were aligned to those of the group) that raised levels of group identification would motivate greater support for efforts the group or its leader might make to increase the group's positive distinctiveness.

Tajfel's basic model has been extended through the work of subsequent researchers (Haslam et al., 2010; Haslam et al., 2011). What is called Social Identity Theory now is much more diffuse, and is sometimes called an approach or a perspective rather than a theory. It is now embedded in a series of explanatory frameworks applied most frequently in the context of organisational and health behaviours (the latter most notably in relation to the way people responded to the strictures of the COVID-19 pandemic; Jetten, 2020).

The development of the model in practice has been primarily concerned with the influence of identification within a group upon attitudes, beliefs, and behaviour. It has elaborated the specification of the antecedent conditions that initiate identification. It has shown how identification, and specifically the individual's motivation to maintain or enhance it, will predict the individual's reactions. For example, a person whose identification with a valued group is challenged is likely to take action to prove the strength of that identification and, as a result, is more likely to ignore the weaknesses of the group or to become an advocate of a leader that is clearly espousing the group's values. This sort of higher-order prediction is of practical value because it encompasses a range of propositions that run from establishing identification through shaping identification to achieving a desired change in thought, feeling, or action. Modelling identification motives provides a tactical tool for interventions to change what individuals do in groups, but also, as a result, to change group dynamics and intergroup relationships. At least, that is what it offers in principle.

The tenets of the social identification model of group behaviours are widely generalisable because the definition of concept of group used is very broad (in terms of the group size, structure, longevity, purpose, etc.). However, this does mean that practical application of the predictions from the model have to be customised to be relevant or appropriate to a specific situation. Customisation, to be done effectively, requires a great deal of information about the specific situation. The specific group will need to be understood in its social context and against its history (including its intergroup context and history). The people in it will each have their own personal history within the group. They will differ in the precise nature of their identification with the group as a consequence of that history. With systematic information about these features of the group, predictions about what it and its members are likely to do can be made using the social identification model. But, even then, the predictions will be probabilistic. The level of confidence in those predictions will vary markedly depending on the quality of the information used.

This is true when any theory is put to practical use. With theories of identity it is particularly relevant because the range of interacting variables that affect the way identity influences thought, feeling, and behaviour is enormous and changes rapidly, as the immediate circumstances shift. Using an intervention designed on the basis of an identity theory in a real-world group context in order to achieve a specific outcome is like trying to hit a rapidly moving target that is camouflaged and is deploying countermeasures.

Theories that have gone through their developmental stages (and have their wings) are likely to have accumulated an evidence base that indicates in which contexts they work and in which they flop. If the theory is very complicated, allowing alternative predictions in any one situation dependent on interacting conditions, it is more likely that the evidence base will be equivocal. Either way, the theory that has been used in practice should be capable of further refinement.

Identity theories that are focused on a single strong theorem (usually linked into a more generic, underlying theoretical orientation), which can be applied because their key construct is open to many interpretations, seem to have a good chance of being widely used. Their simplicity and simultaneous flexibility make them attractive. Their key constructs are also typically amenable to incorporation into other theories, so they get used indirectly. The self-esteem and self-efficacy concepts fall into this category. Such theories accumulate very large and diverse evidence of their usefulness. This means that predictions based on them can be customised to the specific circumstances more effectively because their relevance to similar contexts can be seen in evidence previously collected. Appropriate, systematic collection and use of multiple data sources should mean that a practitioner that is using identity theory to make sense of a new phenomenon or to design a different intervention should not be relying on intuition, guesswork, or a profession's habitual practices. To help practitioners, theories need to be updated and responsive to new data.

Integrative theories, which pull together strong theorems from other models, can be particularly useful in supporting practitioners. If they identify the most predictive features of earlier models, show how they link together, and indicate how they are influenced differentially by conditions in the context where they are applied, integrative theories of identity can be valuable. However, integration of constructs that stem from different epistemologies is hazardous. Often integration involves loosening the link of the key constructs to their underpinning epistemological base. For instance, the concept of 'identity conflict', coined by Erikson, is often used in identity theorising without importing the psychoanalytic assumptions of Erikson. Similarly, the concept 'self-esteem' is used without reference to its early bases in humanism, phenomenology, or social learning theory. What tends to happen is that the construct is imported into a new model because it has proven to have predictive value within the simple theorem. Its epistemological baggage is jettisoned. Mostly this happens deliberately, rather than accidentally. By the time it has happened, amalgamating constructs that have quite distinct epistemological pedigrees seems acceptable. After all, the constructs themselves are perceived to have been changed in the process. It seems likely, in any case, that such philosophical questions will get shelved if the integrative theory proves substantially better at prediction, or more flexible in its application, than its predecessors.

Using Identity Process Theory

Since Identity Process Theory has informed much of this book, it seems only right to consider how it can be used. It is a descriptive, explanatory, and predictive model. Once you think about it, a lot of what it says is not surprising and seems pretty plausible. However, it is somewhat complicated by being an integrative model. It sets out to describe a wholistic concept of identity, spanning the personal and social approaches previously adopted. It uses aspects of earlier and contemporaneous models of self-motivation and group membership dynamics. It lodges its model of identity processes within both the neurophysiological and the cognitive, conative and motivational processes of the individual, but also includes the influence of the interpersonal and group relations and the social representational and ideological processes in that individual's social milieu. It is a complex theory concerned with the construction and maintenance of the identity structure over the lifespan, and with its implications for thought, feeling, and action.

In order for IPT to be recognised as useful in practice, it has been necessary to learn the lessons from past successful popularisations and applications of social psychology theories.

These include focusing on 'relevant' problems and providing an explanatory model that is intuitively plausible and expressed in a few simple tenets that include a few memorable constructs and tested predictions. Dating from the original formulation of IPT, the relevant problem it addressed was how individuals cope with threat to their identities. The theory explains what constitutes a threat. It explains what coping strategies can be used to manage threat to identity. In order to do this, it introduces some key theoretical concepts: the identity processes (assimilation-accommodation and evaluation); the identity principles (self-esteem, self-efficacy, positive distinctiveness, and continuity); levels of coping strategies (intra-psychic to intergroup); and identity resilience. It is notable that this is a theory of identity that grew from being concerned with a particular problem of great social relevance. Yet it is a comprehensive theory of identity. Only a comprehensive theory of the wholistic identity can actually explain how threat operates and what reactions it produces. This now means that IPT can be used to understand identity processes that are not directly concerned with threat to identity. In keeping with its original purpose, IPT provides clear predictions about the occurrence of threat to identity, with specification of the conditions under which it will appear. It also explains how choice of coping strategy is limited both by the status of the identity structure itself and by the social context of the threat.

Initially, IPT was mainly used to understand and predict how people react when they perceive their identity to be threatened and to suggest how they can be supported in coping. For instance, it was used to interpret how women who worked in male-dominated occupations coped with the consequences of breaking gender stereotypes and then to propose how they could be supported (Breakwell, 1985; Mavridi & Breakwell, 2000). In this period, IPT was used in analyses of the effects of unemployment on young people and then in the planning of government youth opportunity policy (Breakwell et al., 1982). Threats emanating from sexuality and sexual orientation have also been researched using the IPT framework. As AIDS/HIV was first identified, research using IPT was conducted on the sexual behaviour of 16–21-year-olds and their willingness to take risks. This was used to support the development of health education campaigns for this age group (Breakwell et al., 1991; Fife-Schaw & Breakwell, 1992). IPT has also been used to explain how gay men react to societal homonegativity (Jaspal, 2019). The practical value of this use of the theory has been manifest in its uptake by gay support networks. IPT has also been used to predict strategies used for coping during public crises, such as the COVID-19 pandemic (Breakwell & Jaspal, 2021; Jaspal, 2021; Jaspal & Breakwell, 2022a).

IPT has also been applied in many contexts to explain or predict how people will respond to aversive change or uncertainty, which may or may not threaten identity. For example, it has been used to explain and predict reactions to some serious societal crises. It has been used to analyse public reactions to climate change (Adger et al., 2011; Barnett et al., 2021) and predict environmental beliefs and activism (Bonaiuto et al., 1996; Breakwell, 2010b; Twigger-Ross et al., 2003). Understanding the psychodynamics that underlie the willingness to be constructively pro-environmental is a basic precursor to finding robust responses to climate change. IPT has also been used to prompt policy makers more generally to incorporate sensitivity to identity processes into their strategies. Its relevance to the effects of nationality and nationalism has also been shown when considering how social upheaval results in the international displacement of people or political reconfiguring (as in the case of the changing membership of the European Union), produces expectations of new allegiances (Breakwell,

2004; Breakwell & Lyons, 1996; Lyons, 1996), and marginality (Breakwell, 1978; Jaspal & Cinnirella, 2010; Timotijevic & Breakwell, 2000).

This work has been tied to a growing body of research, based on IPT, on the way mistrust can affect practical interventions meant to control public hazards and risk (Barnett & Vassileiou, 2014; Breakwell & Jaspal, 2021). Research on the public responses to the COVID-19 pandemic control policies and remediation measures has been used to explore whether IPT can predict mistrust of science and politicians in such a crisis. IPT does predict levels of mistrust and perception of personal risk levels, which in turn predict behavioural decisions about the adoption of behavioural protection or the likelihood of vaccination (Breakwell, Camilo et al., 2022). The genesis and course of mistrust can be interpreted in terms of identity processes that are intimately tied to social representational and ideological processes (Breakwell, 2001a, 2010a; Jaspal & Nerlich, 2020).

As a result of its use in the growing body of research on public crises, IPT is evolving. It has been extended to model mistrust processes (Breakwell, 2020b, 2021b). It has also explicitly examined the role of the status of the identity principles and the efficacy of identity processes in generating identity resilience when facing stress or crisis (Breakwell, 2020a, 2021a). This has resulted in the further development of new studies of variations in mental health, life satisfaction, and creativity during public crises (Jaspal & Breakwell, 2022a, in press; Jaspal, da Silva Lopes & Breakwell, 2021). The identity resilience construct predicts differences between people in responses to both personal and societal uncertainty and threat. The development of a tool to measure identity resilience means that it can be assessed for individuals or groups of individuals. IPT should continue to evolve and incorporate new constructs that deepen and extend its relevance. It is an integrative theory and should not be shy of assimilating and accommodating to new ideas as the societal structure it analyses changes.

Enabling the use of identity theories

In conclusion, it seems that identity theory is being used. Theories of identity are useful in addressing many societal problems because identity is core to the responses that people make to most of those problems. Any identity theorist will tell you that. The problem lies in getting the practitioners and policy makers that should be using the theories to do so.

Some theories have a head start on gaining user interest because they manifestly focus on issues of great public concern. IPT, from its inception, has been concerned with real-world risks and threats. It was developed in order to explain and predict what happens in such situations. Throughout, research using IPT has dealt with responses to salient social issues: unemployment, public understanding of science and new technologies, BSE and Foot and Mouth diseases, bioterrorism, AIDS/HIV, leadership in high-intensity conflict arenas (i.e., war), migration and asylum-seeking, gender and sexuality, and pandemics. It has meant that IPT is seen as relevant and amenable to use by practitioners and policy makers.

Yet it is important when doing such 'relevant' research to work alongside those agencies tasked with dealing with the problem. Social psychologists who are interested in having their work used beyond academe must not only see the world of practice as an outsider looking in;

they must also see the world of practice from the inside. This does not necessitate becoming an 'insider' or losing independence and objectivity. In fact, it is vital to retain objectivity in order to be useful. But it does require detailed knowledge of that world and a willingness to understand its priorities, culture, and knowledge base. With such a perspective it is easier to show how a theory may be useful and can, in fact, be used.

Social psychological theory often influences practice first through the provision of *in situ*, ongoing advice, and later through handbooks, professional development programmes, and codes of practice. Accompanying media popularisation of constructs from the theory may speed its adoption (or, through misrepresentation, derail it). But typically, it takes time and persistence for any theory to gain serious and lasting traction in any practice context. As a theorist, it can be worth all the effort when you see a policy, which you have made even a minor contribution towards, being instituted and lives changed for the better.

More identity researchers should be out and about telling potential users about their theories and findings. There is, however, one really big hazard notice that has to be posted here. Theories are only valuable when people are told the limitations of their applicability. In advising people to use our theories, we have to ensure that they understand in which conditions they are relevant and what they can offer. Do they explain? Do they predict? Do they have recognised and tested implications for the design of interventions? Unfounded generalisations are to be avoided at all costs, even if it means the theory is not used in some cases. Having a theory rejected by a potential user is an interesting way to learn how it needs to be further developed. Although having a theory rejected by a potential user is one way to learn that the theory needs more work, it is much better if the theorist has paved the way for the user to test the theory appropriately by specifying what falls outside the scope of the theory from the outset. IPT is complex and ambitious and has so far responded well to elaboration and testing in a range of real-world scenarios that have fallen within its remit.

10

ADAPTATION AND EVOLUTION

> Intelligence is the ability to adapt to change.
> Stephen Hawking

> Adaptability is not imitation. It means power of resistance and assimilation.
> Mahatma Gandhi

A theory of adaptation

Identity Process Theory tries to describe how the whole identity of an individual is constructed and adapts to change. It is a theory of identity that focuses on the dynamism of identity processes and the adaptability of the coping strategies used to respond to change. It emphasises that the individual is motivated to achieve and optimise certain states of identity principles (self-esteem, self-efficacy, positive distinctiveness, and continuity) as it adapts to change. Intrinsic to the theory is the basic premise that the scope for adaptation of the individual identity is bounded by the capacities of biological organism (particularly by its neuro-physiological characteristics) and the influences of the social structures and social representational system in which it resides. To misquote a common aphorism, IPT assumes 'it is possible to take the individual out of society, but not society out of the individual'.

Theories should evolve

Irrespective of what one might think about the broader Darwinian theory of evolution, Darwin got it right when he proposed that adaptation is the key to survival. Theories in social science should evolve, and should seek to evolve for the following reasons:

- They should respond to the qualitative and quantitative changes that occur over time in the social phenomena that they wish to explain.
- They should capitalise on the developments that occur over time in the information sources that they have at their disposal and in the technologies that permit the collection and analysis of new data streams.
- They should respond to the findings from empirical tests of their propositions. Learning from tests that prove a proposition inadequate or false should be used to refine the theory. Learning from tests that do not falsify the proposition should motivate more robust and rigorous efforts to identify where the limitations of the proposition actually do lie. They may also suggest where weaknesses in the empirical operationalisation of theoretical constructs exist. This all indicates that it is unhealthy only to focus on findings that appear to support a hypothesis.
- They should respond to whether the theory is proving useful when applied. Understanding the limitations in the theory's applicability can result in construct elaboration, refinement, or excision. Pruning and regrowth propagate better theory.
- They should respond to opportunities to integrate new theoretical perspectives that emerge where they are relevant and compatible with the core model. To use another cultivation analogy, hybridisation across theories is an important evolutionary option.

IPT has evolved since its original formulation. It would be strange if it did not, given that its focus is on adaptation. This development of IPT has involved the work of many researchers. Each has made a unique contribution, particularly in showing how the theory can be used in relation to different threats to identity and in proving how different methods can be used to explore its limitations and value.

Many of the developments and adaptations of the theory have been described already in this book. This chapter brings them together to summarise an integrative model of IPT. Clearly, this is only a snapshot of where IPT is now in its evolutionary journey.

A theory evolving

The developments in the theory have occurred primarily in nine areas. Often it has been possible to make these adaptations to the theory by integrating the developments that have been occurring since the original formulation of IPT was produced in other domains within psychology and beyond. It seems likely that in each of these nine areas, there is much further elaboration to be done. The outline of each given here represents the evolving direction of travel:

- The biological organism: IPT has always proposed that identity construction and maintenance depend on the structure and processes of the individual as a biological organism. Memory has been included in IPT as a key feature of the biological organism. More recent work within IPT has elaborated on the role of memory in identity processes and in coping. This has integrated the implications of findings from cognitive psychology on the malleability of memory (e.g., Loftus, 2020). It has also incorporated, in modelling the strategies used in coping with change, the implications of rehearsal and sharing of memories (e.g., Sedikides & Wildschut, 2018). Memory in IPT is now treated both as a medium in which identity resides and as a tool with which identity is adapted.
- Identity principles: IPT originally proposed three identity principles (self-esteem, distinctiveness, and continuity) directed at the adaptation of the identity structure. Early in the evolution of IPT, a fourth identity principle, self-efficacy, was added, as the model integrated the implications of the work of Bandura (1982). Subsequently, a refinement of the distinctiveness construct used in the model was introduced to make it explicit that the motive was to achieve positive distinctiveness, and not just distinctiveness *per se* (Brewer, 2003). Further developments of the specification of the identity principles have focused on the role of optimisation. This acknowledges that the individual's contemporary identity structure and the social context will interact to determine what the individual considers to be an optimal level for each of the identity principles. Optimisation is a continual objective.
- Social influence processes: IPT originally conceived the society in which the individual lived as comprised of two dimensions: the social structure (i.e., interpersonal networks, group memberships, and intergroup relationships) and the social influence processes that establish a prevailing ideological milieu. From the late 1980s, IPT has increasingly

attempted to model these social influence processes. Particularly, it has integrated the major theoretical developments that have occurred with the introduction of social representations theory (Moscovici, 1988). IPT has been elaborated to include proposals about the ways in which the identity principles will influence the access to, and acceptance and use of, social representations. IPT has also been used to explain how and why some individuals become involved in the reproduction and renovation of social representations. Use of social representations (e.g., in the form of conspiracy theories) has been shown to be an important tool within strategies for coping with change (e.g., a public crisis) that threatens identity. This evolution of IPT has suggested the advantages of a more formal linking of identity and social representations theories.

- Social structure: Social structure was the second dimension of society indicated in IPT originally. Structure was envisaged to encompass interpersonal networks, group memberships, and intergroup relationships. One important adjustment to the theory has been to focus critically on the way the nature of any group membership influences the role it can have in the identity structure and the way it will be used by the identity processes in coping strategies for dealing with change. Chapter 7 goes into this in detail. The gist of this development is that group membership, as an influence on identity, must be defined in terms of the extent to which the individual identifies with the group. Mere membership is not enough; the degree of subjective belonging is more predictive of thought, feelings, and action. This development in the IPT model represents a reflection of the social identity 'approach' to social identification (Haslam et al., 2010). IPT is now particularly concerned with the ways in which 'de-identification' can be used in changes to the identity structure and as a strategy for coping with threat.
- Social time: IPT recognises that individuals move through society and are consequently exposed, as they move, to different aspects of its social structures and variations of the social influences (including social representations) that pervade it. The early graphic representations of IPT included this dynamic between the individual and society by including a third dimension: social time. During their lifetime, while they construct their identities, individuals travel simultaneously through chronological and social time. The latter construct reflects how the character of the social structure and social influence nexus continuously alters during the individual's lifespan. IPT has increasingly sought to model how significant changes in social time affect identity structure and processes. Rapid or unexpected modifications in the interactions between the social structure and social influence processes will alter the basis upon which identity continuity is founded. These modifications happen throughout an individual's lifetime. This sort of societal uncertainty has wide-ranging consequences for the feasibility of effective coping with identity threat.
- Expressions of identity: It is important for a theory of identity to consider how identity is expressed. IPT's initial formulation predated even the hint of the concept of the metaverse. The theory has been evolving throughout the growth of cyber reality. The advent of social media and interactive virtual reality has transformed the channels through which identity can be expressed. More importantly, it has radically altered the constraints that previously applied to the expression of identity. Notably, by

undermining the basis for verification or challenge, it has broken or weakened the links between the subjective identity structure and its external expressions. This brave new world of identity-expression changes what coping strategies can be used in order to deal with threat. IPT has begun to examine what this means for the ongoing subjective identity structure over time.

- Coping strategies: Early work on IPT did not explore when or how identity processes might fail to deploy effective coping strategies to deal with change or threat. Chapter 8 dealt with some of the evolving understanding of the limitations that constrain the success of the identity processes. An important conceptual development is the incorporation into the theory of the idea that the way that identity processes operate will be changed by their successes or failures in adapting the identity structure to satisfy the identity principles. People are characterised by differential levels of identity process resilience. Such resilience is a product of the past experience of the consequences of coping efforts. Alongside this integration of the notion of identity process 'learning' is the elaboration of the theory to allow for a much more diverse and hybridised range of coping strategies to be used. The neat classification initially used the clustering of coping strategies into intra-psychic, interpersonal, intra-group, and intergroup. For the purposes of a clear outline of options, this may help. However, what has been found to happen in practice is that people pick and mix across these levels. More importantly, coping tactics from one level will interact with those from another to create what are actually novel, individualised, approaches to the threat. This development in the theory has suggested that much more research is needed on the actual varieties of coping tactic and strategy that are used in different social times.
- Identity resilience: One of the biggest evolutionary steps in the development of IPT has been the introduction of the identity resilience construct. The level of identity resilience depends on the capacity of the biological organism (i.e., primarily memory), the existing configuration of the identity structure (i.e., content and value), and the activity and state of the identity principles. Each of the identity principles contributes to identity resilience through two routes: first, through the amount they motivate the identity processes to adapt the identity structure during change; second, through the extent to which they have already been optimised by prior identity development and can therefore provide a firm foundation for coping activity. These two routes reflect the emphasis in more recent IPT research on separating the motivational power of an identity principle from the subjective perception of the level of satisfaction with that identity principle. Individuals with high levels of self-esteem, self-efficacy, positive distinctiveness, and continuity are deemed to have greater identity resilience. High identity resilience results in two things: the identity structure is less likely to accept weakening adaptations; and the individual is more likely to respond to change with greater self-protection in thought, feelings, and action. Also, identity resilience is likely to be positively correlated with identity processes resilience (since it may enhance their success rate). This concept of identity resilience needs much further specification. It is especially necessary to establish in practice what happens when the identity principles do not motivate adaptation of identity in the same direction as each other. This, in turn, leads to questions about the relative priority of the principles in motivating adaptation and coping. To make matters more complex, there is no reason to believe

that the identity principles would maintain the same priority order across individuals, or the lifetime, or social times. There is plenty of scope for evolving the theory around these issues.

- Indexing identity constructs: Operationalising the constructs in a theory of identity is never easy. There are always too many subordinate variables and too many of them interacting with each other to make it simple. Where possible, IPT has imported and adapted established scales, designed and standardised by earlier researchers (e.g., for self-esteem or self-efficacy). For some variables, IPT studies have been developing new indexes (e.g., with respect to identity resilience). Chapter 5 considered the complexities of developing effective, valid, and reliable indicators of the IPT model constructs. However, the further evolution of the theory will require substantially more work on producing good indicators of its constructs. The Identity Resilience Index is already suggesting that such tools will allow us to greatly improve tests of the theory.

These are the nine broad-ranging evolving aspects of IPT. There are many others in early stages of their development. For instance, one is concerned with examining how far there are describable developmental stages (such as Erikson would recognise) in the use of coping stages. Another is concerned with cross-cultural differences in identity resilience. Of course, there is also the continual effort to determine whether there are other identity principles, besides the usual four, that should be included in the theory. It is healthy to have such new evolutionary pathways being plotted.

Evolving figure of Identity Process Theory

In concluding this chapter, and the book, it may be worth trying to represent the evolving integrated model of IPT figuratively. Having been foolish enough to offer a two-dimensional image of the 1986 version of IPT in Chapter 2, it seems no more foolish to present a revised version of that here.

Figure 10.1 differs from Figure 2.8 in five important ways. It includes the input of the identity principles right from the start of the development of identity (extreme left of the figure, large arrow encompassing the whole trajectory of identity through to identity resilience). At the far right, identity resilience is indicated to be a product of identity value and content, the state of the biological organism, and the endpoint of the impact of identity principles. Identity resilience is shown to impact on both identity processes (assimilation-accommodation and evaluation). The social influence processes arrow at the top explicitly includes social representations (note that the large arrow indicates its influence throughout the development of identity and on both identity processes and identity principles). The social structure arrow at the bottom of the figure now includes social identifications rather than group memberships (note that the large arrow indicates its influence throughout the development of identity and on both identity processes and identity principles).

Anyone with an artistic temperament might think the figure quite alarming. However, if it makes you stop and think about the constructs and processes it represents, it will have done its job. The same can be said about this book.

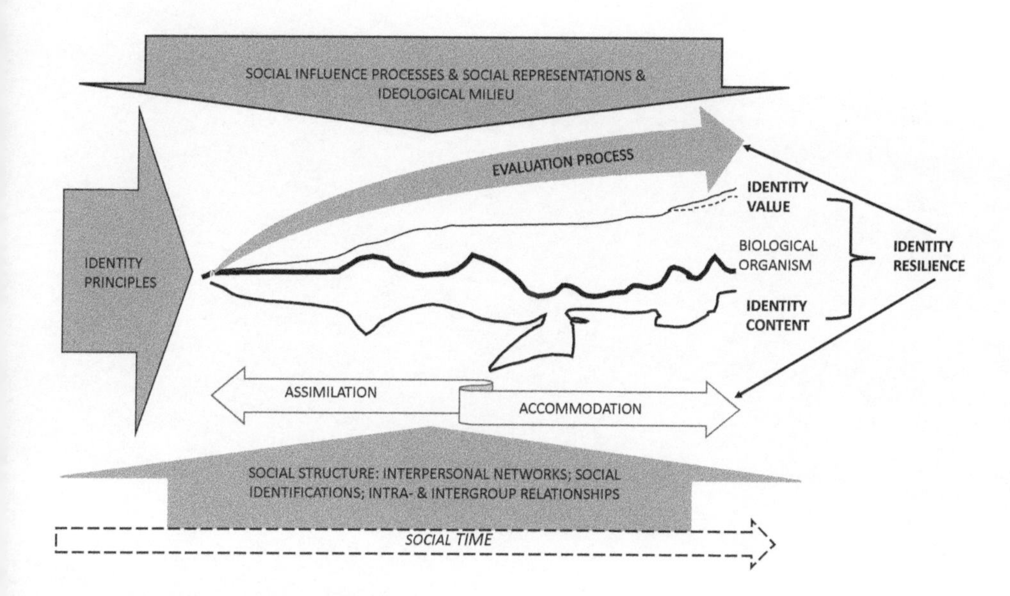

Figure 10.1 Identity Process Theory (2022)

So, is identity unique and shared? The notable thing about Figure 10.1 is that it suggests the complexity of what we study when we look at identity. It illustrates why every identity will be unique. How could it be otherwise, when so many variables are at work in its production? Equally, this unique identity, from its moment of inception, wants to be expressed and so has to be shared. But more importantly, it is shared because the complex interactions that produce it could never occur if it were not shared.

REFERENCES

Abrams, D., & Hogg, M. A. (Eds.). (1990a). *Social Identity Theory: Constructive and Critical Advances.* NewYork: Springer.

Abrams, D., & Hogg, M. A. (1990b). Social identification, self-categorization and social influence. *European Review of Social Psychology, 1*(1), 195–228.

Adger, W. N., Barnett, J., Chapin III, F. S., & Ellemor, H. (2011). This must be the place: Underrepresentation of identity and meaning in climate change decision-making. *Global Environmental Politics, 11*(2), 1–25.

Aguilar, G. K., Campbell, H. A., Stanley, M., & Taylor, E. (2017). Communicating mixed messages about religion through internet memes. *Information, Communication & Society, 20*(10), 1498–1520.

Allport, G. W. (1955). *Becoming: Basic Considerations for a Psychology of Personality.* New Haven, CT: Yale University Press.

American Psychiatric Association (APA) (2013). *Diagnostic and Statistical Manual of Mental Disorders (DSM-5).* Washington, DC: APA.

American Psychological Association (APA) (2020) *Building your resilience.* https://www.apa.org/topics/resilience/building-your-resilience. Accessed 1 November 2022.

American Psychological Association (APA) (2022). Identity. *APA Dictionary of Psychology.* https://dictionary.apa.org/identity. Accessed 2 May 2022.

Anderson, M. (2022). 10 alter egos of the music industry. *Encyclopedia Britannica.* www.britannica.com/list/10-alter-egos-of-the-music-industry. Accessed 15 May 2022.

Angelou, M. (2008). *Letter to My Daughter.* New York: Random House.

Atkinson, P. A., Martin, C. R., & Rankin, J. (2009). Resilience revisited. *Journal of Psychiatric and Mental Health Nursing, 16*(2), 137–145.

Bandura, A. (1982). Self-efficacy mechanism in human agency. *American Psychologist, 37*(2), 122.

Bandura, A. (1997). *Self-efficacy: The Exercise of Control.* New York: Freeman.

Bandura, A. (2005). The evolution of social cognitive theory. In K. G. Smith & M. A. Hitt (Eds.), *Great Minds in Management* (pp. 9–35). New York: Oxford University Press.

Banks, M. H., Bates, I., Breakwell, G., Bynner, J., Emler, N., Jamieson, L., & Roberts, K. (1992). *Careers and Identities.* Milton Keynes: Open University Press.

Baran, L., & Jonason, P. K. (2020). Academic dishonesty among university students: The roles of the psychopathy, motivation, and self-efficacy. *PLoS One, 15*(8), e0238141.

Bardi, A., Jaspal, R., Polek, E., & Schwartz, S. (2014). Values and identity process theory: Theoretical integration and empirical interactions. In R. Jaspal & G. M. Breakwell (Eds.), *Identity Process Theory: Identity, Social Action and Social Change* (pp. 175–200). Cambridge: Cambridge University Press. https://doi.org/10.1017/CBO9781139136983.013

Barnett, J., & Breakwell, G. M. (2003). The social amplification of risk and the hazard sequence: The October 1995 oral contraceptive pill scare. *Health, Risk & Society, 5*(3), 301–313.

Barnett, J., Graham, S., Quinn, T., Adger, W. N., & Butler, C. (2021). Three ways social identity shapes climate change adaptation. *Environmental Research Letters, 16*(12), 124029.

Barnett, J., & Vasileiou, K. (2014). Making sense of risk: The role of social representations and identity. In R. Jaspal & G. M. Breakwell (Eds.), *Identity Process Theory: Identity, Social Action and Social Change* (pp. 357–378). Cambridge: Cambridge University Press.

Bennett, D. H., & Holmes, D. S. (1975). Influence of denial (situation redefinition) and projection on anxiety associated with threat to self-esteem. *Journal of Personality and Social Psychology, 32*(5), 915.

Berg, R. C., Munthe-Kaas, H. M., & Ross, M. W. (2016). Internalized homonegativity: A systematic mapping review of empirical research. *Journal of Homosexuality, 63*(4), 541–558.

Berger, P. L., Berger, B., & Kellner, H. (1974). *The Homeless Mind*. Harmondsworth: Penguin.

Bonaiuto, M., Albers, T., Ariccio, S., & Cataldi, S. (2019). Pride of place in a religious context: An environmental psychology and sociology perspective. In M. Bonaiuto, T. Albers, S. Ariccio, & S. Cataldi (Eds.), *The Psychology of Religion and Place* (pp. 97–129). Basingstoke: Palgrave Macmillan.

Bonaiuto, M., Breakwell, G. M., & Cano, I. (1996). Identity processes and environmental threat: The effects of nationalism and local identity upon perception of beach pollution. *Journal of Community & Applied Social Psychology, 6*(3), 157–175.

Bradford, B., Hohl, K., Jackson, J., & MacQueen, S. (2015). Obeying the rules of the road: Procedural justice, social identity, and normative compliance. *Journal of Contemporary Criminal Justice, 31*(2), 171–191.

Braly, A. M., Parent, M. C., & DeLucia, P. R. (2018). Do threats to masculinity result in more aggressive driving behaviour? *Psychology of Men & Masculinity, 19*(4), 540–546.

Breakwell, G. M. (1978). Some efffects of marginal social identity. In H. Tajfel (Ed.), *Differentiation between Social Groups: Studies in the Social Psychology of Intergroup Relations* (pp. 301–336). Cambridge, MA: Academic Press.

Breakwell, G. M. (1979). Woman: Group and identity? *Women's Studies International Quarterly, 2*(1), 9–17.

Breakwell, G. M. (1983). *Threatened Identities*. Hoboken, NJ: Wiley.

Breakwell, G. M. (1985). *The Quiet Rebel: Women at Work in a Man's World*. London: Century Publishing.

Breakwell, G. M. (1986). *Coping with Threatened Identities*. London and New York: Methuen.

Breakwell, G. M. (1988). Strategies adopted when identity is threatened. *Revue Internationale de Psychologie Sociale, 1*(2), 189–204.

Breakwell, G. M. (2001a). Mental models and social representations of hazards: The significance of identity processes. *Journal of Risk Research, 4*(4), 341–351.

Breakwell, G. M. (2001b). Social representational constraints upon identity processes. In K. Deaux & G. Philogène (Eds.), *Representations of the Social: Bridging Theoretical Traditions* (pp. 271–284). Oxford: Blackwell Publishing.

Breakwell, G. M. (2004) Identity change in the context of the growing influence of European Union institutions. In R. Hermann, T. Risse, & M. B. Brewer (Eds.), *Transnational Identities: Becoming European in the EU* (pp. 25–39). New York: Rowman and Littlefield.

Breakwell, G. M. (2007). *The Psychology of Risk*. Cambridge: Cambridge University Press.

Breakwell, G. M. (2010a). Resisting representations and identity processes. *Papers on Social Representations, 19*(1), 6–1.

Breakwell, G. M. (2010b). Models of risk construction: Some applications to climate change. *Wiley Interdisciplinary Reviews: Climate Change, 1*(6), 857–870.

Breakwell, G. M. (2014). Identity process theory: Clarifications and elaborations. In R. Jaspal & G. M. Breakwell (Eds.), *Identity Process Theory: Identity, Social Action and Social Change* (pp. 20–37). Cambridge: Cambridge University Press.

Breakwell, G. M. (2015a). *Coping with Threatened Identities* (2nd edition). Hove: Psychology Press.

Breakwell, G. M. (2015b). Identity process theory. In G. E. Sammut, E. E. Andreouli, G. E. Gaskell, & J. E. Valsiner (Eds.), *The Cambridge Handbook of Social Representations* (pp. 250–266). Cambridge: Cambridge University Press.

Breakwell, G. M. (2020a). Mistrust, uncertainty, and health risks. *Contemporary Social Science, 15*(5), 504–516.

Breakwell, G. M. (2020b). In the age of societal uncertainty, the era of threat. In D. Jodelet, J. Vala, & E. Drozda-Senkowska (Eds.), *Societies under Threat: A Pluri-Disciplinary Approach* (pp. 55–71). Cham: Springer International.

Breakwell, G. M. (2021a). Identity resilience: Its origin in identity processes and its role in coping with threat. *Contemporary Social Science, 16*(5), 573–588. doi: 10.1080.21582041.2021.1999488

Breakwell, G. M. (2021b). *Mistrust*. London: Sage.

Breakwell, G. M., Camilo, C., Jaspal, R., & Lima, M. L. (2022). Influences of nationality and national identification on perceived dangerousness of COVID-19 variants and perceived effectiveness of COVID-19 vaccines: A study of UK and Portuguese samples. *Journal of Social and Political Psychology, 10*(1), 106–122.

Breakwell, G. M., Fife-Schaw, C., & Clayden, K. (1991). Risk-taking, control over partner choice and intended use of condoms by virgins. *Journal of Community & Applied Social Psychology, 1*(2), 173–187.

Breakwell, G. M., Fife-Schaw, C., & Devereux, J. D. (1989). Political activity and political attitudes in teenagers: Is there any correspondence? *Political Psychology, 10*(4), 745–755.

Breakwell, G. M., Fino, E., & Jaspal, R. (2022). The identity resilience index: Development and validation in two UK samples. *Identity, 22*(2), 166–182. doi: 10.1080/15283488.2021.1957895

Breakwell, G. M., Harrison, A. J. L., Propper, C., & Weinberger, B. (1982). The observation of young people in and out of work: Serendipity and hazard. *Bulletin of the British Psychological Society, 35*, 19.

Breakwell, G. M., & Jaspal, R. (2021). Identity change, uncertainty and mistrust in relation to fear and risk of COVID-19. *Journal of Risk Research, 24*(3–4), 335–351.

Breakwell, G. M., & Jaspal, R. (2022). Coming out, distress and identity threat in Gay Men in the UK. *Sexuality Research and Social Policy, 19*(3), 1166–1177.

Breakwell, G. M., Jaspal, R., & Wright, D. B. (in press). Identity resilience, science mistrust, COVID-19 risk and fear predictors of vaccine positivity and vaccination likelihood. *Journal of Health Psychology*.

Breakwell, G. M., & Lyons, E. (1996). *Changing European Identities: Social Psychological Analyses of Social Change*. Oxford: Butterworth Heinemann.

Breakwell, G. M., Vignoles, V. L., & Robertson, T. (2003). Stereotypes and crossed-category evaluations: The case of gender and science education. *British Journal of Psychology, 94*(4), 437–455.

Breakwell, G. M., Wright, D. B., & Barnett, J. (Eds.). (2020). *Research Methods in Psychology*. London: Sage.

Brewer, M. B. (1979). Ingroup bias in the minimal intergroup situations: A cognitive motivational analysis. *Psychological Bulletin, 86*(2), 307–324. doi:10.1037/0033-2909.86.2.307

Brewer, M. B. (1991). The social self: On being the same and different at the same time. *Personality and Social Psychology Bulletin, 17*(5), 475–482. https://doi.org/10.1177/0146167291175001

Brewer, M. B. (1999). Multiple identities and identity transition: Implications for Hong Kong. *International Journal of Intercultural Relations, 23*(2), 187–197.

Brewer, M. B. (2000). Reducing prejudice through cross-categorization: Effects of multiple social identities. In S. Oskamp (Ed.), *Reducing Prejudice and Discrimination* (pp. 165–183). Mahwah, NJ: Lawrence Erlbaum Associates.

Brewer, M. B. (2003). Optimal distinctiveness, social identity, and the self. In M. R. Leary & J. P. Tangney (Eds.), *Handbook of Self and Identity* (pp. 480–491). New York: The Guilford Press.

Brewer, M. B., & Caporael, L. R. (2006). An evolutionary perspective on social identity: Revisiting groups. *Evolution and Social Psychology, 143*, 161.

Brockmeyer, T., Holtforth, M. G., Bents, H., Kämmerer, A., Herzog, W., & Friederich, H. C. (2013). The thinner the better: Self-esteem and low body weight in anorexia nervosa. *Clinical Psychology & Psychotherapy, 20*(5), 394–400.

Bruner, J. (1997). Celebrating divergence: Piaget and Vygotsky. *Human Development, 40*(2), 63–73.

Campbell, W. K., & Sedikides, C. (1999). Self-threat magnifies the self-serving bias: A meta-analytic integration. *Review of General Psychology, 3*(1), 23–43. doi:10.1037/1089-2680.3.1.23

Cialdini, R. B. (2001a). The science of persuasion. *Scientific American, 284*(2), 76–81.

Cialdini R. B. (2001b). *Influence: Science and Practice* (4th edition). Boston, MA: Allyn & Bacon.

Cialdini, R. B., & Goldstein, N. J. (2004). Social influence: Compliance and conformity. *Annual Review of Psychology, 55*, 591–621.

Clare, A., Camic, P. M., Crutch, S. J., West, J., Harding, E., & Brotherhood, E. (2020). Using music to develop a multisensory communicative environment for people with late-stage dementia. *The Gerontologist, 60*(6), 1115–1125.

Cooley, C. H. (1902). *Human Nature and the Social Order*. New York: Scribner's.

Cooper, J. (2019). Cognitive dissonance: Where we've been and where we're going. *International Review of Social Psychology, 32*(1), 7. http://doi.org/10.5334/irsp.277

Cooper, K., Russell, A., Mandy, W., & Butler, C. (2020). The phenomenology of gender dysphoria in adults: A systematic review and meta-synthesis. *Clinical Psychology Review, 80*, 101875.

Corrigan, P. W., Druss, B. G., & Perlick, D. A. (2014). The impact of mental illness stigma on seeking and participating in mental health care. *Psychological Science in the Public Interest, 15*(2), 37–70.

Cosco, T. D., Howse, K., & Brayne, C. (2017). Healthy ageing, resilience and wellbeing. *Epidemiology and Psychiatric Sciences, 26*(6), 579–583.

Costa Jr, P. T., & McCrae, R. R. (1997). Longitudinal stability of adult personality. In R. Hogan, J. Johnson, & S. Briggs (Eds.), *Handbook of Personality Psychology* (pp. 269–290). London: Academic Press.

Crisp, R. J., Walsh, J., & Hewstone, M. (2006). Crossed categorization in common ingroup contexts. *Personality and Social Psychology Bulletin, 32*(9), 1204–1218.

de Rosa, A. S., Bocci, E., Bonito, M., & Salvati, M. (2021). Twitter as social media arena for polarised social representations about the (im)migration: The controversial discourse in the Italian and international political frame. *Migration Studies, 9*(3), 1167–1194.

Di Paula, A., & Campbell, J. D. (2002). Self-esteem and persistence in the face of failure. *Journal of Personality and Social Psychology, 83*(3), 711.

Doise, W. (1978). *Groups and Individuals: Explanations in Social Psychology*. (Trans D. Graham). Cambridge: Cambridge University Press.

Dumont, M., & Provost, M. A. (1999). Resilience in adolescents: Protective role of social support, coping strategies, self-esteem, and social activities on experience of stress and depression. *Journal of Youth and Adolescence, 28*(3), 343–363. https://doi.org/10.1023/A:1021637011732

Durkheim, E. (1984) *The Division of Labour in Society*. New York: Free Press.

Dziewanski, D. (2020). Leaving gangs in Cape Town: Disengagement as role exit. *Journal of Contemporary Ethnography, 49*(4), 507–535.

Ebaugh, H. R., & Ebaugh, H. R. F. (1988). *Becoming an Ex: The Process of Role Exit*. Chicago, IL: University of Chicago Press.

Einstein, A. (1922). *The Meaning of Relativity: Four Lectures Delivered at Princeton University, May, 1921*. London and New York: Methuen & Company Limited.

Erikson, E. H. (1950). *Childhood and Society*. New York: W. W. Norton.

Erikson, E. H. (1968). *Identity: Youth and Crisis*. New York: W. W. Norton.

Erikson, E. H. (1994). *Insight and Responsibility*. New York: W. W. Norton.

Festinger, L. (1957). *A Theory of Cognitive Dissonance* (Vol. 2). Stanford, CA: Stanford University Press.

Fife-Schaw, C., & Breakwell, G. M. (1990). Predicting the intention not to vote in late teenage. *Political Psychology, 11*(4), 739–755.

Fife-Schaw, C., & Breakwell, G. M. (1991). The class basis of late teenage voting preferences. *European Sociological Review, 7*(2), 135–147.

Fife-Schaw, C., & Breakwell, G. M. (1992). Estimating sexual behaviour parameters in the light of AIDS: A review of recent UK studies of young people. *Aids Care, 4*(2), 187–201.

Finkelstein, S. R., Xu, X., & Connell, P. M. (2019). When variety is not the spice of life: The influence of perceived relational self-threat on variety seeking in snack choices. *Appetite, 136*, 154–159.

Fischer, A., Peters, V., Neebe, M., Vávra, J., Kriel, A., Lapka, M., & Megyesi, B. (2012). Climate change? No, wise resource use is the issue: Social representations of energy, climate change and the future. *Environmental Policy and Governance, 22*(3), 161–176.

Fitch, G. (1970). Effects of self-esteem, perceived performance, and choice on causal attributions. *Journal of Personality and Social Psychology, 16*(2), 311.

Freud, S. (2019). *The Ego and the Id*. New York: Simon & Schuster.

Freud, S. (2021). *A General Introduction to Psychoanalysis*. Phoemixx Classics Ebooks.

Furnham, A., & Ribchester, T. (1995). Tolerance of ambiguity: A review of the concept, its measurement and applications. *Current Psychology, 14*(3), 179–199.

Gardner, D. G., & Pierce, J. L. (1998). Self-esteem and self-efficacy within the organizational context: An empirical examination. *Group & Organization Management, 23*(1), 48–70. https://doi.org/10.1177/1059601198231004

Ginting, N., Rahman, N. V., & Nasution, A. D. (2018). Distinctiveness, continuity, self-esteem, & self-efficacy in tourism of Karo Regency, Indonesia. *Asian Journal of Quality of Life, 3*(13), 29–38.

Graumann, C. F. (1983). On multiple identities. *International Social Science Journal, 35*(2), 309–321.

Harding, J., & Hogrefe, R. (1952). Attitudes of white department store employees toward Negro co-workers. *Journal of Social Issues, 8*, 18–28.

Hartmann, A. S., Thomas, J. J., Greenberg, J. L., Matheny, N. L., & Wilhelm, S. (2014). A comparison of self-esteem and perfectionism in anorexia nervosa and body dysmorphic disorder. *The Journal of Nervous and Mental Disease, 202*(12), 883–888.

Haslam, C., Haslam, S. A., Knight, C., Gleibs, I., Ysseldyk, R., & McCloskey, L. G. (2014). We can work it out: Group decision-making builds social identity and enhances the cognitive performance of care residents. *British Journal of Psychology, 105*(1), 17–34. doi: 10.1111/bjop.12012

Haslam, S. A., Ellemers, N., Reicher, S. D., Reynolds, K. J., & Schmitt, M. T. (2010). The social identity perspective tomorrow: Opportunities and avenues for advance. In T. Postmes & N. R. Branscombe (Eds.), *Rediscovering Social Identity* (pp. 357–379). Hove: Psychology Press.

Haslam, S. A., Reicher, S. D., & Platow, M. J. (2011). *The New Psychology of Leadership: Identity, Influence, and Power*. Hove: Psychology Press.

Hayman, K. J., Kerse, N., & Consedine, N. S. (2017). Resilience in context: The special case of advanced age. *Aging & Mental Health, 21*(6), 577–585.

Hegel, G. W. F. (1977 [1807]). *Phenomenology of Spirit*. Oxford: Clarendon Press.

Hirschman, A. O. (1974). 'Exit, voice, and loyalty': Further reflections and a survey of recent contributions. *Social Science Information, 13*(1), 7–26.

Hoffmann, B. (2010). Bringing Hirschman back in: 'Exit', 'voice', and 'loyalty' in the politics of transnational migration. *The Latin Americanist, 54*(2), 57–73.

Hogg, M. A. (2000). Subjective uncertainty reduction through self-categorization: A motivational theory of social identity processes. *European Review of Social Psychology, 11*(1), 223–255.

Hogg, M. A. (2007). Uncertainty–identity theory. In M. P. Zanna (Ed.), *Advances in Experimental Social Psychology* (Vol. 39, pp. 69–126). San Diego, CA: Academic Press.

Hogg, M. A. (2016). Social identity theory. In S. McKeown, R. Haji, & N. Ferguson (Eds.), *Understanding Peace and Conflict through Social Identity Theory* (pp. 3–17). Cham: Springer.

Hogg, M. A., Terry, D. J., & White, K. M. (1995). A tale of two theories: A critical comparison of identity theory with social identity theory. *Social Psychology Quarterly, 58*(4), 255–269. https://doi.org/10.2307/2787127

Hogg, M. A., van Knippenberg, D., & Rast III, D. E. (2012). The social identity theory of leadership: Theoretical origins, research findings, and conceptual developments. *European Review of Social Psychology, 23*(1), 258–304.

Hornsey, M. J. (2008). Social identity theory and self-categorization theory: A historical review. *Social and Personality Psychology Compass, 2*(1), 204–222.

Hume, D. (2019). David Hume. In *Stanford Encyclopedia of Philosophy Archive* (Summer 2019 Edition). First published 26 February 2001. https://plato.stanford.edu/archives/sum2019/entries/hume/. Accessed 17 May 2022.

Ingraham, M. E. (2022). *'Being Believed, Being Seen, Not Being Questioned': Bisexual Women's Experiences of Validity while Passing as Heterosexual*. Doctoral dissertation, Seton Hall University.

Jackson, T., Wang, Y., Wang, Y., & Fan, H. (2014). Self-efficacy and chronic pain outcomes: A meta-analytic review. *The Journal of Pain, 15*(8), 800–814.

Jahn, H. (2022). Memory loss in Alzheimer's disease. *Dialogues in Clinical Neuroscience, 15*(4), 445–454.

James, W. (1890) *The Principles of Psychology*. New York: Henry Holt.

Janis, I. L. (1982). *Groupthink: Psychological Studies of Policy Decisions and Fiascos*. Boston, MA: Houghton Mifflin.

Jaspal, R. (2019). *The Social Psychology of Gay Men*. London: Palgrave.

Jaspal, R. (2021). Identity threat and coping among British South Asian gay men during the COVID-19 lockdown. *Sexuality & Culture, 25*(4), 1428–1446.

Jaspal, R., & Breakwell, G. M. (Eds.). (2014). *Identity Process Theory: Identity, Social Action and Social Change*. Cambridge: Cambridge University Press.

Jaspal, R., & Breakwell, G. M. (2022a). Identity resilience, social support and internalised homonegativity in gay men. *Psychology & Sexuality*, 13(5), 1270–1287. https://doi.org/10.1080/19419899.2021.2016916

Jaspal, R., & Breakwell, G. M. (2022b). Socio-economic inequalities in social network, loneliness and mental health during the COVID-19 pandemic. *International Journal of Social Psychiatry, 68*(1), 155–165.

Jaspal, R., & Breakwell, G. M. (in press). Identity processes and musicians during the COVID-19 pandemic. *Musicae Scientiae*.

Jaspal, R., & Cinnirella, M. (2010). Coping with potentially incompatible identities: Accounts of religious, ethnic, and sexual identities from British Pakistani men who identify as Muslim and gay. *British Journal of Social Psychology, 49*(4), 849–870.

Jaspal, R., da Silva Lopes, B. C., & Breakwell, G. M. (2021). British national identity and life satisfaction in ethnic minorities in the United Kingdom. *National Identities, 23*(5), 455–472.

Jaspal, R., Lopes, B., & Rehman, Z. (2021). A structural equation model for predicting depressive symptomatology in Black, Asian and Minority Ethnic lesbian, gay and bisexual people in the UK. *Psychology and Sexuality, 12*(3), 217–234. https://doi.org/10.1080/19419899.2019.1690560

Jaspal, R., & Nerlich, B. (2020). Social representations, identity threat, and coping amid COVID-19. *Psychological Trauma: Theory, Research, Practice, and Policy, 12*(S1), S249.

Jetten, J. (2020). *Together Apart: The Psychology of COVID-19*. London: Sage.

Jetten, J., Haslam, C., & Haslam, S. A. (2012). *The Social Cure: Identity, Health and Well-Being*. Hove: Psychology Press.

Johnson, C. (2002). Heteronormative citizenship and the politics of passing. *Sexualities, 5*(3), 317–336.

Johnstone, M., Jetten, J., Dingle, G. A., Parsell, C., & Walter, Z. C. (2015). Discrimination and well-being amongst the homeless: The role of multiple group membership. *Frontiers in Psychology, 6*, 739.

Josselson, R., & Harway, M. (Eds.). (2012). *Navigating Multiple Identities: Race, Gender, Culture, Nationality, and Roles*. New York: Oxford University Press.

Kaakinen, M., Sirola, A., Savolainen, I., & Oksanen, A. (2020). Shared identity and shared information in social media: Development and validation of the identity bubble reinforcement scale. *Media Psychology, 23*(1), 25–51.

Kanuha, V. K. (1999). The social process of 'passing' to manage stigma: Acts of internalized oppression or acts of resistance? *The Journal of Sociology & Social Welfare, 26*(4), 3. https://scholarworks.wmich.edu/jssw/vol26/iss4/3

Killian, L. M. (1952). The significance of multiple-group membership in disaster. *American Journal of Sociology, 57*(4), 309–314.

Krasner, B. (2019). *Historical Revisionism*. New York: Greenhaven Publishing.

Lane, J., Lane, A. M., & Kyprianou, A. (2008). Self-efficacy, self-esteem, and their impact on academic performance. *Social Behavior and Personality: An International Journal, 32*(3), 247–256. https://doi.org/10.2224/sbp.2004.32.3.247

Lee, C. S., Choi, K. S., Shandler, R., & Kayser, C. (2021). Mapping global cyber-terror networks: An empirical study of al-Qaeda and ISIS cyberterrorism events. *Journal of Contemporary Criminal Justice, 37*(3), 333–355.

Leonardelli, G. J., Pickett, C. L., & Brewer, M. B. (2010). Optimal distinctiveness theory: A framework for social identity, social cognition, and intergroup relations. In M. P. Zanna & M. Olson (Eds.), *Advances in Experimental Social Psychology* (Vol. 43, pp. 63–113). San Diego, CA: Academic Press.

Lewin, K. (1943). Psychology and the process of group living. *The Journal of Social Psychology, 17*(1), 113–131.

Licata, L., & Mercy, A. (2015). Collective memory (social psychology of). In J. D. Wright (Ed.), *International Encyclopedia of Social & Behavioral Science* (2nd edition, pp. 194–199). https://doi.org/10.1016/B978-0-08-097086-8.24046-4

Lightsey Jr, O. R., Burke, M., Ervin, A., Henderson, D., & Yee, C. (2006). Generalized self-efficacy, self-esteem, and negative affect. *Canadian Journal of Behavioural Science, 38*(1), 72–80. https://doi.org/10.1037/h0087272

Locke, J. (2008 [1847]). *An Essay Concerning Human Understanding*. Philadelphia, PA: Kay & Troutman.

Loftus, E. (2003). Our changeable memories: Legal and practical implications. *Nature Reviews Neuroscience, 4*(3), 231–234.

Loftus, E. (2020). *The Fiction of Memory*. Presented 27 February. Georgia Institute of Technology. https://smartech.gatech.edu/handle/1853/62483?show=full

Lyons, E. (1996). Coping with social change: Processes of social memory. In G. M. Breakwell & E. Lyons (Eds.), *Changing European Identities: Social Psychological Analyses of Change* (pp. 31–40). London: Butterworth Heinemann.

Maalouf, A. (2000). *On Identity*. Harmondsworth, Penguin.

Marlowe, C. M., Schneider, S. L., & Nelson, C. E. (1996). Gender and attractiveness biases in hiring decisions: Are more experienced managers less biased? *Journal of Applied Psychology*, 81(1), 11–21. https://doi.org/10.1037/0021-9010.81.1.11

Mavridi, K., & Breakwell, G. M. (2000). Women's coping strategies for workplace gender discrimination: The role of individual differences. In A. Kantas, T. Velli, & A. Hantzi (Eds.), *Societally Significant Applications of Psychological Knowledge*. Athens: Hellinika Grammata.

McAdams, D. P. (2001). The psychology of life stories. *Review of General Psychology, 5*(2), 100–122.

Mead, G. H. (1910). What social objects must psychology presuppose? *The Journal of Philosophy, Psychology and Scientific Methods, 7*(7), 174–180.

Mead, G. H., & Mind, H. (1934). *Self and Society*. Chicago, IL: University of Chicago Press.

Minard, R. D. (1952). Race relations in the Pocahontas coal field. *Journal of Social Issues, 8*(1), 29–44.

Mograbi, D. C., Huntley, J., & Critchley, H. (2021). Self-awareness in dementia: A taxonomy of processes, overview of findings, and integrative framework. *Current Neurology and Neuroscience Reports, 21*, 69. https://doi.org/10.1007/s11910-021-01155-6

Morrissey, B., & Yell, S. (2016). Performative trolling: Szubanski, Gillard, Dawson, and the nature of the utterance. *Persona Studies, 2*(1), 27–40.

Moscovici, S. (1988). Notes towards a description of social representations. *European Journal of Social Psychology, 18*(3), 211–250.

Moscovici, S. (2001). *Social Representations: Essays in Social Psychology*. New York: New York University Press.

Nam, S. J. (2021). Deviant behavior in cyberspace and emotional states. *Current Psychology, 3*(9), 45–51. https://dx.doi.org/10.22098/jrp.2022.10801.1101

NHS (2022). *Dementia*. www.nhs.uk/conditions/dementia/symptoms/ Accessed 9 June 2022.

Orth, U., & Robins, R. W. (2022). Is high self-esteem beneficial? Revisiting a classic question. *American Psychologist, 77*(1), 5–17. doi.org/10.1037/amp0000922

Parker, C. M., Hirsch, J. S., Philbin, M. M., & Parker, R. G. (2018). The urgent need for research and interventions to address family-based stigma and discrimination against lesbian, gay, bisexual, transgender, and queer youth. *Journal of Adolescent Health, 63*(4), 383–393.

Parkinson, B. (2020). Intragroup emotion convergence: Beyond contagion and social appraisal. *Personality and Social Psychology Review, 24*(2), 121–140.

Philpott, G. (1982). Consciousness raising: Back to basics. In M. Rowe (Ed.), *Spare Rib Reader*. Harmondsworth, Penguin.

Piaget, J. (1965). The stages of the intellectual development of the child. *Educational Psychology in Context: Readings for Future Teachers, 63*(4), 98–106.

Piaget, J. (2000). Piaget's theory of cognitive development. In K. Lee (ed.), *Childhood Cognitive Development: The Essential Readings* (pp. 33–47). Oxford: Wiley-Blackwell.

Piccoli, V., Carnaghi, A., Grassi, M., Stragà, M., & Bianchi, M. (2020). Cyberbullying through the lens of social influence: Predicting cyberbullying perpetration from perceived peer-norm, cyberspace regulations and ingroup processes. *Computers in Human Behavior, 102*, 260–273.

Pidgeon, N., Kasperson, R. E., & Slovic, P. (Eds.). (2003). *The Social Amplification of Risk*. Cambridge: Cambridge University Press.

Ritchie, T. D., Sedikides, C., & Skowronski, J. J. (2016). Emotions experienced at event recall and the self: Implications for the regulation of self-esteem, self-continuity, and meaningfulness. *Memory, 24*(5), 577–591. https://doi.org/10.1080/09658211.2015.1031678

Robins, R. W., Trzesniewski, K. H., Tracy, J. L., Gosling, S. D., & Potter, J. (2002). Global self-esteem across the life span. *Psychology and Aging, 17*(3), 423–434.

Rogers, C. R. (1947). Some observations on the organization of personality. *American Psychologist, 2*(9), 358–368.

Rosenberg, M. (1965). Rosenberg self-esteem scale (RSE). In J. Ciarrichi & L. Bilich, *Acceptance and Commitment Therapy: Measures Package, 61*(52), 18.

Rosenberg, M. (1989). *Society and the Adolescent Self-Image*. Princeton, NJ: Princeton University Press.

Rosenberg, M., Schooler, C., Schoenbach, C., & Rosenberg, F. (1995). Global self-esteem and specific self-esteem: Different concepts, different outcomes. *American Sociological Review, 60*(1), 141–156. http://www.jstor.org/stable/2096350

Rubin, M., & Hewstone, M. (1998). Social identity theory's self-esteem hypothesis: A review and some suggestions for clarification. *Personality and Social Psychology Review, 2*(1), 40–62.

Sadeh, N., & Karniol, R. (2012). The sense of self-continuity as a resource in adaptive coping with job loss. *Journal of Vocational Behavior, 80*(1), 93–99. https://doi.org/10.1016/j.jvb.2011.04.009

Sali, A. W., Anderson, B. A., & Courtney, S. M. (2018). Information processing biases in the brain: Implications for decision-making and self-governance. *Neuroethics, 11*(3), 259–271.

Saxe, R. (2013). Theory of mind: How brains think about thought. In K. N. Ochsner & S. Kosslyn (Eds.), *The Oxford Handbook of Cognitive Neuroscience, Volume 2: The Cutting Edges*. Oxford: Oxford University Press. https://doi.org/10.1093/oxfordhb/9780199988709.013.0013

Schwartz, S. J., Luyckx, K., & Vignoles, V. L. (Eds.). (2011). *Handbook of Identity Theory and Research*. New York: Springer.

Schwarzer, R., & Warner, L. M. (2013). Perceived self-efficacy and its relationship to resilience. In S. Prince-Embury & D. Saklofske (Eds.), *Resilience in Children, Adolescents, and Adults* (pp. 139–150). New York: Springer. https://doi.org/10.1007/978-1-4614-4939-3_10

Sedikides, C., & Alicke, M. D. (2019). The five pillars of self-enhancement and self-protection. In R. M. Ryan (Ed.), *The Oxford Handbook of Human Motivation* (pp. 307–319). Oxford: Oxford University Press.

Sedikides, C., & Wildschut, T. (2018). Finding meaning in nostalgia. *Review of General Psychology, 22*(1), 48–61.

Sharma, S., Åkerlund, H., Liao, H. W., & Bluck, S. (2021). Life challenges and resilience: the role of perceived personality continuity. *Aging & Mental Health, 25*(11), 2090–2099.

Sharma, S., Mukherjee, S., Kumar, A., & Dillon, W. R. (2005). A simulation study to investigate the use of cutoff values for assessing model fit in covariance structure models. *Journal of Business Research, 58*(7), 935–943. https://doi.org/10.1016/j. jbusres.2003.10.007

Sharma, S., & Sharma, M. (2010). Globalization, threatened identities, coping and well-being. *Psychological Studies, 55*(4), 313–322.

Singh, A. A., Meng, S. E., & Hansen, A. W. (2014). 'I am my own gender': Resilience strategies of trans youth. *Journal of Counseling & Development, 92*(2), 208–218.

Sodian, B., & Kristen, S. (2016). Theory of mind. In J. A. Greene, W. A. Sandoval, & I. Bråten (Eds.), *Handbook of Epistemic Cognition* (pp. 80–97). Abingdon: Routledge.

Sowislo, J. F., & Orth, U. (2013). Does low self-esteem predict depression and anxiety? A meta-analysis of longitudinal studies. *Psychological Bulletin, 139*(1), 213–240. https://doi.org/10.1037/a0028931

Stroebe, W., & Stroebe, M. (1996). The social psychology of social support. In E. T. Higgins & A. W. Kruglanski (Eds.), *Social Psychology: Handbook of Basic Principles* (pp. 597–621). New York: The Guilford Press.

Stryker, S., & Burke, P. J. (2000). The past, present, and future of an identity theory. *Social Psychology Quarterly, 63*(4), 284–297.

Sutherland, S. (1989). Consciousness. In S. Sutherland (Ed.), *Macmillan Dictionary of Psychology*. Basingstoke: Macmillan

Swift, V., & Peterson, J. B. (2018). Improving the effectiveness of performance feedback by considering personality traits and task demands. *PLoS One, 13*(5), e0197810.

Tajfel, H. (1974). Social identity and intergroup behavior. *Social Science Information, 13*(2), 65–93. doi:10.1177/053901847401300204

Tajfel, H. (Ed.). (1978). *Differentiation between Social Groups: Studies in the Social Psychology of Intergroup Relations*. London: Academic Press.

Tajfel, H. (1981). *Human Groups and Social Categories*. Cambridge: Cambridge University Press.

Tajfel, H., Billig, M. G., Bundy, R. P., & Flament, C. (1971). Social categorization and intergroup behaviour. *European Journal of Social Psychology, 1*(2), 149–178. doi:10.1002/ejsp.2420010202

Taliaferro, L. A., McMorris, B. J., Rider, G. N., & Eisenberg, M. E. (2019). Risk and protective factors for self-harm in a population-based sample of transgender youth. *Archives of Suicide Research, 23*(2), 203–221.

Taylor, K. (2006). *Brainwashing: The Science of Thought Control*. Oxford: Oxford University Press.

Thoits, P. A. (1985). Social support and psychological well-being: Theoretical possibilities. In I. G. Sarason & B. R. Sarason (Eds.), *Social Support: Theory, Research and Applications* (pp. 51–72). Dordrecht: Springer.

Timotijevic, L., & Breakwell, G. M. (2000). Migration and threat to identity. *Journal of Community & Applied Social Psychology, 10*(5), 355–372.

Trzesniewski, K. H., Donnellan, M. B., & Robins, R. W. (2013). Development of self-esteem. In V. Zeigler-Hill (Ed.), *Self-Esteem* (pp. 60–79). Hove: Psychology Press.

Turner, J. C. (1978). Social categorization and social discrimination in the minimal group paradigm. In H. Tajfel (Ed.), *Differentiation between Social Groups: Studies in the Social Psychology of Intergroup Relations* (pp. 235–250). London: Academic Press.

Turner, J. C. (2010). Social categorization and the self-concept: A social cognitive theory of group behavior. In T. Postmes & N. R. Branscombe (Eds.), *Rediscovering Social Identity* (pp. 243–272). Hove: Psychology Press.

Turner, J. C., & Haslam, S. A. (2001). Social identity, organizations, and leadership. In M. E. Turner (Ed.), *Groups at Work* (pp. 39–80). Hove: Psychology Press.

Turner, M. E., & Pratkanis, A. R. (1998). Twenty-five years of groupthink theory and research: Lessons from the evaluation of a theory. *Organizational Behavior and Human Decision Processes, 73*(2–3), 105–115.

Turner, R. H. (1976). The real self: From institution to impulse. *American Journal of Sociology, 81*(5), 989–1016.

Twigger-Ross, C., Bonaiuto, M., & Breakwell, G. (2003). Identity theories and environmental psychology. In M. Bonnes, T. Lee, & M. Bonaiuto (Eds.), *Psychological Theories for Environmental Issues* (pp. 203–233). Aldershot: Ashgate Publishing.

Twigger-Ross, C. L., & Uzzell, D. L. (1996). Place and identity processes. *Journal of Environmental Psychology, 16*(3), 205–220.

Valle, A., Massaro, D., Castelli, I., & Marchetti, A. (2015). Theory of mind development in adolescence and early adulthood: The growing complexity of recursive thinking ability. *Europe's Journal of Psychology, 11*(1), 112.

Vess, M., Arndt, J., Routledge, C., Sedikides, C., & Wildschut, T. (2012). Nostalgia as a resource for the self. *Self and Identity, 11*(3), 273–284.

Vignoles, V. L. (2011). Identity motives. In S. J. Schwartz, K. Luyckx, & V. L. Vignoles (Eds.), *Handbook of Identity Theory and Research* (pp. 403–432). New York: Springer.

Vignoles, V. L., Chryssochoou, X., & Breakwell, G. M. (2000). The distinctiveness principle: Identity, meaning, and the bounds of cultural relativity. *Personality and Social Psychology Review, 4*(4), 337–354.

Vygotsky, L. S., & Cole, M. (1978). *Mind in Society: Development of Higher Psychological Processes*. Cambridge, MA: Harvard University Press.

Wang, C. C., Chang, Y. P., Yang, Y. H., Hu, H. F., & Yen, C. F. (2019). Relationships between traditional and cyber harassment and self-identity confusion among Taiwanese gay and bisexual men in emerging adulthood. *Comprehensive Psychiatry, 90*, 14–20.

Wang, S., & Xu, H. (2015). Influence of place-based senses of distinctiveness, continuity, self-esteem and self-efficacy on residents' attitudes toward tourism. *Tourism Management, 47*, 241–250. https://doi.org/10.1016/j.tourman.2014.10.007

Warburton, S. (Ed.). (2012). *Digital Identity and Social Media*. Hershey, PA: IGI Global.

Watson, G. (1970). *Passing for White*. London: Tavistock.

Wildschut, T., Sedikides, C., Routledge, C., Arndt, J., & Cordaro, F. (2010). Nostalgia as a repository of social connectedness: The role of attachment-related avoidance. *Journal of Personality and Social Psychology, 98*(4), 573–586.

Wilkinson-Ryan, T., & Westen, D. (2000). Identity disturbance in borderline personality disorder: An empirical investigation. *American Journal of Psychiatry, 157*(4), 528–541.

Williams, D. (2010). Theory of own mind in autism: Evidence of a specific deficit in self-awareness? *Autism, 14*(5), 474–494. doi:10.1177/1362361310366314

Windle, G., Bennett, K. M., & Noyes, J. (2011). A methodological review of resilience measurement scales. *Health and Quality of Life Outcomes, 9*(8). https://doi.org/10.1186/1477-7525-9-8

World Health Organization (WHO) (2022). *Mental Health in Emergencies*. www.who.int/news-room/fact-sheets/detail/mental-health-in-emergencies. Accessed 15 May 2022.

Zandersen, M., & Parnas, J. (2019). Identity disturbance, feelings of emptiness, and the boundaries of the schizophrenia spectrum. *Schizophrenia Bulletin, 45*(1), 106–113. https://doi.org/10.1093/schbul/sbx183

Zare, S., Aguilar-Vafaie, M. E., & Ahmadi, F. (2017). Perception of identity threat as the main disturbance of Iranian divorced women: A qualitative study. *Journal of Divorce & Remarriage, 58*(1), 1–15.

Ziglar, Z. (2013). *Be firm on principle but flexible on method*. Facebook post, 4 March. www.azquotes.com/quote/613436

INDEX